A Season with Coach
Dick Bennett

A Season with Coach Dick Bennett

Eric Ferris

PRAIRIE OAK PRESS
Madison, Wisconsin

First edition, second printing, 1998
Copyright © 1997 by Eric Ferris

Prairie Oak Press
821 Prospect Place
Madison, Wisconsin 53703

Typeset by Quick Quality Press, Madison, Wisconsin
Printed in the United States of America by BookCrafters, Chelsea,
    Michigan

Library of Congress Cataloging-in-Publication Data

Ferris, Eric, 1962–
    A season with coach Dick Bennett / Eric Ferris. -- 1st ed.
        p.   cm.
    ISBN 1-879483-48-3 (alk. paper)
    1. University of Wisconsin--Madison--Football--History.
2. Bennett, Dick, 1943–   . I. Title.
GV958.U587F47 1997
796.332'63'092--dc21   97-36449
[B]   CIP

Contents

Not all rewards of an individual's life are reaped by the sower.
I, for one, am the beneficiary of my parents' life of exremely hard work.
For that, I am forever indebted and, therefore, lovingly dedicate
this book to my mother and father, Bill and Linda Ferris.

Acknowledgments

This project would never have reached conclusion without the help of some very talented and gifted individuals. I would like to thank Kim O'Brien and Kelly Jeffers for their initial review of the material and their continual words of encouragement. In addition, Nora Smith, a long time friend and mentor, provided invaluable literary insight and direction. Her contributions to this project have been tremendously helpful. I would also like to thank Coach Bennett, the basketball staff, the players, and the Bennett family for providing me with the opportunity to tell this story. And finally, I must acknowledge the contributions of Jerry Minnich and Prairie Oak Press who have been so helpful in bringing this book to fruition.

The Coaches of the 1996–97 Season

Dick Bennett, Head Coach

Bennett spent eleven years coaching at the high school level in Wisconsin, compiling a 168-60 record between 1965 and 1976. He then moved into the college ranks as head coach at the University of Wisconsin-Stevens Point. In his nine-year tenure at Stevens Point, Bennett compiled an impressive 174-79 overall record, and his teams made three consecutive trips to the NAIA national tournament during his final three seasons. Bennett's team posted a 28-4 mark in the 1983-84 season and finished second in the national tournament, earning him NAIA National Coach of the Year honors. One year later, Bennett accepted his first Division I challenge when he agreed to take over the 4-24 University of Wisconsin-Green Bay Phoenix. He spent the next ten years building the UWGB program into a perennial winner, and along the way built a national reputation for himself. He compiled a 187-109 record between 1985 and 1995 and his teams reached post-season play in five of his last six seasons. Bennett was voted Mid-Continent Conference Coach of the Year in 1990 and 1992, NABC (National Association of Basketball Coaches) District Coach of the Year in 1992 and 1995, and the *Basketball Times* Midwest Coach of the Year in 1994.

Bennett assumed control of the University of Wisconsin-Madison men's basketball program in the spring of 1995. UW Athletic Director Pat Richter explained his decision to recruit Bennett for the job. "Dick Bennett was hired because he was the best person to bring stability and credibility to our program." Bennett's colleagues obviously agreed with Richter. Earlier that spring, the *Seattle Post-Intelligencer* reported on a survey that they had conducted among the 113 college basketball coaches who attended the 1995 Final Four. Bennett ranked second nationally as the coach "who does the best job in a difficult situation," and was surpassed by only Indiana's Bob Knight, North Carolina's Dean Smith, and Duke's Mike Krzyzewski in "strategizing the game."

Bennett and his wife, Anne, have three grown children. Kathi, the oldest, is the head women's basketball coach at the University of Evansville; Amy is a speech therapist in Green Bay; and Tony, UWGB's all-time leading scorer, currently plays professionally in New Zealand.

Brad Soderberg, Assistant Coach

Soderberg grew up in Stevens Point, Wisconsin, and attended Pacelli High School, where he was coached by his father. He attended the University of Wisconsin-Stevens Point and was a team captain and starting guard for Bennett's 1984 NAIA national runner-up team.

Soderberg began his coaching career as an assistant for Bennett during the 1984-85 season, as he completed course work for his undergraduate degree. Bennett moved on to UWGB the following season and Soderberg accepted a graduate assistant position at Colorado State University. Upon completion of his master's degree in physical education, he moved on to Fort Hayes State for one season as an assistant, and then to Loras College in Dubuque, Iowa. After only one year, in 1988, he was promoted to the head coaching position. Soderberg guided the Duhawks to a cumulative 79-45 record over the next five years. In 1993 he moved up to the Division II level when he accepted the head coaching position at South Dakota State University. He compiled a 36-18 mark with the Jackrabbits before rejoining his former coach at the University of Wisconsin in the spring of 1995.

Soderberg's primary responsibilities include recruiting and on-the-floor coaching.

Shawn Hood, Assistant Coach

Hood grew up in Boston and attended Don Basco High School. He led his team to two state championships before playing collegiately at Cleveland State University. He lettered in all four of his seasons at CSU between 1983 and 1987. The 1985-86 CSU team posted a 29-4 record and advanced to the "sweet 16" of the NCAA Tournament. Hood also served as captain for his team during both his junior and senior seasons.

After graduating in 1988 with a degree in social services, he joined the CSU coaching staff. His reputation as a recruiter grew as he gained experience, and in his final season he was named the senior assistant on the staff. He then joined the Badger staff in 1994, a year prior to Bennett's arrival in Madison.

Hood's primary responsibilities include recruiting and on-the-floor coaching.

Brian Hecker, Assistant Coach

Hecker, a native of Milwaukee, graduated from Indiana University in 1990 with a sports marketing/management degree. He returned to Milwaukee and served as an assistant basketball coach at Nicolet High School before joining the Badger staff in 1991 as Stu Jackson's administrative assistant. In 1993 he was promoted to assistant coach.

Hecker's primary responsibilities include summer camps, video coordination, scouting of opponents, and underclass recruiting.

Paul Costanzo, Administrative Assistant

Costanzo graduated from the University of Wisconsin-River Falls in 1984 with majors in physics and chemistry. He got his start in coaching in 1984-85 when he served as assistant basketball and baseball coach at Madison Memorial High School. He then moved on to Verona High School and served in the same capacity for the next three seasons. In 1988 he returned to UW-River Falls and served as the associate head coach with the basketball program before joining the Badger staff in 1995.

Costanzo has developed and marketed a computer software package designed to assist in the basketball recruiting process.

The Players of the 1996-97 Season

Hennssy Auriantal
6'1" Sophomore Guard, Montreal, Quebec

Auriantal played at Dawson College, a Canadian prep school, before attending Wisconsin. He was the league's leading scorer at Dawson, averaging 26.7 points per game, and was named to the first-team all-Canada squad his senior season. However, it was his defensive prowess that prompted Bennett to play him in all thirty-two games as a freshman at Wisconsin, including twenty-one starts.

Major: Kinesiology.

David Burkemper
6'1" Junior Guard, Hubertus, Wisconsin

Averaged 7.2 points, 9.1 assists, and 3.1 rebounds for a Marquette High School team that won the state title with a 25-1 record his senior season. Holds the school's all time assist record. Burkemper joined the Badgers at mid-season in 1995-96 as a practice player. Saw three minutes of action in three games.

Major: Undecided.

Ty Calderwood
6'0" Junior Guard, Joliet, Illinois

The only new face in the Badger program for the 1996-97 season. Averaged 14.8 points a game while guiding his team to a 30-1 mark his senior season at Carbondale High School. Spent the next two years playing for Coach Pat Klingler at Joliet Community College and Palm Beach Community College in Florida. Though he shot 44 percent from the three-point line and averaged 12.9 points a game during his sophomore season, his 8.3 assists per game and leadership ability on the floor prompted the UW staff to recruit him as a point guard.

Major: Agricultural journalism.

Booker Coleman
6'9" Junior Center/Forward, Erie, Pennsylvania

Played high school basketball at Cathedral Prep in the Erie Metro League. Named first team all-state as a senior. Averaged 17 points and 10 rebounds to help his team to a 24-7 record and a second place finish in the Class 4A state tournament. Coleman has served as a reserve for most of his UW career. A gifted athlete, Coleman's strength as a player is his defense ability and rebounding.

Major: International relations.

Sean Daugherty
6'10" Junior Forward, Vincennes, Indiana

A graduate of Lincoln High School in Vincennes, Daugherty averaged 19 points and 10 rebounds his senior year and was named first-team all-state by the Indiana Basketball Coaches Association. His high school team posted a 56-16 record during his three-year varsity career. At Wisconsin, played in all but one game as a freshman, starting five times while averaging 4.6 points and 3.8 rebounds. Daugherty started 31 of the team's 32 games as a sophomore, and scored in double figures in 17 games. Daugherty has the ability to play either inside or out, and possesses an exceptional shooting touch from the perimeter for a player of his size.

Major: Biological aspects of conservation.

Duany Duany
6'4" Freshman Forward, Bloomington, Indiana

Originally from Juba, Sudan, Duany was selected first-team all-state in Indiana as a senior. He became Bloomington North High School's all-time leading scorer his senior season. His freshman season at UW was cut short when he broke a bone in his foot in a late November practice and was forced to redshirt. Duany's strength is his jumping ability and his shooting touch from beyond the three point arc.

Major: Undecided.

Paul Grant
7'0" Senior Center, West Bloomfield, Michigan

Grant chose to play his final season at the University of Wisconsin after spending his first three seasons at Boston College. While at BC, he played in 88 games, including 34 starts, and averaged 4.3 points and 2.8 rebounds. Grant played high school basketball at Brother Rice High

School in Birmingham, Michigan, where he averaged 23 points and 9 rebounds a game in his senior season, on his way to earning all-state honors. Grant's greatest asset as a player is his physical strength. He carries 245 pounds on his 7'0" frame.

Major: English.

Mike Kosolcharoen
6'1" Sophomore Guard, Adams, Wisconsin

Kosolcharoen averaged 22.3 points per game in his senior season at Adams-Friendship High School and was named first team all-state by the *Milwaukee Journal Sentinel*. Was a walk-on (non-scholarship) Badger player as a freshman and spent most of his time developing his skills on the red team (the practice squad), although he did see action in eighteen games. Despite his lack of overall quickness and height, he developed into one of the team's best defenders at the small forward position.

Major: Undecided.

Sean Mason
6'2" Junior Guard, Olympia Fields, Illinois

A graduate of Rich Central High School, Mason was named to the *Chicago Tribune* and *Chicago Sun-Times* all-area teams. Averaged 21 points a game his senior season. Played in 25 of 27 games as a UW freshman and averaged five points a game. Started the first thirteen games of his sophomore season for the Badgers, averaging nine points a game, before suffering a season-ending knee injury against the University of Michigan. Mason's forte is his exceptional quickness and scoring ability.

Major: Agricultural journalism.

Sam Okey
6'7" Sophomore Forward, Cassville, Wisconsin

Led his high-school team to back-to-back state championships and was named the state's player of the year by the Associated Press and *Milwaukee Journal Sentinel* as a junior and senior. Fourth leading scorer in state high school league history with 2,539 points. Okey became the first player in Big Ten history to lead his team in points, rebounds, assists, and blocked shots in one season, on his way to being voted the 1996 Big Ten Freshman of the Year. His greatest asset as a player is his physical strength and athletic ability.

Major: Undecided.

Mosezell Peterson
6'4" Junior Guard, Louisville, Kentucky

Peterson was voted first team all-state by the *Louisville Courier-Journal* and *Lexington Herald-Leader.* Averaged 19.9 points as a senior before becoming the first Badger basketball recruit from the Bluegrass State. Played in 18 games as a UW freshman and scored in double figures on four different occasions. As a sophomore, he started 21 of 30 games and averaged 11.5 points per game. Peterson suffered a season-ending knee injury in an NIT post-season game against Manhattan ans was redshirted for the 1996-97 season.

Major: Special education.

Matt Quest
6'6" Sophomore Forward, Watertown, Wisconsin

Averaged 22 points and 10 rebounds his senior season at Watertown High School. He did not play competitive basketball during his freshman season at college and walked on to the 1996-97 Badger squad.

Major: Construction administration.

Adam Shafer
6'4" Junior Guard, Downers Grove, Illinois

Shafer transferred to Wisconsin from Villanova University and joined the UW team as a redshirt walk-on in January of 1996. He played in eleven games as a freshman at Villanova, and averaged 1.2 points a game. In high school, he set a career scoring mark with 1,811 points and was a consensus two-time all-state selection in the state of Illinois.

Major: Philosophy.

Brian Vraney
6'6" Junior Forward, Valders, Wisconsin

Vraney served as captain on his high school team and earned all-Olympian conference and all-area team honors as a senior. Averaged 21 points and 10 rebounds a game. Was a walk-on at UW and has played a total of 31 minutes, scoring 23 points, in two seasons. His primary contribution to the team is his relentless work ethic in practice.

Major: Kinesiology.

Preface

> *It is not the critic who counts, not the*
> *man who*
> *points out where the strong man stumbles*
> *or where the doer of*
> *deeds could have done better.*
> *The credit belongs to the man who is actually*
> *in the arena;*
> *whose face is marred by dust and*
> *sweat and blood; who*
> *strives valiantly; who errs and comes*
> *short again and again;*
> *who knows the great enthusiasm, the*
> *great devotion, and*
> *spends himself in a worthy cause; who,*
> *at the best, knows in*
> *the end the triumph of high achievement;*
> *and who; at the worst,*
> *if he fails, at least fails while daring*
> *greatly so, that his*
> *place shall never be with those cold and*
> *timid souls who know*
> *neither victory nor defeat.*
>
> —Theodore Roosevelt

This famous quotation was a constant companion as I wrote the book you are about to read. Though I had read it many times before, its words became more important, a constant reminder that the real story I longed to tell lay beneath the surface of the meetings, practices, and games I observed. My ultimate goal, then, was to look within.

Introduction

The resurrection of my career was not going as I had planned. Sun broke through the low-hanging gray clouds as I reached for the phone and dialed the number of a man I knew only by reputation, Dick Bennett. He was then head basketball coach at the University of Wisconsin-Green Bay.

"Green Bay Basketball," a soft, feminine voice answered.

"May I speak with Coach Bennett, please?"

"Just one moment."

Breath grew shallow in my lungs as I realized I was ill prepared for the call. Of course I wanted to talk to Bennett, but about what? I knew him only through his instructional video tape on pressure defense. Thoughts raced through my mind before I settled on a plan to meet with him in person. That way, I would have time to formulate at least a few intelligible questions before I attempted a discourse with him.

"This is Coach Bennett," I heard through the receiver.

"Hi Coach, my name is Eric Ferris," I heard myself say, "I coach at the College of St. Scholastica in Duluth, Minnesota, and I was hoping to meet with you sometime in the near future to discuss your defensive philosophy."

"Sure, when were you thinking about coming to Green Bay?"

"As soon as possible. Is next week O.K.?"

"How is next Monday at 11:00 A.M.?"

"That would be great. I'll see you then," I said, surprised by his availability. I hung up, put pen to paper, and wrote out a long list of questions I wanted to ask.

The grounds of the University of Wisconsin-Green Bay (UWGB) are atypical among college campuses. UWGB is isolated from the rest of the city in a remote location which seeks to maintain the natural habitat, both forested areas and fields of indigenous grasses. The buildings are concentrated at the center of the acreage. Driving the winding roads around the periphery, lined with brown wooden signs giving directions to the different structures, I finally came upon the Phoenix Sports Center. It looked simple in design, functional, but smaller than I had expected for a Division I program. My original thought was that it must be a difficult task attracting recruits with such modest playing facilities. I also wondered whether Bennett ever saw it in that light. Impressing eighteen-year-old kids with flashy surroundings was not consistent with his reputed personality. My contemplation turned out to be pointless, however, as I later learned that the team held their home contests at Brown County Veterans Memorial Arena, a 5,800-seat facility located adjacent to Lambeau Field, home of the NFL's Green Bay Packers.

I pulled into a nearly vacant parking lot and walked into the field house. There was no one in sight, so I looked around the entranceway for a directory. I found it just inside the double glass doors, studied it for a moment, and then headed toward the sound of muffled voices down the right corridor. I passed an open set of doors on my left and took a moment to study the gym. Two small sets of bleachers pushed back into their storage position and green sidelines bordered the heavily used wooden surface. There were lines for every net game imaginable on the floor, making it nearly impossible to distinguish the free throw lane or the half-court line. "Not what I expected," I thought to myself as I continued down the hall. The voices were resonating from the basketball office, so I stepped inside and the secretary greeted me warmly. After introducing myself and informing her that I had a meeting with Coach Bennett, she said that he was expecting me and led me down a narrow hallway and through a doorway on my right. Bennett, seated behind the desk, stood to extend a welcoming handshake. I couldn't help but notice that his office was obviously a workstation, not window dressing. Boxes of camp T-shirts and basketballs filled the corner, a television and tape deck sat adjacent to the desk, and there were stacks of books and folders everywhere. It wasn't necessarily messy, just busy and practical. We exchanged pleasantries. I inquired about Tony's progress on making the roster of an NBA team. (Tony is Bennett's son who had been an outstanding guard at UWGB for the previous four seasons.) His face lit up as he spoke about Tony. There was pride in his voice, of course, but there was something more. He spoke of how blessed Tony, he, and the rest of his family had been for the opportunities they had been given. He also spoke of Tony's recent back injury, commenting, "If it is God's will, everything will turn out fine."

Our discussion then turned to basketball. I located the list of questions I had attached to a clipboard and asked Bennett if he minded if I went through them to serve as a guide for our discussion. He agreed to the format. I wrote careful notes on a separate notebook as he answered each question and placed a check next to each question when he had finished. His answers were technically precise, but were without the emotion I assumed would accompany them. After all, this was the foundation that his reputation and career were built on, so I thought. I was befuddled by his lack of enthusiasm for the intricacies of the game, nonetheless, I listened intently, taking notes when I thought appropriate. Only when we talked about other aspects of the game, those not constrained by style, tempo, or rules, did our conversation seem to interest him. An explanation on fronting the post became a deliberation on the concept of TEAM.

One hour had passed, which I thought might be the longest time appropriate for such a meeting, so I excused myself even though I felt that my inquiry had just begun. Bennett walked me out to the front door and then left me to digest our conversation. In doing so, I realized that basketball was this man's vocation, not his obsession. It was evident there were other aspects of his life that were at least as important as the game of basketball, primarily faith and family. The crunching of gravel under my shoes broke the still summer silence in the air as I walked back to my car. Sun reflected off the key as it slid into the lock, and I looked back at the building and thought of a motto that should be written above the front doors: *Excellence comes from within.* Why else would you attend this school if you were a basketball player? There was no fanfare or flash to be found anywhere.

Five years later, the University of Wisconsin-Madison athletic director, Pat Richter, had just hired his third basketball coach in four years. Twice before, he had passed over Dick Bennett's application for the position. The first time he did so to hire Stu Jackson, a high profile coach with NBA head coaching experience. When Jackson left to become the general manager of the expansion Vancouver Grizzles, Richter promoted assistant Stan Van Gundy to the top spot. Van Gundy's team, featuring future NBA first-round draft pick Michael Finley and seven-footer Rashard Griffith, finished below .500 for the season and Van Gundy's contract was not renewed. Dick Bennett, however, did not throw his name into the selection process after Van Gundy's departure. He had decided to spend the rest of his career in Green Bay. But Richter had finally decided that Bennett was his man. He convinced Bennett in a telephone conversation that he owed it to himself to at least hear what Richter had to say, since he had been interested in the position in the past. Bennett obliged Richter and a meeting was set up in the Bennett home. The meeting itself was not enough to convince Bennett to leave Green Bay. The UWGB program was in great shape and the incoming freshmen had him excited about the future.

A meeting was called with his team to announce his final decision, but just one hour before the meeting was to occur, Richter asked Bennett to hold off telling his team or the media until they could speak one final time. Out of respect for Richter, he again agreed to his request, though it was too late to cancel the meeting with his players. The meeting with the players went ahead as planned. He explained to the players that he was leaning heavily toward staying, but wanted their input. Gary Grzesk spoke first, then Jeff Nordgaard, and they essentially said he had the right to leave if that was what he really wanted to do.

The team's comments took him by surprise. The players recognized all that he had done for them and the UWGB program, and that all the goals they had set had either been reached or surpassed. The players understood, more than anyone, that he had to go, he had to take the job. Bennett returned home from the meeting, walked into the kitchen where his wife was standing, kissed her, and told her that he was taking the Wisconsin job. Richter had his new coach and Bennett had the opportunity to fulfill a dream. At fifty-two years of age, and after thirty years on the sideline, he was the head coach of the University of Wisconsin Badgers.

Bennett arrived in Madison in the spring of 1995 and was greeted by a team in transition. Rashard Griffith, the seven-foot sophomore center, was deciding whether or not to declare himself eligible for the NBA draft. All indications were that he would not be returning. Still, Bennett welcomed the opportunity to work with the exceptionally talented Griffith and instill some of the traits that had made his less talented UWGB players successful. The awesome potential of the combination was staggering. Bennett never got that chance. Soon after Bennett was hired, Griffith declared himself available for the draft. Gone also were three other starters, Andy Kilbride, Brian Kelly, and Michael Finley, who soon would be an NBA rookie-of-the-year finalist. The bulk of the experience on the roster was gone. Darnell Hoskins was the only player returning with playing experience. The rest of the team was comprised of a group of young and unproven role players. The only notable exception was the highly recruited and talented freshman, Sam Okey.

The summer was exceptionally busy, filled with fund-raisers and speaking engagements. The demands of his new job required him to speak at numerous social events, to a diverse group of audiences, promoting his basketball team and UW athletics. In addition, he occasionally spoke to Christian groups about his spirituality. Around campus, he extended friendly greetings to those he met, often taking the time for impromptu conversations with fans and colleagues, and his friendly nature became widely recognized. A public persona of a kind and generous man developed as he became more familiar to Badger fans. When the Bennetts purchased a townhouse on Cherokee Golf Course and his wife Anne joined him in Madison late in the summer, he embarked on preparing for his first Big Ten season.

Along with five hundred other coaches, I sat in the Field House bleachers at the University of Wisconsin-Madison, attending the inaugural Dick Bennett Badger Coaches Clinic. Tony Bennett, sporting a cast on his left foot, was also in attendance. While at the Cleveland Cavaliers training camp, he had torn the *plantar facia* in his right foot. The *plantar facia* is a large band of connective tissue running the entire length of the foot. The injury brought an early end to his NBA season for the second straight year. (He had suffered the same injury to his left foot in the previous season while playing for the Charlotte Hornets.) Bennett had watched his son excel on the basketball court for nearly twenty years and the two had developed a special bond as a father and son while Tony played at UWGB. Bennett understood that a significant part of his early success at Green Bay was attributable to Tony's outstanding play. Tony's injury allowed him to spend time in Madison and lend moral support to his father as practice started.

We watched Bennett take his new team through its first practice; first introductions and warm-ups, then defensive drills, shooting and scrimmaging. The play was crisp and aggressive, players trying to impress both their new coach and the educated spectators in the stands. The enthusiasm, however, soon gave way to fatigue. Old habits plagued the team. Bennett's patient demeanor quickly grew assertive and direct as he stepped out onto the floor.

"We must *outlast* the offense on every possession! Great defense takes consistent effort and a commitment to excellence, every second of every practice and every game. It is not good enough to just go through the motions, to give the impression that you are trying, that you care. You must take pride in your defense, in your effort, and be committed to *outlasting* your opponent." He implored, almost pleaded, "You have to believe that! Anything less gives our opponent the edge. Gentlemen, we must *outlast* the offense on every possession. That must be our foundation."

Bennett dropped his head in thought and walked to the sideline. Play resumed with renewed vigor. His message was unmistakably clear. His words proposed wisdom applicable far beyond the basketball court. After all, it was that exact personal trait, relentless determination, that had finally landed him the head coaching job at the University of Wisconsin, a school on its fourth coach in five years. Bennett's continued success at Green Bay, taking his teams to two NIT and three NCAA post-season appearances between 1989 and 1995, made it virtually impossible for the UW administrators to pass him over once again when filling the vacancy. He had simply outlasted all the other applicants for the job.

Convinced that there was something "different" about Bennett's leadership style, I decided to return to the University of Wisconsin for an entire season and investigate the origin of these "differences." After several preliminary discussions, Bennett cautiously agreed to let me pursue this endeavor on an ongoing basis. "At the very least, this will improve my self-awareness, and give me another perspective on the team. We'll leave it at that, and see how it develops." With those "resounding" words of encouragement, I began my extensive analysis of Dick Bennett as a coach, and as a man. Bennett himself, his staff, players, and family, have all provided invaluable insights into the understanding of this seemingly indiscernible man that is Dick Bennett. This book, then, is the compilation of the subsequent months of interviews, observations, and interactions.

Chapter 1

I'm Just One Person

Traffic on Gorham Street was heavier than usual. Thousands of students joined downtown businessmen and women on their daily commutes into Madison. A sleek new Porsche darted dangerously close to a slow-moving 1973 Dodge Dart, rusted nearly to the frame. Cars, people, bikes, and mopeds all converged on the heart of the city, a few square miles of real estate, home to both the State Capitol and the University of Wisconsin-Madison campus. Lake Mendota to the west, and Lake Monona to the east, squeeze the traffic to a narrow isthmus at the Capitol building. Out-of-town visitors and freshman were easily spotted in the rush of activity, as their heads pivoted back and forth on tense, rigid shoulders.

Diversity gives this midsize community its personality. This is the one place in the state where outrageous behavior, dress, or attitudes are tolerated, often ignored, sometimes even admired as the close proximity of the Capitol and the university melds students, politicians, shoppers, vagrants, professionals, lobbyists, street vendors, protesters, street musicians, artists, wanna-bes, yuppies, and immigrants into one colorful blur of activity. On a much smaller scale, Madison is Wisconsin's New York City. Nowhere else in the state is there so much diversity and activity in so small an area.

Camp Randall Stadium, named after the Civil War training camp once located on the grounds (Alexander W. Randall was a Civil War governor), is located in the southwestern part of the campus. Granite soldiers and bronzed cannons still guard the premises. The combatants who prepare behind the the stadium's stone walls now, however, are student-athletes instead of Union soldiers. Camp Randall is home to the University of Wisconsin-Madison Athletic Department, whose offices are located under the stadium stands. The venerable Field House, which holds nearly 12,000 for basketball, sits directly behind the south stands at the open end of the horseshoe. I circled the stadium four times before I finally found a place to park, then made my way to the men's basketball office. The sprawling complex, housed on the third floor, was impressive by any standards.

Bennett reclined in his chair, hands folded behind his head, as I entered his office. Fatigue showed on his face. Silence and a pensive demeanor replaced his usual warm greeting of previous meetings. Questioned about his lethargic behavior, he apologetically sat forward, rubbed his eyes and forehead with the heals of his hands, and explained that he had not been sleeping well. The only agenda for the day was to discuss my access to him and the team. My boundaries for the next several months were established. I was to attend practices and coaches meetings, conduct regular personal interviews, and attend any other pre-approved activities that were appropriate for my book. The discussion then fell into idle chatter. The source of his sleepless nights became apparent when the topic of recruiting came up.

Bennett stared at a framed poster of his 1993-94 UWGB team, a group that won twenty-seven games and upset Jason Kidd's California Bears in the NCAA tournament. He shook his head slowly, two index fingers pressed against his chin, and said, "One of our top recruits informed us that he no longer wants to make a campus visit."

"What reason did he give?" I asked.

"Well, it seems he didn't think that I called him often enough. Our assistants called every week, and I called every other week, but that was not enough to convince him that we were committed to him as a player."

He rubbed his eyes with the palms of his hands, fending off both fatigue and anxiety, and rested his elbows on his desk. "I don't like calling a player that often," Bennett said, disgruntled. "I'm not good at all that small talk. I'm just not very good at playing the game."

"What game is that?"

"The recruiting game."

Bennett had just suffered one of his toughest losses of the year, but no one other than the staff would know about it. College basketball really has two competitions, two games, the actual game on the floor and the recruiting game. An established truth of competition, all else being equal, is that talent will win out every time. Therefore, recruiting is the game within the game of college athletics that has no beginning and no end. The process is intense and the competition for the best high school and junior college players can be vicious at times. Losing the recruiting game can devastate a program. Coaches write letters daily to top recruits, a routine and meaningless ritual of college athletics. Phone calls can be made once a week, as regulated by the NCAA, except in limited and pre-scribed circumstances. Tales of overzealous coaches calling recruits on a daily basis, however, are as common as sand on a beach. Parents, high school coaches, and girlfriends of recruits get special attention, as well. There are many influences which might affect a recruit's decision, so no chances are taken and no stones left unturned. The bulk of the work (assessing talent, daily letters, phone calls, and networking) falls on the shoulders of the assistant coaches. The recruiting wars are the proving grounds for the assistants, and recruiting often makes or breaks careers. Still, it is the role of the head coach to close the deal, to get the recruit to sign the letter of intent. If he fails to do so, he not only fails himself, he also fails his assistants.

"It does hurt to be rejected like that," Bennett admitted. "When I learned it was because I personally hadn't called enough, my face went flush and I could feel the sting in my whole body.

"The sting I have felt hundreds of times in my twenty years of college coaching, but I'm certainly not going to buddy up and say all kinds of goofy things to them [recruits], the things that their brothers, sisters, friends or girlfriends say. I can't coddle a recruit, build him up into something he is not." Bennett's face was stern and he sat erect in his chair. "What happens when he shows up for the first practice with fifteen other guys?"

Bennett mimicked an imaginary recruit with turned-up palms and raised eyebrows. "Holy cow! Who the heck is this guy? Where is the guy who recruited me?"

"That is what he will say to himself, and that is not fair to him or to me."

The office fell silent. Bennett glanced out the window at the sparse white clouds drifting across the warm fall sky. Turning back to the conversation, he added, "I do not want the players to get the wrong idea of who I am and how I coach. That is not my style." He shook his head slowly from side to side. "I just don't know how to do it without compromising my own personal standards. I can't sacrifice integrity for talent."

"Whose integrity?" I inquired.

Bennett seemed taken back by the question. He sat back in his chair and stared directly at me with furrowed brow. "Both, I suppose, mine and the recruit's. I don't believe in recruiting as it is today, so if I buy into that style, I sacrifice my integrity. But, as your question suggests, there is more to it than that.

"There is a perception that exceptionally talented players lack personal integrity, and unfortunately, in some cases, that is true," Bennett continued. Footsteps and muffled voices outside the partially closed office door interrupted his speech. He shifted his eyes toward the direction of the noise while gathering his thoughts, then continued. "I believe in the synergy of the group, believe that the sum of the parts is greater than the individual talents of the members. Therefore, I have always tried to recruit players with great character, players who are selfless and committed to the team first. But great talent is an easy seduction. It is awful easy to look at a kid with that kind of talent and think that it really doesn't matter that he won't go to class, that he will lie, that he is lazy or selfish. That doesn't matter because I can teach him integrity. Yet, in reality, I know I can't. Not in the short amount of time I have to spend with him. Therefore, I want to hold character in the highest regard." Bennett smirked. "When that one particular requirement is met, I really get excited about talent."

I asked, "When you look at a potential recruit, what are you really looking for?"

"It probably is not as hard as I make it," explained Bennett. "It's not hard to see a really good player. A player who is a smart basketball player and also a really good athlete. That's easy. Plus, a really solid basketball player is typically solid off the court, valuing the same intangibles both on and off the basketball court—intangibles such as selflessness, intelligence, and intensity. So finding those players is an easy call. Unfortunately, there are not many players like that." Coach sat forward at his desk, his voice growing more convincing. "The question becomes, what type of player you want. Do you want a kid who is a great athlete but is not a solid player? Or do you want the kid who is not a great athlete but is a solid basketball player all the time? It really comes down to physical ability versus mental ability."

Bennett had built his reputation coaching teams full of slightly less talented players, but with a great mental toughness. However, he remained guarded about his optimism of whether or not that philosophy could succeed at Wisconsin. "You have to recognize that I have not won consistently at this level with the less athletic players. That is yet to be proven. I have only one doubt left with coaching at this level. How much can we move away from the intangible characteristics we talk about, toward talent, and still make it happen? That is the only hang-up I have. I have no more hang-ups about the way we play, but I have doubts about who we can be successful with. Only more success will remove those doubts."

"How do you work with players who are not considered your type of player, as you previously indicated were on the team, specifically those who lack passion and who are selfish?" I asked.

"I keep reminding myself that I do not want to turn them off. I want them to just keep plugging away. Hopefully, when they start to turn the corner, I can fan the flames a little. I will continue to stay patient with them as long as they do not place demands on me. If they act up or disturb the team, then I give up on them. If they do not cause trouble, I remain patient and try to keep in mind they have a different approach. Shawn [Hood] has taught me to accept players where they are, and move them forward from there."

To understand Dick Bennett's personal philosophies, all areas of his life—his work, his family, his friends—and considering his reputation as a religious man, his faith, had to be investigated. When questioned about his willingness to discuss those areas of his personal life, Bennett's response rolled off his tongue.

"I only have one life. I can't separate my personal life from basketball. If I can't bring my faith and family into the office, I feel fragmented."

Chapter 2

Begin with the End in Mind

The first day of fall classes marks more than the start of another academic year for college basketball players. It is the beginning of a long and grueling seven-month journey. Mandatory weight training, conditioning, and practices continue unabated through March, longer if the team reaches post-season play; a schedule and routine that is rarely interrupted for more than forty-eight hours at any point during the season. Nonetheless, the players greet the first day of practice with enthusiasm and optimism. Some players have put in a great deal of time working on their game and are anxious to show the coaches and their teammates how much they have improved. The new players simply want to prove to the coaches, and themselves, that they belong at this level. And finally there are the returning redshirt players who just can't wait to get back into the action.

Optimism fills the air in nearly every basketball arena in the country. New coaches bring a rejuvenated enthusiasm to programs that have been perennial losers. Championship teams dream of hanging another banner on the rafters. Last year's middle-of-the-pack also-rans vow that this year will be different. Injured players eagerly retake the floor hoping to regain their previous level of play. Head coaches, assistant coaches, and players get caught up in the dream of becoming the next legends. Regardless of the previous season's record, recruiting losses, or injuries, every coaching staff has the opportunity to lead their team to an undefeated season. Likewise, each player, regardless of ability or minutes played, has the opportunity to win a starting job. Theoretically, on that first day of practice, it is everyone's year. Everyone is undefeated and everyone starts!

The concourse around the basketball court and bleachers is wide at both ends of the Fieldhouse. The cavernous north concourse, separating the basketball court from the south end zone of the football stadium, was filled with the echoing sounds of dribbling basketballs. This concourse, separated in the middle by concrete pillars painted white below and red just above eye level, is illuminated primarily by numerous soda machines. Here, vintage photos and trophies commemorate the glory of Wisconsin's past NCAA championships in boxing and its rich wrestling tradition. The working apparatus of the building—cast iron plumbing pipes, aluminum electrical tubing, and gray sheet metal air ducts—forms an overhead maze that diminishes the significance of those historic accomplishments. At the opposite end of the Fieldhouse, vacant concession stands, blank scoreboards, and silent television sets await the arrival of a new season to spring back to life. In the preseason, they lie dead in the shadows of the dimly lighted corridor. Only the occasional student, using the corridor to pass through to avoid the extra two-hundred-yard walk around the building, invades this space. Bennett and assistant coach Shawn Hood walked side by side up the narrow ramp leading from the home team's locker room to the concourse. They turned sharply to their right at the top of the incline and Hood pushed aside the large red plastic curtain which veils the concourse from the basketball court.

Paul Grant, a seven-foot transfer from Boston College, was busy putting himself through a series of offensive moves under the north basket. He had added twelve pounds of body weight, dropped his body fat from twelve to ten percent, and added thirty pounds to his bench press in the weight room during his mandatory redshirt season. Though he carried a disproportionate amount of muscle on his upper torso, his 245-pound body was ready for the bruising Big Ten. Moments later, Booker Coleman, an exceptionally athletic 6'9" junior from Erie, Pennsylvania, casually strolled onto the floor, picked up a ball and headed to the south basket. Bennett glanced at his watch as Sean Daugherty, a silky-smooth 6'10" junior from Vincennes, Indiana, appeared from behind the curtain. Bennett and Hood walked onto the hardwood floor and gathered the group together on the large "W" at center court. Bennett spent several minutes giving the trio and Hood instructions on what he expected from the workout and then made his way to the sideline bleachers. Hood proceeded to take the three post players through a vigorous twenty-minute shooting workout.

This routine repeated itself every twenty minutes over the following hour and a half. Sophomore forwards and Wisconsin natives, 6'7" Sam Okey from Cassville and 6'1" Mike Kosolcharoen from Adams, were joined by 6'4" redshirt freshman Duany "Doc" Duany of Bloomington, Indiana. Assistant coach Brad Soderberg joined them on the floor. Bennett met the group at half-court for instructions and then returned to the bleachers. Twenty minutes later the guards took the floor. Ty Calderwood, a six-foot, street-smart junior college transfer, the only newly recruited player on the team, joined six-foot sophomore Hennssy Auriantal and 6'2" junior Sean Mason, still slowed by knee surgery, at half-court with Bennett and assistant Brian Hecker. Bennett again gave instructions and returned to the sideline to watch Hecker take the guards through an identical shooting workout. The practice session concluded with Hecker leading a group of four walk-ons, 6'6" Brian Vraney, 6'6" Matt Quest, 6'4" Adam Shafer, and 6'1" David Burkemper, through their paces. However, there was no meeting at half-court with Bennett and Quest was instructed to take a seat while the others worked out, as only three were allowed to be on the floor at one time.

Bennett walked slowly to the exit as he watched the last group get started. Shafer's eyes followed him as he departed. A high school standout in the Chicago area, Shafer had scored 1,811 points in four seasons at Downers Grove South High School and was a two-time consensus all-state selection in Illinois. He attended Villanova on a basketball scholarship for one year before moving back to the Midwest and transferring to the University of Wisconsin. His facial expressions made it clear that he realized how difficult it was going to be to start all over again, and, in addition, how humbling it was to be a walk-on in a major college basketball program.

Preseason practice in college basketball, until just recently, was a time for conditioning and weight training. For the 1995-96 season, however, the National Collegiate Athletic Association (NCAA) adopted a rule which allowed any coaching staff to work with players, in groups of no more than three, for two hours a week. In his first season at Wisconsin, Bennett led the majority of those workouts himself, ensuring that his philosophy and techniques were accurately taught to his new team. After a year of observation and Bennett's mentoring, however, the assistants stepped to the forefront in practice. Bennett distanced himself from the teaching activities and observed, contemplating the task of leading this

Chapter 3

End with the Beginning in Mind

Exhaust fumes poured out of the poorly-maintained diesel engines of the huge cranes as they moved steel. The engines raced, generating power, further poisoning the polluted sky, as the cranes stacked the newly molded I-beams. John Bennett's skin was darkened with the combination of the summer sun, swirling dust and dirt, and diesel fumes that filled the air. His shirt sleeves were damp and soiled from wiping the sweat from his brow. A loud air horn blew in the background, signifying the shift change. John froze for a moment, took a deep breath, and removed his hard hat as the air slowly escaped from his lungs. He set the protective headgear on a stack of pallets. He then carefully slid his hands out of his protective leather gloves and laid them gently across the battered headgear. Finally, without looking back, he walked toward the gate of the fence surrounding the periphery of the steel yard. He paused momentarily at the gate, looked briefly to the sky, and continued on.

The 1955 Ford Fairlane sedan crept out of the deep Ohio River valley and the smog of the steel mills winding its way up into the residential areas of Pittsburgh. A breeze blew through the open window and cooled John as he drove through the narrow hilly side streets of the Italian neighborhood of McKees Rocks. He passed the Sportsman Bar and Grill, where he held a second job as a part-time bartender for his good friend Tony Mussman, Dick Bennett's godfather, and continued home. A small group of boys played a game of pick-up basketball on the street. They had nailed several 1x8-inch wood planks together, attached a rusted hoop, and mounted it onto a light pole to serve as a basket. Concrete and asphalt provided the only open spaces for the youngsters to play among the steep hills and tightly packed row houses. Pulling slowly to the curb, brakes squeaking, John rolled down his window and called to one of the boys, "Dick, your mom will have supper ready in a few minutes. Head home and get cleaned up for dinner." His tone was firm but caring. The young boy took the tattered basketball in his hands, playfully tossed it at the makeshift hoop, and jogged home to join his father. There were no clues in Dick's actions, nor in those of his friends, to indicate that he would not be returning the following day to resume the ongoing competition. Their immigrant fathers handled such moments through stoic and brave facades, and in that tradition they veiled their emotions as best they could.

The morning sun cleared the hilltop and cast a warm light across the table as John and Rosalyn Bennett shared breakfast with their sons. Dick, then eleven years old, and Jack, five, listened intently as their parents planned the events of the day. After breakfast, the boys carried the remaining boxes of household goods out to their father to pack in the rented moving truck. The Bennetts stood hesitantly by the curb, visiting with family and friends who had gathered to send them off and wish them luck on their journey. With tears in her eyes, Rosalyn hugged and kissed her loved ones goodbye. John shook hands, saying little. Dick and Jack, brave in their departure, remained quiet and returned a handshake extended by one of the adults. Finally, there were no more goodbyes to be said. John positioned himself behind the wheel of the truck as Dick jumped into the passenger seat. He set a bag of fruit, three sandwiches, and a thermos of hot coffee on the seat between him and his father. Rosalyn took Jack by the hand and led him to the Fairlane, which was also packed full.

The boys looked back and waved goodbye to friends and family as the vehicles pulled away from the curb. Rosalyn looked into the rear-view mirror, bit her lip, and waved goodbye over her shoulder as their old house disappeared from view behind the rising blue clouds of tailpipe smoke. John, however, focused his eyes straight ahead. There was no looking back for such a proud and quiet man. He would miss the closeness of his family and friends, but he knew that Pittsburgh would limit his sons' opportunity for a better life. A life which could be had only if he had the courage to seek it elsewhere, regardless of the personal sacrifice.

Lansing, Illinois, was the first stop for the Bennetts. John got a job building railroad cars for the Press Steel Company and Rosalyn enrolled Dick and Jack in St. Anne's Elementary School. Having been raised in strict Catholic families, the Bennetts were committed to parochial educations for their children. Alas, within six short months John realized that although the location had changed, and the job had changed, he was still mired in a dead-end blue-collar job.

John's boyhood and lifelong friend, Phil Lareno, was living in Clintonville, Wisconsin at the time, working for the Four Wheel Drive Company. Phil landed a job for John, working in the shipping department and, for the second time in six months, the Bennetts were uprooted. Snow covered the ground and the lakes were frozen when the Bennetts drove toward the small town of 5,400 people in northeastern Wisconsin. Without a place to live, John accepted Phil Lareno's offer to stay at his cabin on Clover Leaf Lake, a few miles west of Clintonville. The stark late winter landscape provided little reassurance that this move would be any different from the last. Nonetheless, a young Dick Bennett tried to make new friends at St. Rose's Elementary, his third school in less than a year.

The sense of identity he had among his family and friends back in the Pittsburgh area had been lost with the movement of the family. He felt alone and despondent with each successive move. The sports programs of Clintonville, however, provided him an avenue to fill the void of lost relationships, come to terms with his new unfamiliar surroundings, and re-establish his own identity.

Three months later, winter had turned to spring. The lakes were deep blue, the grass bright green, and the trees were in full bloom. The Bennett family settled into a house of their own. Only then did John realize that the vision he held for his family was finally within his grasp. He worked hard at the Four Wheel Drive Company, advancing through the ranks of shipping foreman and general foreman, and was ultimately rewarded for his diligence and work ethic by being promoted to Director of Manufacturing. The successful growth of his career was mirrored by the successful growth of his family. John and Rosalyn added two sons, Bob and Tom, to the family while in Clintonville.

Dick Bennett's developing personality and values were heavily influenced by his family and his environment. He is, in large part, a product of his past. Therefore, his personal insights into his own history are revealing. In addition, it is interesting to note that there are many coaches who have a wealth of knowledge about the game of basketball, and who also work endless hours, whose basketball experience, in other words, is similar to Bennett's. Yet, their intellect and efforts do not, in and of themselves, guarantee professional success. This suggests that there are other important, albeit perhaps elusive and intangible, characteristics that might be present.

The conscious and subconscious mind (psychology), and the pursuit of truth in existence (philosophy and spirituality), provide the foundational belief system that guides an individual's actions and behaviors. Examining the origin of Bennett's personality and belief system, then, illuminates a few of these intangible characteristics. The work of Erik Erickson, a highly respected 20th-century psychoanalyst who studied under Sigmund Freud, provides an interesting, and telling complement to Bennett's journey through life. Erickson developed a model which identified eight stages (infancy, early childhood, play age, school age, adolescent, young adult, adulthood, and mature age) of a person's psychological development (psyche). Erickson's theory is based on the belief that each stage of the "life cycle" develops either positive or negative personality traits. Optimally, when fostered by a healthy environment, a person successfully "matures" through these stages and attains "integrity."

The cornerstones of an individual's psyche, his/her personality, are the cumulative effect of the socialization process with families, friends, and life experiences. Presented in his own words, Bennett's life journey illuminates the richness of his progression toward, and regression away from, this often elusive characteristic.

The mid-September Wisconsin weather had grudgingly relinquished its grip on summer. The low gray sky inhibited the warming rays of the sun and the temperature struggled toward sixty degrees. True basketball enthusiasts eagerly welcomed the first cold fall day. The climate change suggested that the sounds of bouncing basketballs and squeaking sneakers emanating from the gym were soon to follow. There was a second seasonal change occurring in Dick Bennett's office. The warmth of his off-season personality had quickly, like the summer sun, retreated to the background. Bennett was ill at ease discussing his background. Living in the public eye was intrusive enough. The act of voluntarily recounting his personal history made him uncomfortable. Reluctantly, however, he began to open up as we talked.

Infancy, the first stage of development, cultivates either a deep rooted trust or mistrust of the world and those in it. This important first task of the budding personality develops as a direct result of the "quality" of the maternal relationship the infant has with his/her mother in the first year of life. Quality being the consistent and appropriate treatment of the child and unconditional love. Trust, then, is the foundation that all other personality traits are built upon. (Erickson)

"Well, I was born [April 20] in Pittsburgh, Pennsylvania, in 1943. I had a good childhood, a good family. I was the oldest of the four sons, and my brother Jack was not born until I was six, so my early childhood was like that of an only child." Bennett's eyes suddenly opened widely. "My mother, Rosalyn, was a very intense, fiery Italian woman. She was very, very outgoing. She just had a way of making people feel good, that was her special gift. She was a very easy person to love."

Rosalyn Bennett was the sole parent to Dick during his first three years of life, a time in which her husband served in the Air Force during World War II. She did, however, have a great deal of help from both sets of grandparents and the large extended family living in the neighborhood. Bennett's words began to come more freely. "We had a very close extended family that lived throughout Pittsburgh. My grandparents immigrated to Pittsburgh from Italy and spoke very little English, and in those settings, everyone lived in neighborhoods." Bennett reclined in his chair, placed his hand to his chin and looked off into space. "One of my earliest memories was taking the trolleys every week into downtown Pittsburgh with my grandmother and aunt to the Roman Catholic cathedral. It was a trip we made for six years."

Bennett added with a hearty laugh as his thoughts returned to his "Mum." "She would have been a remarkable recruiter. She was high-strung to be sure, but she felt very passionately and she showed it. When she came to my games she was very vocal. They still laugh about her at Ripon. (They had all the parents sitting on the sideline of the football field during parents' day.) Well, I ran a kickoff back for a touchdown and she ran all the way with me. There was another time when I was in high school, a guy was criticizing me during a basketball game, so she went down and rapped him over the head with her purse. She was just that way." His smile broadened as he shook his head.

Bennett's enthusiastic description of his mother faltered only once when he explained, "The unfortunate thing was that Mum was not healthy for a long time. She was very asthmatic and later on she developed diabetes, which eventually robbed her of most of her health for her last ten years. She passed away six years ago [October 8, 1990] of heart failure brought on by the diabetes."

> *A person's autonomy, which is a person's self-sufficient will to become "an independent individual who can choose and guide his own future," develops in the **early childhood** stage of the life cycle. The role of the mother is still vital at this stage, however, the father takes on an integral role in the developmental process. Unlike the instinctual love an infant feels for the mother, the father becomes the first person whom the child loves on a spiritual, as opposed to physical basis. (Erickson)*
>
> *A father's love is contingent love, conditional upon the adoption of certain values, standards, and modes of conduct which are acceptable to him, the father. (Erickson)*

"It is amazing, almost eerie, how parallel our professional careers were," Bennett explained. "He started at the bottom of the Four Wheel Drive Company as a shipping clerk and stayed with the same company, working his way up, until he retired as the Director of Manufacturing. I was a small-town high school coach, who stayed in the state and worked my way up to this level. I think the seeds were sown early. He wasn't highly educated, he wasn't particularly bright, but he was hard-working and honest. He has impacted me more than I ever sensed at the time. I do not know how a son cannot be influenced heavily by his father, especially when you grow up in the environment I did with our extended family. We were taught values and respect for authority and I have never lost that. So to watch him as I did was extremely important to me."

The source of Bennett's own quiet and private nature revealed itself as he continued. "Dad was quiet, felt very deeply, but just didn't express himself an awful lot. There was never a more appropriate use of the saying that still waters run deep than my father."

Bennett became quiet and his eyes focused on his hands folded in his lap. "I did not prepare for Dad's death. For some reason I thought he would go on for many more years. He was healthy, he walked, he gardened, he wanted to play more golf, and even though he was 77, he looked very young. He had been out in the yard swinging the golf club, then went back into the house complaining of a headache, took a seat, and had a massive stroke. He died on March 24th of this year [1996]. It just came so suddenly!"

Bennett's voice wavered as his eyes moistened with emotion. "There was no closure and that bothers me to this day. I was so busy, I guess I took him for granted."

He sat silent for many seconds before clearing his voice and continuing. "There was so much more than just sadness when he died. I realized that I am the way I am largely because of his influences. All the stuff I had to do growing up came rushing back at me. He was a very demanding man. He pushed me hard and there was pressure, always! Most of the things I did growing up I did seeking his approval. My desire to please my father started after we moved away from Pittsburgh. I could feel the need to do well in sports for my dad, so it was important for me to be very good in sports. And I wanted to, I loved it, but I could sure tell when he was proud of me or when I had disappointed him. Very rarely would he say anything, but he just had a way of letting me know with his body language. He wasn't the kind to sit me down and tell me what I should have done or replay the game. Sometimes I wish he would have done that, but he was a quiet man and if I disappointed him, he would just get quieter. I find that is the way I react."

Bennett reflected on the source of his father's disapproval. "He always used to say, 'You know, it hurts me when you hurt.' So maybe the disappointment I detected in him was really his hurting for me. Now having been a father and having gone through that with my own children, I guess it was so, I understand that."

Bennett spoke of the quiet relationship between father and son. "Even though we had always been close, living near each other, we said very little to one another of an intimate nature. It was almost like I didn't want to know and he didn't want to tell me. I never wanted him to be uncomfortable around me and he didn't want me to be uncomfortable around him." Bennett's eyes again focused on his hands as he contemplated his father's unforeseen passing. "If I were not grounded in faith, I would have been blown away. That is ultimately what kept me going through it all." Silence again filled the room as Bennett took several deep breaths before returning to his family history.

*A healthy child, advancing through the **play age**, will develop initiative, or self-motivation. The **school age** stage, signified by the onset of formal education, fosters the acquisition of industry, which is the desire to learn and to produce. (Erickson)*

"The first years of my life were greatly influenced by my extended family and the neighborhood." Bennett's face finally softened. "We had a big group of friends who played football, baseball, and basketball all day in the street. There wasn't any place else to do it, so we converted the street to whatever we needed, a baseball diamond, a football field, and we even nailed a make-shift basketball hoop to a light post to play basketball.

"My father moved us to Wisconsin when I was twelve. He did it to get away from the limitations we faced. He worked in a steel yard, and I think he just wanted a better life for his family. So he just picked up me, my brother Jack, and my mother and moved away; in a time when you just didn't do that, leave your [extended] family. A big part of the move was his wanting his kids to have the opportunity to play sports, because he loved sports but never had the opportunity to play himself. He was the only boy, the middle child, of nine kids, went to a large inner-city school in Pittsburgh, and sports were just something the family did not do."

He diverted his eyes from mine and shook his head slowly back and forth. "I have much more admiration for him now than I did then, because I did not understand. I now realize he left that just so he could carve out a better life for his family."

Adolescence, the fifth stage of psychological growth, is where an individual distinguishes a personal identity through feedback of their academic, athletic, social, and personal endeavors. (Erickson)

The sense of identity Dick Bennett had among his family and friends back in Pittsburgh had been lost with the movement of the family. He felt alone and despondent with each successive move. The sports programs of Clintonville, however, provided him an avenue to fill the void of lost relationships and come to terms with his new unfamiliar surroundings, and to reestablish his own identity.

"Moving to Wisconsin allowed me to be involved in everything. I was involved in Pittsburgh as well, but it wasn't organized. I played football and baseball with the neighborhood kids, but once I got here [Clintonville] I participated in organized football, basketball, and baseball year 'round. I know that impacted everything I did in junior high, high school, and even college, where I played all three sports. As I think back on it, my father's willingness to pick up and move really opened the doors for me. He had a very permissive attitude when it came to sports. I could do anything I wanted as long as it was sports-related. Otherwise he was pretty strict on other social kinds of things. He was very interested in how well I did when we moved to Wisconsin."

Dick Bennett is without a doubt a product of his parents' collective personalities. His father's influence is apparent in his reserved nature and dedication to an ideal, while his mother's impact is evident in his fiery and competitive demeanor on a basketball court, as well as his interest in culture off the floor.

"Mum was very charismatic, played the piano, very gifted and talented. She was everything that dad wasn't. They were a very complementary and good combination. I used to think of them as fire and ice. Mum passed on her love of everything cultural to all of the boys. She instilled the love of culture—music, plays, and reading—in me. I don't do that much of it, other than reading, but when I do I truly enjoy it.

"Dad passed on the passion for 'doing the job' to us. He passed on this fierce desire to succeed. In those days it wasn't 'be the best you could be,' it was *be the best!* Sometimes it would get him in trouble because he would keep things inside of him and then he'd blow up, and I'm sort of the same way. Still, his passion was unlike any I had seen in other people and he had a pride that was unmistakable regarding his job and his family. He also taught us that everything we had, everything we did, had to be earned. He had his principles and expectations, and if you didn't measure up, he had a way of letting you know in that quiet, nonverbal way. However, his stance softened as time went on, and when my mother got sick, he became a very caring and nurturing person. Almost all of the hardness left him. In his eulogy, I said that instead of becoming a grumpy old man, he became a kinder, gentler old man. That had a major impact on me and I have moved in that direction. I am not as intense, I have become much more forgiving. He impacted me as much during that time in my life as he did in my early years."

Young adult, the stage for developing intimacy or the ability to establish complementary and committed relationships, which necessitate significant compromise and sacrifice for another. (Erickson)

The traits that his parents instilled, and the lessons learned, would be tested soon and often as Dick Bennett started his journey into adulthood. He graduated from Clintonville High School in 1961 and enrolled at Ripon College, a small liberal arts college in Ripon, Wisconsin, where he could continue to play all three sports. He played halfback on the football team, guard on the basketball team, and third base in baseball while at Ripon. As in high school, Bennett found it hard to prioritize school over athletics and struggled to maintain average grades in his first two years. In his junior and senior years, however, that finally changed as his academic success took on a new level of importance.

"I was a much better student in my last two years of college and graduated with a major in physical education and a minor in English," Bennett noted proudly as the conversation moved from his youth to adulthood. "I actually ended up teaching English in high school for nine years. It was a good escape from basketball. I still like to read good fiction, something that grabs you and pulls you in. I find it quiets me and I need that fictional adventure." His eyes focused attentively ahead, awaiting the next question.

"When did you get married?" I asked.

"Too soon!" he said with a start.

What a strange response from a man with a purported reputation as a strong family man. "Would you like to elaborate?" I questioned.

"My generation got married very early." he explained. "Anne [Donaldson], my high school sweetheart, and I got married the summer after my freshman year in college. I was only twenty and she was nineteen." He chuckled, "We didn't even live together the first year of our marriage. I lived on campus in the dorms and Anne lived at home with her parents. I didn't even plan on going back to Ripon for my second year of college because Anne had gotten a job at the Four Wheel Drive Company in Clintonville, so I planned on staying there and getting a job as well. Then my football coach, John Storzer, and my basketball coach, Kermit 'Doc' Weiske, convinced me it was in my best interest to return to Ripon."

In addition, a close friend of the Bennett family from Clintonville, Sam Holmes, stepped forward to assist the newlyweds. Sam had a successful insurance agency in Ripon, and used his community connections to help Anne get a permanent job as secretary at Ripon High School and to find the Bennetts affordable housing.

The tale of the youthful marriage took on the tone of a great romance novel as he reminisced. "In my junior year, Anne and our newborn daughter Kathi moved to Ripon after Anne got a job in the high school office.

It was really something. Here we were, married with a child, Anne working full time, I was carrying eighteen credits and working in the college dish room and admissions office. I also had another job off campus as the floor manager at the local theater and competed in three sports." The recounting of the story amused him and he concluded with a wry smile and the shake of his head, " I still can't believe Anne and I did that. It was crazy! I think it has helped us to appreciate everything since."

> *In **adulthood**, stage seven, further development includes the realization that one is not the center of the universe and, thus, become committed to the passing on of life's wisdom to ensuing generations. (Erickson)*

Upon graduation from Ripon in the spring of 1965, Bennett moved his family to West Bend, Wisconsin, where he accepted a job as physical education instructor, varsity tennis coach (though he had never played tennis), ninth-grade boys basketball coach, and assistant ninth-grade football coach. The Bennetts moved the following year to Mineral Point, Wisconsin, where Dick got his first taste of coaching varsity basketball. However, in addition to his basketball coaching duties, he was also head baseball coach, taught grades 7-12 physical education and health, assisted in football, and served as the school's athletic director. On May 25, 1967, Anne delivered the Bennett's second child, Amy, into the world. Six days later, the family moved to Marion, Wisconsin. Anne was obviously not thrilled with the timing. "It was very hectic and tough. I was trying to nurse, pack, and move all at the same time. It was not easy!" Nonetheless, as both her family and her husband's reputation as a coach grew, she knew more moves were inevitable.

The Bennetts stayed in Marion for two years and added a son, Tony, to the family. One month after Tony's birth, Dick once again moved his family to New London in pursuit of a better coaching job. After three seasons in New London, he accepted his final high school job at Eau Claire Memorial, where he spent four years as basketball coach. In eleven seasons as a high school coach, Bennett accumulated a 160-68 record from 1965-1976. In his last season at Eau Claire Memorial, his team won twenty-two of twenty-five games and finished second in the state tournament.

At thirty-three years of age, Bennett was a seasoned coach with a sterling record, and yet his father's teaching of *"be the best"* drove him to accept yet another challenge. He began his college coaching career in the fall of 1973 when he accepted a position at the University of Wisconsin-Stevens Point.

Bennett's first season at UW-Stevens Point was difficult. Not only did he feel the stigma of a high school coach moving into the college ranks, but he worked with an untalented and non-responsive team. The 9-17 season record was almost unbearable.

"That year was a nightmare," Bennett recalled with a chuckle. "I made very little money, $15,000, and we had nothing as a family. I didn't have my masters degree, so I had to be going to school year round; I took seven credits per semester. Twelve was a full load. I was Sports Information Director (SID) for the entire athletic department, and I was the head basketball coach. I kept wondering to myself, 'What am I doing!'"

Bennett found little support from some of his colleagues. Initially there was resentment. "At my very first meeting, a senior faculty member stood up and asked how the school could hire someone with my qualifications. The situation got so difficult that I didn't think I was going to make it." Indeed, he even talked with then-athletic director Paul Hartman about the possibility of resigning at the end of that inaugural season. Hartman, in turn, reassured him that he was the man for the job and even eased Bennett's workload the following academic year by taking away his SID responsibilities. Bennett also knew that his woes on the court would be improved significantly with the addition of his first recruiting class. The program improved to a 13-14 record the following season, the last losing record Bennett would suffer while at Stevens Point. Five years later, while compiling a 26-4 record, his Pointers team made their first appearance in the NAIA National Tournament. The starting back court on that team was Brad Soderberg, current UW top assistant under Bennett, and a talented 6'3" guard from Milwaukee, Terry Porter. Porter went on to a long and successful NBA career with the Portland Trailblazers and currently plays for the Minnesota Timberwolves. Porter remains a close friend with the Bennett family.

The following two seasons included return trips to the NAIA National Tournament before little-known UW-Green Bay enticed Bennett to try his hand at the Division I level. After a humbling 5-23 record in his first year, amidst much heckling from the sparse crowds at the Phoenix home games, Bennett resurrected the dilapidated program. Once again, the experience was very unpleasant.

"I was very unyielding in my style of play as well as my treatment of players in that first year. I was rather inflexible, which was a blessing because I stuck to my guns and eventually got what I needed, but it also made those first years miserable. I demanded players accept my defensive philosophy, the type of discipline I wanted offensively, and play with the type of team attitude I wanted. If the players didn't measure up, if they were selfish or wouldn't do things the way we wanted, I just eliminated them from the program. I lost some very good players by being so demanding, but I did it the only way I knew."

Bennett made it his top priority to find players that fit his style—intelligent, hard working, and selfless—to help him succeed in a difficult situation. He built his teams around mostly local Wisconsin players who were high on enthusiasm, desire, and work ethic, but often lacking in size and innate basketball ability. Nonetheless, he drilled them day after day, week after week, month after month, and year after year on the basics of his half-court containment defense, patient screening offense, and the concept of selfless team play. Though his teams were rarely the most talented on an individual level, he often succeeded in getting the whole of his team to be greater than the sum of the parts, or the parts of the opponents. In his last six seasons at UW-Green Bay, Bennett's teams combined for a 135-49 record, including the 13-14 rebuilding season of 1992-93. In that same period of time, his teams went to the NIT post-season tournament twice and the "Big Dance," the NCAA Tournament, three times. That level of success nearly defied logic and became the ultimate motivation for this book.

Bennett reminisced as the cool November wind blew outside his window at Camp Randall. "What I always wanted was to teach and coach in high school. Once I got into the college ranks, however, I realized I would really like the chance to coach at this level. So this became the place I yearned to be."

That yearning became a reality in the spring of 1995. Thirty-one years of preparation had finally landed him the head coaching job at the University of Wisconsin-Madison, the flagship institution of the state where he had spent his entire professional career. Bennett decided to take a different approach in his first season at Wisconsin than he had at Stevens Point or Green Bay.

"I took the lessons from Point and Green Bay and met the players here halfway. I gave a little. I played guys who had different ways of doing things. We took a lot of bad shots, I let them dribble more than I like, I let them bust out on breaks. I brought kind of a watered-down disciplinary approach. None of that was allowed where I was before and the result is that we got more out of the kids here. That made my first year here, professionally, much easier."

"Will you move back to being more demanding and disciplined?" I inquired.

"No. I am maintaining that position now because I think today's college game requires a bit more flexibility, and I understand that. Coaching my son Tony really began to loosen me up. I knew he was a kid who had paid his dues and he could do so many things that I had to let him do it. If I made him a clone of the other guards I had coached, he would never have been as good as he was."

Bennett's first season at Wisconsin, though deemed successful on the floor with the team winning seventeen games and making it to the second round of the NIT tournament, was filled with loss on a personal level. The team Bennett took over was not totally lacking in talent, but they were young and needed direction. Several of them were playing for their third coach in three years. The consensus among local sports media personnel was that the Badgers would struggle to win ten games in Bennett's first season. Color commentator and former UW basketball coach John Powless was even less optimistic, suggesting the Badgers might win only six games.

Bennett had built a reputation, indeed a career, on weaker foundations; however, he proceeded to go right to work with his new team and began to mold them in his image. The skeptics waited.

Tough half-court defense and a deliberate motion offense made up the bulk of the early practice sessions. Even though Bennett's reputation as a half-court basketball coach preceded him, he knew that convincing his new team to abandon the up-tempo basketball of former Badger head coaches Stu Jackson and Stan Van Gundy would be a delicate task. The players showed grit and determination as they slowly learned Bennett's deliberate style. The transition to "Bennett Ball" was going well by most accounts, even with the loss of 6'4" freshman guard Duany "Doc" Duany to a foot injury on November 25. The early season injury allowed him to redshirt, thereby giving him an additional year to develop the strength that he sorely lacked. On December 18, with a surprising 5-4 record, Darnell Hoskins, the team's point guard and only returning starter, left the team. He cited the lack of social opportunities for African-Americans in Madison as the motivating factor for his departure. Hoskins transferred to the University of Dayton where he went on to have a successful junior season in 1996-97. Bennett was disappointed with Hoskins' decision, but later learned that Hoskins had "other personal and compelling reasons for returning home" that he would not discuss.

Wisconsin responded to the abandonment by reeling off four victories. On January 3, an exhilarating comeback victory over heavily favored Michigan capped the win streak that pushed the Badgers' record to 9-4. Bennett's successful inaugural game in the conference was not without cost. Sophomore starting guard Sean Mason crumpled to the floor late in the second half. He had torn the anterior cruciate ligament in his left knee while driving to the basket. His season was over. Bennett found himself without his top two guards, and only seven scholarship players, as he faced the bulk of the Big Ten season.

His personnel problems, however, were not the only things weighing on his mind. His youngest brother Tom, only thirty-seven years of age, was slowly dying in Boston from the opportunistic diseases that accompany the later stages of full-blown AIDS. Tom was a physician who had dedicated his life to the treatment of Boston's poorest citizens. Tom was also gay. He had contracted the virus through unprotected sex. On December 11, while the team was in Providence for a game, Bennett rented a car and made the one-hour drive to Boston to visit Tom. It was an emotionally charged day as Bennett grappled with questions about Tom's sexuality, his impending death, his own religious beliefs on the subject, and the wonderful man he knew as his brother.

Bennett shifted in his seat as I questioned him about Tom's lifestyle and eventual death. Through squinted eyes, he explained his thoughts and feelings about his brother.

"I was disturbed by Tom's sexuality, but as I viewed Tom, he was very accomplished professionally and he was as wonderful a human being as you can be. He was generous, sensitive, and anyone who dealt with him loved him. I had trouble with his sexuality and I was trying to work through it, but when the AIDS illness took over, all those questions just faded away. I try not to judge anyone anymore. I am far less judgmental now than I have ever been, and my brother helped me through that. I would not be so presumptuous as to suggest anything about anybody's lifestyle. I may be uncomfortable, but that is me, I am not in a position to judge and I refuse to do so."

Bennett had shared those same sentiments with his team when he returned to them after visiting Tom in Boston. That experience, combined with a heartbreaking last-second loss to Providence College that evening, left Bennett emotionally drained and thoughts of Tom lingered long after Bennett returned to Madison.

The next month and a half saw the young Badgers struggle with a Jekyll and Hyde personality, as they worked their way through the Big Ten schedule. Poor performances on the road at Penn State, Indiana, and Northwestern all produced losses, while home games produced wins over eleventh-ranked Iowa, Michigan State, and Minnesota. While Dick Bennett was losing his battle against the Ohio State Buckeyes, 63-55, Tom Bennett lost a much more costly battle with AIDS when he died on January 31, 1996. Assistant Coach Brad Soderberg assumed head coaching duties as Bennett attended his brother's funeral in Boston. The Wisconsin players rallied around Soderberg and pulled out a last-second victory over Illinois, their first road win during the Big Ten season and their first in Champaign since 1981. Bennett returned to Madison hoping to put the despairing events of the past week behind him, but an embarrassing 33-point home-court loss to Purdue, 75-42, left him nearly catatonic in the post game press conference. He sat motionless with his shoulders sloped forward and his head hanging down. Brad Soderberg later commented, "I was genuinely concerned for his well-being as I saw him sitting there, but I knew there was nothing I could do." The emotional upheaval was taking its toll on Bennett, but as he later explained, basketball was his lifeline.

"I really needed basketball at that point, even as consuming and taxing as it was, or I think I would have sunk into a deep depression. I had the kids [players] to worry about and I needed to get them prepared for each game, which really was my salvation at the time. I think those closest to me understood that."

The Badgers played sub-.500 basketball for the remainder of the season, going 3-5 in their last eight games, but Sam Okey established himself as the Big Ten Freshman of the Year and sophomore guard Mosezell

Peterson developed into the team's marquee perimeter player. Wisconsin's 15-15 overall record, 8-10 in the Big Ten, earned them an invitation to the NIT post-season tournament.

A first-round victory over Manhattan at the Field House was overshadowed by a grotesque knee injury suffered by Mosezell Peterson. His totally dislocated right knee left both his teammates and the Field House crowd in stunned silence. The loss of Peterson left the guard core undermanned and the season closed out with a lethargic 62-77 loss to Illinois State in the second round. Little did Bennett know, the worst for him was yet to come. Less than one week later, on March 24, his father suffered a massive stroke and died soon after. That loss and the stressful events of the previous twelve months finally took their physical toll on the coach. When his energy level did not return to normal by May, Anne finally convinced Bennett to see a physician, and he was diagnosed with a bleeding ulcer. His decline in health was just one more loss in a year full of personal losses.

> *Passage into the final stage,* **mature adult,** *is not signified by old age, rather, by the characteristics of integrity. "Only he who in some way has taken care of things and people, and has adapted himself to the triumphs and disappointments of being, by necessity, the originator of others and the generator of things and ideas—only he may gradually grow the fruit of the seven stages. I know no better word for it than integrity." (Erickson)*

Bennett's first season (his self-proclaimed "cross to bear") influenced how he went into his second season at Wisconsin. Calmness washed over his face as he explained, "The loss was, and remains, the staggering element in my life. I was not big into a lot of relationships, so the loss of those closest to me has left me staggering to this day. I think every day of what I could have done better in my relationships with dad, mom, and Tom. The other losses have also affected me. The loss of Tony's professional career because of injuries, and my loss of physical activity with my two hip replacements, have added to the heartache. However, the sadness, the heartache, is the other side of the joy and the happiness. In order to experience one, you have to experience the other. There was an Emily Dickinson poem which I enjoyed even when I was young. I don't recall the name of it, but the idea was that 'to comprehend a nectar required a sorest need.' I do feel that heartache teaches you how to enjoy and appreciate those special moments. I would have to say I am happier now than I have ever been, but I am also sadder now than I have ever been. I can say that in all honesty."

Bennett pulled himself in toward his desk, sat up straight, and ended our meeting on an optimistic note. "That year has really made me appreciate what happened in high school, at Point, and at Green Bay. It just proves something I've always known, it is the process that counts, not the destination. I have thought a lot more about the special times in those other places."

He also thought about the special players on his first Wisconsin team; Mosezell Peterson, Sean Daugherty, Shawn Carlin, Sam Okey, Hennssy Auriantal, Sean Mason, Jeremy Hall, Osita Nwachukwu, Brian Vraney, Booker Coleman, Mike Kosolcharoen, David Burkemper, and redshirts Duany Duany and Paul Grant. Given little chance of success, and with ever-increasing adversity, the team became only the seventh team in Wisconsin's ninety-eight year basketball history to win at least seventeen games. Bennett rewarded the team by leaving it virtually intact, recruiting only one player, and awarding the returning walk-ons full scholarships.

I walked out of the basketball office into the cold November wind to find an Emily Dickinson poem I had never read.

> *Success is counted sweetest*
> *By those who ne'er succeed.*
> *To comprehend a Nectar*
> *Requires sorest need.*

> *Not one of all the purple host*
> *Who took the flag to-day*
> *Can tell the definition,*
> *So clear, of victory,*

> *As he, defeated, dying,*
> *On whose forbidden ear*
> *The distant strains of triumph*
> *Break agonize and clear.*

Chapter 4

Man Not Alone

It is not good for the man to be alone; I will make him a helper suitable for him.

Genesis 2:18

While I analyzed Bennett's background, it became obvious that his wife Anne has been a vital part of his life. They had both been integral parts of each other's lives for more than four decades, since meeting in the sixth grade when he, the new boy in town, flirted with her at the local skating rink. Though Bennett had joked that Anne would not be particularly pleased to visit with me, as she was a very private person, she was quite cordial and friendly when I visited her at their home. She politely greeted me at the door, helped me with my jacket, and led me into a tastefully decorated living area where we took our places in front of the lit fireplace. Pleasantries were exchanged before we moved on to the "business" of my visit, discussing her influence on, and her participation in, her husband's basketball success.

"How important have you been in your husband's coaching success?" I began.

She raised her eyebrows at the directness of the question. She pondered her answer for several seconds before answering modestly, "I would hope I have been important. He [Dick] knows that I have always supported him in everything he does. I suppose I have been a balancing force, keeping things in perspective." She then turned her attention to her role with the family. "I really wanted to stay at home because of his commitment to coaching. He needed that to concentrate on his job. He knew he didn't have to worry about anything at home. I wanted to be a stable force at home for our entire family."

Indeed, Bennett had informed me in our previous meeting about his family that he had spent an inordinate amount of time away from the family during the early part of his career.

He had said, "In my early years I was so busy forging a career that I didn't pay enough attention to my daughters and didn't help Anne enough. I was such a workaholic for the first years that I coached. I just didn't do anything but teach and coach. I didn't take any time off in the summer. I worked every camp, went to every clinic, and opened the gym as much as I could. It was pretty much my life early on. By the time Tony was born, though, a lot of that had begun to change."

Our discussion continued. I asked open-ended questions, to give Anne the opportunity to take her answers in any direction she wanted.

"Why do you think Dick has been so successful at his profession?" I asked.

"I think it is because of his passion for it. He loves the game and he likes to bring the team together to be its best. Sort of like an artist pulling a painting together. His passion for putting it together in just the right way is wonderful to watch in action." Her comments stirred her memory and she revealed with laughter, "What has amazed me over all the years is the amount of time he will spend each night putting a practice together. I would think after all these years it would be automatic." She then interrupted herself, displaying a thorough understanding of the intricacies of the game. "But it isn't . . . I understand that he has different teams, players, and injuries to contend with. The situation is always different, but boy, what a process!"

"What do you believe is the source of his passion?" I questioned.

"I think he got it from his father." Her answer confirmed Bennett's own account. "He and his dad had a wonderful relationship, but his dad was very hard on him. I remember when he played high school ball; if he did not play well, he did not even want to go home. It probably wasn't real healthy, but somehow some good came out of that. It instilled a desire in him to go for whatever he wanted and to never give up, no matter what the circumstance."

Keeping a balance in one's life is important for personal happiness, but difficult to do when striving to excel at one's profession. Curious as to how Anne perceived Dick's commitment to his career, I asked, "What does being a basketball coach mean to Dick Bennett?"

"Without a doubt being a coach is third on his list. The Lord is first, his family is second, and then it would be his job." Pausing to reflect for a moment, she qualified her answer, "At this level, winning is paramount, but to him coaching is so much more than that. I know he struggles with feeling that basketball (and winning) becomes too consuming. I know he wishes it were not like that. He sees the 'ugly' side of his profession and it bothers him. He is very competitive and he understands that side of the game, but it is just a bit too much of the 'world' sometimes. He will ask himself if this is what he should be doing with his life. Is it right for him to be in the profession? Is this what the Lord wants him to be doing?"

Anne and I spent the better part of two hours discussing basketball, success, leadership, faith, and her family. She has without a doubt played a mighty role in the personal and professional success of her husband. But Anne herself summarized their relationship best when she responded to my question, "Who is Dick Bennett to you?"

"He is my husband and my lover, he is the father of my children, and he is a wonderful human being."

My impression of Anne Bennett was that she, too, is a wonderful human being.

Chapter 5

My Curse is My Greatest Blessing

Fanatic. God squad. Jesus Freak. Bible Banger. All these labels connotate a certain belief system, mainly fundamental Christianity. Bennett may or may not be all of the above, depending on the perspective of the reader. I had heard some of those terms used to describe Bennett in the past. Still, I wondered if they were appropriate. The well-read Bible sitting on his desk, the inspirational scriptures posted around his office, and his casual references to Jesus Christ had caught my attention at earlier meetings. To judge him on such limited information, however, would have been ill-informed. I had not spent enough time with him in his private life to make that distinction by pure observation. Therefore, I decided to go right to the source and confer with him on the issue. Faith was obviously an aspect of his life that needed to be explored for a complete picture of him as a person and coach.

Three weeks into the preseason, Bennett sat in the bleachers as the assistant coaches took the players through another shooting workout. The team's Achilles heel had been inconsistent shooting during the 1995-96 season, so an inordinate amount of time had been set aside to improve this particular skill. The aroma of popcorn filled the Field House as concession attendants prepared for the following day's football game against Penn State. Bennett's eyes studied the rhythm of the players' shots. "Sam," he hollered, "legs, elbow, reach." Okey turned to Bennett, copied the motion without a ball, and Bennett nodded his head in approval.

Bennett was very calm as he sat in the bleachers during those workouts, only rarely commenting to a player or assistant. The majority of the time he sat at the far end of the court in quiet, relaxed observation. His demeanor resembled a meditative state. His eyes did not meet mine until

I was only a few steps away from him as he sat on the first row of bleachers under the south basket. He blinked his eyes rapidly and raised his eyebrows as I sat down next to him. When he sat back out of his "thinker's pose" I again noticed his Bible resting on the bleacher next to him. We shared greetings and idle chatter about the events of the day before I decided to initiate an impromptu dialogue about his spirituality.

"Coach," I asked, "I've heard through the grapevine that you are a religious man. Would you mind explaining your spirituality to me?"

He was not at all surprised by the question. "My grandmother was very spiritual and I think those trips to the Cathedral in Pittsburgh were my first experience with genuine spirituality," he explained. "My mother and father attended church and raised us to be God-fearing, so I developed the values and habits of my religion from my family. By that standard, I was always religious, but my faith wasn't always that strong. I believe I developed my real relationship with Christ after I started coaching, as several people during my early coaching years influenced me greatly in that area."

I waited for him to elaborate.

"One of them was a former player I had coached at New London High School, Mark Meshnick. He was also a volunteer assistant for me at Eau Claire Memorial. There was just such a gentle nature about him. That always impressed me and little by little we began to talk about what it was that gave him the peace he seemed to have. I think he was naturally that way, but he'd start speaking of the relationship he had with Christ, and as time went on we began to talk about different scriptures. That was my first real taste of spirituality, and I believe it was because of his gentle persuasion that I accepted it.

"I slip back because of the nature of my job," he continued. "I am thrust heavily into a world where you tend to close spiritual doors. I do some things out of intensity, a desire to win, and other pressures that make me look anything but Christian. So I end up slipping, wandering away, but there always seem to be people in my life who pull me back."

The guards replaced the forwards on the floor. Bennett took a few minutes to greet them under the north basket before he rejoined me in the stands. Upon Bennett's return, he offered insight into Calderwood's role on the team and his unorthodox shot. The team had not yet accepted Calderwood as a full member of the team, and that concerned Bennett. He defended Calderwood's addition to the team. "So many people judge an offensive player's ability by their shot, but that is such a small part of the game. He will give this team so much more than scoring. He was recruited to run this team, and that is what he can do, his shot is so unimportant."

Though I expected Bennett to resume his discussion on his faith, he did not. Bennett became quiet and watched Auriantal and Mason. I sought to entice him to elaborate on his scant reply. "Coach, the one word I continually hear when others describe you is humility. Is that tied to your faith?"

"I hope it is," he replied emphatically, "but I am not a humble person. I am a prideful person. I have excessive pride!

"I learned my pride from my father, always teaching me to believe in myself, compelling me to believe I could do what I set out to do. Sometimes I get carried away with that and it gets in the way of what I believe I am called to do as a Christian. Christ was very humble, so I have gone out of my way to develop at least a humble approach. That doesn't mean I'm humble. But like most behaviorists teach, if you conduct yourself in a certain way long enough, that characteristic will become yours. That is essentially what has happened, but I'm still way too prideful."

Calderwood shook his head in disgust as his shot clanked off the rim. "Use your legs Ty," Bennett encouraged.

"I've always said there is a great blessing in vulnerability, especially if that vulnerability is understood. I'm vulnerable because of my pride, and I know that. So I have to be vigilant almost all of my waking hours, because I know that if I let myself go, I would be more prideful than anybody. That is what I mean by the blessing of vulnerability, and pride is my vulnerability. For example, it is like the athlete who can't shoot the ball. He better know that. There is nothing worse than a kid who can't shoot the ball but thinks he can! And so, self-knowledge in this case, as with my pride, is invaluable. My pride wells up inside of me and I have to bite my tongue and walk away more times than I would care to admit."

Bennett continued to watch Calderwood struggle with his shot. "At any point in time in my coaching career you'll find people who have seen my prideful side. I'm sure they'd say, 'Boy is he an arrogant guy.' I'm sure I was that way a lot. However, the desire to conquer it, or be assisted in conquering it, has been in my heart from the beginning. I have worked at it, but I don't always win the battle."

"What are some examples of when you feel the most prideful?" I asked.

"When someone challenges me, whether it is a player, parent, the media, a fan, my wife, or even a friend. I also feel prideful when we lose a game or a player when recruiting. Remember the day we talked about the recruit that chose not to visit campus? The sting I felt was mostly about my pride." Bennett laughed. "That kind of runs the gamut, but I feel the sting of pride when any of that happens."

The three guards moved to the next phase of their shooting workout, penetrating jump shots. With the use of the dribble, Calderwood made baskets at an ever increasing frequency. Bennett paused to watch, then continued, "There are two incorrect ways that my pride manifests itself when I'm affected by it, particularly after a loss or criticism. Sometimes I react passionately and lash out, in which case, I almost always develop an incredible guilt over that action. Other times, I will just take everything inside and blame myself, and really suffer for that period of time following the rebuke or loss. At my best, I'm able to look at the situation and say I did my best, it wasn't good enough, so I have to learn from it and move on. That way, the third, is the way I have worked to develop over the years."

In self-reflection of his comments, he continued. "The people who pay most are my players. Sometimes I will get a little personal with a kid, I'll put the team down, I may be sarcastic, or even swear. I mean I'm almost out of control. Sometimes they need to hear what I have to say, but I don't know that my approach as a coach is always appropriate. I recognized early that this was not the right way to act, so if I explode like that, the next day is a horrible day. I'm just filled with guilt."

"How do you recover from that?" I inquired.

"I apologize. I say I'm sorry, forgive me, and so far they have forgiven me on every occasion."

Calderwood, Auriantal, and Mason walked to the water cooler, dripping with sweat, and glanced at Bennett as they walked by. Bennett did not return their glance as he stared at a spot on the floor in deep thought. "As I became more in tune with the Christian teachings, I realized there was no better lesson of humility than in the life of Christ. That is why the Christian principle of thankfulness is so vital. When I can remain thankful, for all that happens, I can retain a degree of humility in a most natural way. Then I say to myself, 'I needed to hear that criticism,' or 'we needed this kind of a game.' We're told throughout the Bible to be thankful, always. That is the way I want to do it, and I try to do it, but sometimes I don't.

"My fire is my strength and my weakness, it is my blessing and my curse. It is a constant battle, but now it's easier for me, most of the time, because it is so linked with my Christian beliefs."

Mason and Auriantal sat emotionless on the first row bleachers, recovering from their aggressive workout. Calderwood, meanwhile, playfully handled the ball between his legs and behind his back as he implored them to join him in the weight room. They slowly rose to their feet, tossed the paper cups into the large plastic trash can, and followed him out of the Field House.

"Why did you choose to coach basketball over football or baseball?"

"I thought basketball was the one sport played where the whole could almost always be greater than the sum of the individual parts." Leaning back in his chair, he relaxed and his speech became freer, the tension visibly passing out of his body. "I wasn't sure about that in baseball where you had to have pitching. I wasn't sure about that in football because aspects like size and speed are so important. In basketball, I'd seen five small guys come together and play big and I'd seen five slow guys outplay quick guys just by being smart. Overall, I had seen a lot more variables that could be used to offset disadvantages in basketball. I just gravitated toward basketball because I felt like I might be able to make more of a difference."

Basketball is a more complicated game than it first appears. There are a wide variety of offenses, ranging from highly structured patterns to loosely regulated free movement, also known as "motion offense" or "passing games." Offenses are not unlike automobiles. They all have the same primary function, transportation, yet manufacturers package vehicles in a variety of different ways to fit the tastes of the drivers. Coaches choose offenses that fit their personal tastes, though all of them have the same goal of scoring points. Likewise, defenses all have basically the same function, preventing the other team from scoring, yet approach that task from a variety of different strategic angles: full-court presses, full-court zones, half-court traps, half-court zones, pressure or sagging man-to-man, trapping or containment zones, etc. Different defenses require different sacrifices, sort of like choosing a car. Playing a full-court defense will open up fast-break opportunities for the opponent. Choosing a high-performance car will waive high gas mileage. A sagging half-court defense will give up fewer easy shots but will not create any turnovers. A luxury car will increase the driver's comfort, but the cost to operate it will be significantly higher than that of an economy car. All in all, a big step in any coach's career is to settle on an overall philosophy of how to coach, and then design offenses and defenses consistent with that philosophy.

Bennett glanced out the window again. The muscles of his face lifted his cheeks and brow nearly to a smile as he became aware of the beauty of the day. "When I first started coaching I didn't have a neat and tidy coaching philosophy." He used his right hand to count out the number of years, "one, two, three . . . seven. It took seven years. The first six years I did what I had learned to do in my high school and college playing days, as well as what I had picked up at clinics. I did a lot of different things with those teams—multiple defenses, patterned offenses, and set plays." He shook his head in disbelief and continued. "Even from the beginning, though, I had a high regard for team defense, taking care of the ball, and shot selection. Those three ideas have always stayed with me. However, I have been inclined to seek team defense through man-to-man procedures, and shot selection through motion offense almost entirely since then."

There have been only a few truly revolutionary changes in the game of basketball in the past half-century. Legendary coaches such as Adolph Rupp, Hank Iba, Phog Allen, Pete Newell, and John Wooden were some of the "giants" largely responsible for the schemes of today's modern basketball. Yes, the game of basketball is played differently today, but that has more to do with the athletes than the schemes. Bennett identified what he believed that difference to be.

"Coaches now provide more individual freedom for guys who can do more things. That is where I think the game has changed most dramatically. The game has begun to favor the more gifted athletes who can run the floor and jump. I think there has been a much greater emphasis, and rightfully so, in those areas, but the concepts of the game remain the same."

Many of today's most accomplished college coaches, Bob Knight, Dean Smith, and Rick Pitino, have adapted and advanced those same philosophies of their predecessors. In turn, they have spawned their own generation of disciples. Mentoring is a time-honored tradition among basketball coaches that eliminates the necessity of reinventing the wheel with each successive generation. But where does a new coach begin to develop a philosophy? Where does he or she find a mentor?

"I think mentoring is critical and getting off to a good start is extremely important," Bennet explained. "When we begin coaching we tend to relate almost everything to our former coaches, so having solid people that you look to early is vital. However, I think the problem with mentoring occurs when a young coach chooses only one person to learn everything from. I have told younger coaches that for years. 'Do not copy one coach.' With all the videos, books, and clinics now, we have access to so many teachers that it is foolish to emulate just one.

"I learned from guys like Hank Iba. He reminded me of the source. He had so much soundness in his approach." Iba, a tough and fiery coach, became a legend at Oklahoma State, winning several national championships. "There were also several other great theorists when I started out, but the guy who brought them all together, the man who could articulate the most practical approach, for me, was Knight. He just made sense of it all. He verbalized and demonstrated that like no one else has. As a young coach, I read and listened to Bob Knight every single chance I had. I used to hang on every word he spoke. Almost from the beginning, I found it remarkable for me to see a guy who thought and taught so much that I believed. Thankfully for me, he was the same age as I was, and in a position where people could learn from him. Still, there are other modern-day giants who advance theories also: John Wooden, Dean Smith, Pitino. Most everyone else is an offshoot.

"The rest of my philosophy really came from discussions with friends. I had a very dear friend named Don Colbert who coached high school ball for a long time. I coached against him when he was in Waupaca and I was at both Marion and New London. We used to talk about everything, even to the extent that when we played each other, we would compare scouting reports before the game." Bennett folded his hands behind his head, chuckling as he recalled those days. "He was such a solid coach, such a great sounding board. I bounced every idea off him."

Bennett's style of play is similar to Knight's, but upon closer analysis there are significant differences. Bennett emphasized the development of his team's defense to a greater degree than does Knight, and Bennett's offense, the blocker-mover passing game, has far fewer rules than Knight's patented IU passing game. Bennett modifies his offensive sets to take advantage of the individual talents and limitations of his players. In essence, he designs the offense around his players. Though Knight's offensive system does utilize various "sets" which capitalize on the strengths of individual players, the cuts, screens, and movements are much more regimented in his "system." Bennett explained the departure in offensive strategy. "I've listened to Coach Knight so much, read so much, that I knew I wasn't as bright as him," he attested, "So, I knew that for me to use the same style as he taught, it would have to be more simple. I couldn't teach all that he taught. I don't have the ability to teach all that. This is something I have known about myself since the start and I'm thankful I have been able to come face-to face with my limitations. I love what his teams do, but I had to find a simpler way to do it, even if it wasn't quite as efficient. That was my quest. Also, because I always seemed to be coaching from a disadvantage, smaller high schools, smaller colleges, and rebuilding programs, I had to find ways

Head Coach Dick Bennett

Opposite page, top-left:
Growing up in Pittsburgh.
Top-right: At Ripon College, 1965.
Bottom: A Bennett family portrait with
wife Anne, son Tony, and daughters
Kathi and Amy.

This page, above: UW coaches
Brian Hecker, Shawn Hood,
Dick Bennett, Brad Soderberg,
and Paul Costanzo before a
Badger game. *Right:* Coach Bennett
exhorts his team to victory.

Overleaf: Jubilant fans mob the
floor after UW's upset win over
Minnesota, March 8, 1997, earning
the Badgers a berth in the NCAA
post-season tournament.

Joe Jackson/The Capital Times

that our more limited players could use the system. That ultimately helped me as a coach. It turned my weakness into a strength as a teacher."

The general perception, though not completely accurate, is that, at Wisconsin, Bennett would have top-flight athletes and players to work with for the first time in his career. "How do you coach your current players here at Wisconsin, compared to how Knight coaches at Indiana?"

Bennett leaned forward in his chair and rubbed his chin, his eyes cast downward in thought. "I think the kids that play at Indiana can do more things, they're taught to do more things." He considered his answer further before continuing in a confident tone. "I teach our players to do fewer things. Maybe in the end they [IU] are better players, but I'm not sure about that. Regardless, the major difference is I take less time teaching offense than I do defense. I clearly found, for me to succeed at the levels I was at, we had to be way above average defensively and the only way to be above average was to spend an inordinate amount of time working on that. It is my opinion that Indiana spends a lot of time teaching offense. I couldn't teach all of what they do with the passing game in the amount of time I give to teaching offense." Bennett squinted his eyes and shook his head for effect. "For years I was critical of myself because I saw how well they executed, and they were also so good defensively. I just couldn't teach that. So, indeed, I needed to discover an easier way."

The current popular brand of basketball features up-tempo offenses, trapping and gambling defenses, and Bennett has expressed uncertainty about the perceived differences from his deliberate style of basketball. He fears he is a dinosaur in coaching. "The athletic influence on the game has caused me more self-doubts than anything. The Georgetowns and Kentuckys have forever changed the game at the top levels of college basketball. I'm almost in culture shock when I watch those games on TV. They play a game I am not familiar with, and I do worry about that. I don't know if I can compete with those types of teams with my style."

"Has it made it difficult to stay consistent with your philosophy?" I asked.

"I used to go back to my assistants a lot, especially in Green Bay, and ask them if I had missed the boat. Had the game really passed me by as much as it appeared to me? Mike Hideman and Steve Swan always buoyed me up and reinforced what we were doing. That helped me incredibly." Bennett shifted his focus to the current Badger team. "What tempts me to change more than anything is watching how hard it is for a lot of our players to learn our system, to accept the discipline, the demands." His voice turned assertive and he pounded his fist on the desk as he reminisced. "Our approach in Green Bay was very, very cerebral, we just outlasted people. We were so mentally tough and each player knew his role in what we were trying to do as a team. So many kids would sacrifice themselves offensively in order to be totally committed to screening. I expected to be able to teach them [the UW players] to be the same way."

The intensity of his voice waned as he refocused on the original question. "The thing that would never let me change is the fact that we were different, we were enjoying success, often from a disadvantaged position and against heavy odds. That has always convinced me that this is the way my teams have to play."

The University of Wisconsin had a different type of player than he had ever coached before. The UW players had more physical ability than those he had coached at UWGB and UW-Stevens Point, and with that ability came a different attitude. Most, if not all, of the top nine players on the team were not grateful simply to receive a Division I basketball scholarship. They had known since a relatively young age that they had the ability to play at that level. The recruiters noticed them as juniors, sophomores, and even freshmen in high school. For many of them, it was not enough to just be another member of the team; they wanted to be major contributors. Bennett was keenly aware that he was still unfamiliar with the mentalities of the young men he had not personally recruited. When unsure of the best method of handling a player, he took a more lenient approach than he would have previously. "That's part of it, you know, me moving toward them in my approach," Bennett noted.

Bennett's unspoken desire to win a national championship surfaced as he continued to speak. "I'm not going to beat [those at] Kentucky with the same kind of an athlete, only one who is just a little less of a player and athletically gifted, just not quite as good as theirs. That is a disaster waiting to happen. I couldn't recruit players like [those at] Kentucky while at Green Bay, obviously, and I can't do it here, either. If I can't recruit those types of players, then I have to find another way to compete against them. So the only way I am going to compete is to get an athlete who is different from that."

Translation: You don't challenge a world class thoroughbred and expect to win. You have better odds if you get a plow horse, train him well, and force the thoroughbred into a tree-pulling contest. However, as

Bennett pointed out, it is not necessarily easy to find the right plow horse. "The demand for me to get the kind of player I want is just as demanding as for North Carolina or Kentucky to get the top-caliber player. My way to beat the best is to find players who believe in what we are doing, who buy into it whole-heartedly. That is what Green Bay taught me that no other place could. Those kids were so tough mentally, so skilled, and so smart, they parleyed their lack of athleticism into a strength. The Gary Grzesks, Jeff Nordgaards, Tony Bennetts, Dean Vander Plases, and many others, taught me that we could compete with anybody." Bennett sat forward on his chair and pounded his fist on the desk again. " That is where I am hung up now. I don't have that here, yet. I'm stuck in between. I don't have Kentucky's athletes and I don't have Green Bay's smartness and intensity, so here I am, in between, trying to make the best of this."

"Are you getting closer?" I persisted.

"Nope, not yet." Realizing the harshness of his tone, he amended his statement. "It really is not fair to say no. It was our heart that allowed us to hang in there last year, but I still don't have those types of players. I don't think many of our kids right now understand what I think good basketball is. Either that or they don't agree with me. They'll pay lip service to it and go through the motions on the court, but there are very few who are willing to go to the wall with it. They still are not my kids." Bennett had been through similar situations before in his career and realized it was his responsibility to move the players toward his philosophy. "It doesn't do me any good to say I'm disappointed in their mental toughness. I just have to accept where they are and then move ahead. I have to do the best I can to make them my kids."

"How do you do that?" I asked.

"Through repetition. I'm going to take a very simple approach to offense and defense. Try to place an emphasis on execution and minimize the decisions they have to make, enabling them to make good ones. I'll emphasize taking care of the ball, taking good shots, hitting the glass hard, and being very sound as a team defensively. That is all I can do. I have no other recourse." The plan was grounded in a philosophy that had changed little in his twenty-one seasons as a college coach.

There are other aspects of Bennett's philosophy that are less well-known than his style of play, such as motivation. Bennett explained the importance he places on motivating his team. "I think motivation is the link that makes it all possible. There isn't anything more important. I think it may be more important than the teaching. It's what makes the X's beat the O's, not superior talent and certainly not superior strategy, but motivation."

"What is your favorite style of motivation?" I probed.

"I will choose any method to motivate. Everything I do is with a mind to motivate each player to try as hard as he can, to commit to the team, and to give himself up for the benefit of the team. That is what motivation is to me."

In his response on motivation, Bennett failed to note the lengths he will go to drive a point home. He failed to mention how he had cracked two ribs diving for a loose ball, even though he had two replaced hips, in his first season at Wisconsin, while speaking to the team about aggressiveness. Nor did he mention the time he had a manager approach him and slap him in the face while lecturing his UWGB team about the importance of poise during a physical game. A slap that was so hard it left a red hand print on his cheek. Bennett's "gimmick" techniques are not simply for the moment, however, they are carefully thought out and orchestrated to make a specific point. His other most prominent form of motivation, critical feedback, is more spontaneous. Bennett's face took on a remorseful look as he spoke of his sometimes harsh appraisal of players.

"For most of my coaching life I have been very hard on the young men that I have coached. The right kid can be ridden hard. The kid that is good and tough-minded. The kid who's a little oversensitive, though, will break down if you ride him too hard. Motivation certainly includes encouragement, it's not just pushing and criticism. Everybody needs encouragement. Everyone needs constructive criticism, too, but not everyone can handle confrontation. Most of the criticism of me, by my players, has been that at times I have crossed over and made them feel like they haven't measured up."

Bennett understood that critical and harsh appraisal of a player's inability to perform can ultimately be very detrimental to the player-coach relationship. Players understand that it is in their best interest to do as the coach desires. Yet, when players are faced with the combination of failure and criticism, they sometimes protect their egos by acting as if they do not care, when in reality they care a great deal. "That hurts them when I cross the line," he explained. "I am aware of that and quickly try to repair it, but some damage has been done nonetheless. That is why I have moved away from that style as of late and have been seeking to find alternatives that don't always require that constant push and confrontation."

Bennett sat back in his chair and relaxed with his hands folded in his lap. "I think I have clearly mellowed. I know I've mellowed."

A transformation that had been a continuing process.

Chapter 7

Prepare to Succeed by First Eliminating Failure

The team took the floor as a complete unit for the first time on October 15, 1996. Each member clad in a new set of red practice gear, all except Okey, who had his reversible jersey turned inside-out to white to match his dyed-blond hair. Bennett walked onto the playing surface a few minutes before one o'clock wearing a wrinkled gray T-shirt, mid-thigh-length red cotton coaching shorts, and an old pair of white leggings that showed below the shorts. The only way he could have looked more like a prototypical gym teacher/coach was if he had a silver whistle tied around his neck with a white shoelace, and a baseball cap that read "COACH" on the brim.

Brad Soderberg walked by, neatly attired in his professionally designed '90s-style sportswear, and joked affectionately under his breath, "Sometimes I think Coach tries to look corny on purpose." He laughed as he broke into a jog and joined the team that had gathered at the center circle. Bennett's presence was noticeably different than during the early fall. He was invigorated standing amongst his team. He was back in his element after a six-month layoff, and with a little luck he could throw himself full-force into his second season without having to deal with the continual personal tragedies of the previous season. Bennett's pose amid the towering players was stately and wise as all eyes focused on him. He infused the team and staff with a few inspirational thoughts before breaking the huddle and enthusiastically exclaiming, "It's a great day for basketball, boys!" With that, they jumped directly into their initial warm-up and stretching session.

The opening day of the season saw a typical Dick Bennett practice. It began with twenty minutes of individual shooting drills, reinforcing the work they had done in the preseason. A forty-five minute session of individual and team defensive fundamentals followed the shooting, and the benefit of retaining the bulk of the 1995-96 team was immediately evident. Bennett expended very little time explaining the purpose and execution of each drill. The players instinctively picked up where they had left off the prior season. Only the new players needed an inordinate amount of instruction. Ty Calderwood, a junior college transfer from Palm Beach Community College, struggled to execute the disciplined technique of defending a player with the ball, specifically keeping his hands held high as he moved toward the offensive player. Most junior college players will be playing for their third coach in four years when they step onto the court to compete in their junior seasons. Coaches inevitably have differences in the way they want moves performed, which takes time to learn as a player. That down-side of a junior college transfer was playing out as Ty struggled to learn the intricacies of yet another coach, losing valuable time in his development as a player in the program. Coaches prefer that their players clearly understand the system and are major contributors by their junior seasons. That was rarely the case with JC transfers, as they were again at the front end of a learning curve.

The defensive segment of practice concluded with one of Bennett's favorite drills, the three-on-three "get back" drill. It is a full-court, up-tempo activity that emphasizes a quick conversion from offense to aggressive half-court defense. Bennett stopped the exercise after several minutes to emphasize that the purpose of the exercise was to pull together all the fundamental defensive skills they had developed. He concluded his message by stating, "If you can do this drill well, fellas, then we can start feeling pretty good about our defense." Play resumed, but the quality of their execution did not improve. Indeed, their performance deteriorated with increasing fatigue. There was a great deal of fouling and easy uncontested shots. With each missed assignment, Bennett's feedback became more critical until he finally stopped the workout and harshly lectured from half-court.

"Fellas, I can tell you one thing for certain, I have never had a great defensive team that wasn't really good at this drill. I have also never had a poor defensive team that was great at this drill." Bennett paused and scanned the lethargic players. "Right now, you're not very good at this drill." The challenge inspired the players, and within five minutes their lethargy was replaced with exhaustion. Pleased with the effort, Bennett instructed them to get a drink and shoot free throws.

The players were partnered up, two at a basket, where they shot free throws continuously for fifteen uninterrupted minutes.

Bennett then divided the players into two teams, Red and White, for the offensive segment of practice. He and assistant Brad Soderberg led the White unit of Okey, Grant, Daugherty, Auriantal, Calderwood, and Mason to the north basket, while assistants Hood and Hecker escorted the remaining players, including a visibly disappointed Duany, to the south basket. Twenty minutes of a 5-on-0 screening and cutting drill was followed with a 5-on-5 half-court scrimmage session. Offense is rarely given equal time in a Bennett practice, and therefore he prefers teaching his offenses as a whole, with all five players involved at the same time in either the 5-on-0 or 5-on-5 setting. Breakdown drills, which isolate a single skill, are rarely used. Play during the scrimmage was energized but marred by the ineffective play that often accompanies most early practice sessions—poor passing, poor shooting, and blown defensive assignments. Bennett watched without comment, unimpressed and unconcerned by the poor quality of play. Another short meeting at center court and the players were dismissed for a shower and training table, a catered meal held after each practice in the Reinke Room of the Field House.

Day two. The staff discussed the status of one of their top recruits, Mark Vershaw, who had just returned home from his campus visit to Indiana University. As the staff reviewed their efforts to sign him, Administrative Assistant Paul Costanzo inquired whether it was worth the effort to get him back on campus on an unofficial visit to see a practice. Bennett responded, "My approach to practice would make us look poor compared to Knight. Knight is an encyclopedia, he is the consummate teacher, and I am not. I teach teams. I don't teach players. My strength is tying things together. I don't think a recruit would grasp my strengths in watching a practice, a coach maybe, but not a player. I think we would come off poorly by comparison to Indiana, if you want to know the truth."

Sitting in on a University of Wisconsin practice is very interesting at first, but the average person who visited would probably get bored after a few days. A casual observer would walk away thinking that the daily practice routine rarely changed. To do so, however, would be to misunderstand what a Bennett practice is all about. Each practice is unique, and there are significant subtle differences, even though the routine does not change much. Bennett was not admitting that his practices were not as effective as Knight's, just that they were different, less impressive to the casual observer.

"To be impressed by us, you need to follow us for a while. You'd have to watch us over an entire week because our practices are virtually the same, with only slight modifications. It is not complicated. We have to execute a number of things well, so at the end of practice I look at what we have not done particularly well that day and I will put a heavy dose of drills and emphasis on those areas in the next session. It is just that simple, and that is how I've always done things," Bennett explained.

Bennett also did not buy into the idea of moving quickly from one drill to another, giving the false impression that his team was fine-tuned and well-prepared. He preferred to execute a few drills for an extended period of time, simulating game conditions and game intensity. For example, a simple three-on-three rebounding drill might continue for ten to fifteen minutes, until the players are playing basketball, intensely, "within" the exercise.

"I am not so sure that short, quick-hitting drills serve a purpose because I think sometimes kids drill for drill's sake. They do not let the lesson sink in and relate it to the game as a whole. So when I see that, if they do not do it well, I am not going to move on. I am going to make them hammer away until they understand the importance of what they are working on. With all due respect to those short quick-hitting drills, I think there is a time when emphasis is more important, and my refusal to move on clearly tells them, 'Hey fellas, this is important and we are not stopping until you get it.' "

The uniqueness of Bennett's daily approach, then, is found in his preparation and execution of each practice plan. A closer look at the process reveals two very important and successful teaching techniques he employs: simplicity and thoroughness. Assistant Brad Soderberg stated it most precisely. "That is coach's greatest strength, aside from his humility—his commitment to simplicity in his approach to coaching."

The simplicity of his approach is seen mostly through his use of repetition. His primary goal as a teacher is to approach mastery of his system through the use of repetition. An example is the twelve to fifteen minutes he dedicates in the middle of practice to shoot free throws. The purpose of this is two-fold; to practice free throws, obviously, and to simulate the energy flow of a game. The opening five minutes of the second half in a closely contested college basketball game are considered to be the key to victory by most coaches. Listen to any televised college basketball game and the announcers invariably stress the importance of coming out of the locker room ready for the second half. Bennett understands this as well as anyone, and simply prepares his team to do so. He doesn't leave it to chance.

In reality, each practice of the early season simulated a game: a pre-practice talk, a team stretch, and shooting drills to simulate the warm-up. The intensity of practice elevates quickly as the defensive drills start. Play is fast, furious, and competitive for forty-five to sixty minutes, much like the first half of a game. The free throws follow the defensive work and slow the players down and cool them off, thus simulating halftime. Practice resumes by having the players go through team lay-ups for two or three minutes, getting loosened up for the second half of practice. Finally, the players go directly into a scrimmage situation following the lay-ups. This is the exact sequence of events that occur during a game. This is a simple, yet effective, method of preparing the team to play well in the critical opening minutes of the second half in games.

An observer at Wisconsin's practices would also notice that Bennett is silent most of the time. He typically stands on the sideline, very near his coaching position in games, and watches intently. When he does stop the action and step on the floor to instruct his players, his point emphasizes some critical aspect of his system. He rarely "over-coaches," giving the players more information than they can process. Only by watching him over time does one realize the consistency of his emphasis on specific details in his philosophy. During his 1995 coaches clinic he said, almost in passing, "Your players will do what you emphasize, not what you teach them." His comment, which ironically was stated rather quickly and without emphasis, was likely glossed over by many of those in attendance because of the simplicity of the idea. Nonetheless, that simple code is the primary driving force behind his personal coaching style for practices.

More subtle, but no less important, is the second teaching method employed in each practice session, thoroughness. Tony Bennett had mentioned that his father wrote daily in a journal. He noted that his dad used the journal as a method of contemplation, reflection, and prayer. At an early season meeting, Bennett produced the journal, demonstrating his reliance on his reflective writing as a coaching tool, and carefully reflected on the events of the previous day. He then shared the insights with his assistant coaches. The depth of his thought process, to know and understand his team, as demonstrated in his writings, was impressive. The staff discussed the validity of his observations and reached a consensus of thought. That consensus became the "emphasis" for practice on that day. Finally, Bennett constructs a practice plan for each day. The entire process is simple, yet thorough, and is repeated on a daily basis. That recurring attentiveness to the continual development of the team is what gives each practice its uniqueness.

Bennett was in a particularly good mood the morning of October 25. He could hardly wait for the assistant coaches to get settled in their chairs before he started reading to them from his journal. He said that he had spent the better part of the previous evening and that morning thinking about defeat, more specifically, preventing defeat. "I know playing not to lose gets a bad rap," he said, "but I think that is exactly how my teams have been so successful in the past. I also think we have to do that with this team, first, before anything else," Bennett enthusiastically explained to his attentive assistants. "I thought about it for a long time and I came up with six things that we must do 'not' to lose." He hesitated momentarily as he opened the journal sitting in front of him, a red 6x9-inch spiral notebook, tattered on the corners from use. "You let me know if you can think of any others. I couldn't." He then listed the following six things:

What to do to keep from losing:
1. Prevent turnovers.
2. Take good shots.
3. Don't give up uncontested shots to the opponent.
4. Make free throws.
5. Don't foul, thus giving up free throws and negating pressure.
6. Don't give second shots to the opponent, don't give offensive rebounds.

Bennett looked around the table at the assistants and tapped the pages of the journal while exclaiming, "Only after we take care of those six things can we concentrate on doing things to win. Do you all agree?"

His premise was contrary to a popular coaching perspective and sports cultural trend. "No Fear" sports attire and "in your face" machismo spewed out by many of today's celebrity athletes, not to mention coaches, promote being the aggressor at all times. "Go for the throat," "Killer instinct," "beat your opponent into submission" are the more accepted themes of generation X. Bennett's methodology, preparing not to fail, not to lose, takes a passive approach to competition by comparison. Passivity in competition virtually guaranteess defeat, right? Nonetheless, the assistants agreed with their head coach and left the implementation of "extreme sport" philosophies to others.

"What then?" Bennett continued. "After taking care of the things I have just mentioned, what do we do to win?"

The assistants produced several suggestions, but Bennett was more concerned with his own list. He again turned his attention to the journal and read from a second list. "Here's what I came up with: get open to score, get second shots, and force turnovers with ball pressure." He lifted his head and raised his eyebrows. "Are there others?"

Leaning back in his chair, his mood elevated by the revelation, he provided two humorous analogies to support his claims. "You guys know I try to ride my bike every morning. It is my goal to burn two hundred calories in twenty minutes and I make a game out of it. I have to burn ten calories a minute to be winning. Each morning I inevitably fall behind, but I know what it takes not to lose. I know that if I stay relatively close in the first fifteen minutes, do what it takes not to lose, that I can do what it takes to win in the last five minutes. And I haven't lost yet. The only way I can be relatively assured that I won't win, is if I don't pay attention to 'not losing' in the first part of my ride. By putting not losing as a priority, I always win. I always burn at least 201 calories in twenty minutes."

Bennett's second tale also centered around his morning exercise session. "While I was riding my bike this morning, I noticed a deer in the yard eating apples that had fallen off the trees. Only after it stood there for a long time making sure there was no danger around, would it finally eat, and then only for a little while. This went on the entire time I was riding. I realized he was spending about nine out of every ten minutes trying not to be killed." Between the chuckles of the assistants, he concluded, "We need to be more like that deer. We need to spend a disproportionate amount of time preventing being killed, preventing defeat."

The entire staff agreed that those nine points of emphasis, six not to lose and three to win, provided a solid foundation for what the 1996-97 team would be all about. When the Badgers met for practice later that afternoon, Bennett discussed these points of emphasis with his players.

Paul Costanzo handed out a graphic highlighting the same points. The ensuing practice, similar in routine to the prior day, had an entirely different atmosphere because of the new priority.

The process, taken as a whole, was simple and thorough. Boring? That would depend on the individual.

Identity?. . . Unity? . . . Team?

Bennett had yet to get a feel for his team three weeks into practice. He sat alone one evening contemplating the makeup of this team on a piece of paper. He wrote down the projected starters: Sean Mason, Hennssy Auriantal, Sean Daugherty, Paul Grant, and Sam Okey. Next to that group, he wrote down the names of the five recruits in that year's recruiting class, a group that Bennett had described as his type of players: Mike Kelley, Maurice Linton, Charlie Wills, Andy Kowske, and Mark Vershaw. Having done so, he sat back and compared the potential of each team.

He shared his thoughts on that particular exercise with his assistant coaches the following morning. "I was looking at this and I thought to myself, we should be a pretty good team this year." He looked up with raised eyebrows, giving the impression that he was a bit surprised by his own appraisal. "If we're excited about this group of guys, which we are," pointing to the list of recruits, "then we should really be excited about this year's team." Bennett again raised his eyebrows, furrowing his brow, and shook his head in disbelief at his conclusion. "If you would have told me last year at this time, that one year later, I could feel good about a team after only one year, I would have said I didn't think it was possible."

Bennett realized the 1996-97 Badger basketball team was a fairly talented group of players. "I like this team. We have quality and competition in each spot." Paul Grant, with his chiseled body, provided a presence in the middle, yet had the mobility to run the floor. Sean Daugherty, a silky-smooth shooter at 6'10", had demonstrated the ability to play inside or step out to the perimeter. Sean Mason, Hennssy Auriantal, and Ty Calderwood were all athletic and quick with the ability to provide solid perimeter play, though Calderwood and Auriantal were limited on offense. Duany Duany and Mike Kosolcharoen would provide solid play from the bench, Duany for offensive scoring and Kosolcharoen for defense. At the heart of this group was Sam Okey, an exceptionally gifted athlete who could, at times, dominate a basketball game on either end of the floor.

The team had size, depth, bulk, speed, adequate scoring ability, quick perimeter defense, and strong post defense. The team appeared to have no weaknesses on paper. The unanswered question for Bennett and his staff, however, was whether or not the group could play as a team, whether the whole could be greater than the sum of the parts. Bennett knew that individual talent and potential were meaningless unless the group could play as a unit, as a team.

The apparent abundance of talent had Bennett questioning something else—his ability to lead them. "For the first time in my career I can say that we have enough talent. I'm used to working as a real underdog, and we still may be an underdog, but there is sufficient talent on this team to do about anything we want." Clarifying his primary concern, he added, "The question is, what do we want to do? That is the dilemma that has reared its head quickly. It sort of caught me by surprise because last year we were just hanging on. There is a real legitimate chance to be good. So what do we do?" Shawn Hood spoke first, "You'll have to bring them as close to the way you want to play as you possibly can. It's going to take incredible energy." There was a smattering of other comments, but the staff agreed that building the group into a cohesive unit on the floor would be paramount to any success. But how? That question was still unanswered.

Bennett's tone of voice and expressions during the dialog confirmed that he was genuinely perplexed by this team. The pieces seemed to have fallen in place. Yet, as individually talented as this group appeared to be, they had rarely shown the ability to "jell" as a cohesive unit. Without cohesiveness, there was no reason for him to feel optimistic about their chances. Most of his twenty-two years as a college coach had been spent working with players that were lacking in size and athletic ability. His UW-Stevens Point and UW-Green Bay teams made up for their physical limitations by developing a great knowledge of the game and in their team play. The 1996-97 Badgers, however, appeared to be just the opposite of that. Bennett's pensive demeanor that morning suggsted that he had reservations about coaching such a team. "I am convinced more than I ever have been that success in this game is mental, much more so than physical." The team's performance under gamelike conditions did little to ease his mind.

The team held an intra-squad scrimmage on Sunday, October 27, to help promote the season and get the feel of competition in front of a crowd. The event was open to the public without charge and the stands were full of young families with their children, hardcore Badger basketball fans, and plenty of students. The festive environment allowed the players to loosen up and have a little fun. After a very short practice to get warmed up, the players conducted a three-point shooting contest, a slam-dunk exhibition, and then scrimmaged for twenty minutes. The teams were evenly matched for the scrimmage and the action was intense. Both teams shot the ball exceptionally well and even got out on a few fast breaks for crowd-pleasing dunks. The red team, led by Okey, pulled ahead late and won by three points. Bennett enjoyed the action as he watched from the scoring table, and even the excessive number of turnovers and loose play did not dampen his enthusiasm. The evening's finale, an autograph signing session, sent the fans, young and old, out of the Field House entertained and excited about the upcoming season.

On the morning following the scrimmage, however, Bennett's perspective changed from that of a fan to a concerned coach. "I saw very little of what we have been working on in the first two weeks of practice. There was very little discipline by either team." He identified what he believed the problem to be.

"It is a paradoxical statement, but it takes incredible personal discipline to play with great freedom. We don't have that with our team right now and we must develop that. These kids know everything we have taught them. It is a matter of getting them to do it. I don't think drilling is as important to this team as playing is. I believe we need to get them into more whole [scrimmage] situations where they have to execute, be disciplined."

Bennett used the opportunity to teach his young staff a vital lesson, because up until that point, his extensive experience and thorough knowledge of his own system made the solution evident to him alone. "These kids can be very impressive when they drill, but they break down when they have to go from a drill to a game situation. You just can't teach discipline in drills, you can't teach decisions, and that is the point." Basketball theory is useless unless it can be translated into action on the court, so Bennett turned to his most successful UWGB team to make his point. "When I had Tony, Martinez, and Nordgaard, I had to drill. They were so sharp on the floor they could cover up for so many mistakes. I had to put them into drill situations to improve them." Brian Hecker flipped through his legal pad, which he carried to every meeting, and began to write as Bennett clarified his point. "I think that the smarter you are as a team, the better feel you have for the game, the more you can improve through drills. If you are weak in those areas, as this team is, I believe you have to play and execute in that situation." The "smart" that Bennett referred to was basketball savvy, instinct, which only develops through playing the game. His style of team defense and motion offense takes exceptional awareness and basketball intelligence by the players to be effective. Therefore, to achieve that end, this team would have to play as much as possible.

A new direction in the development of the team had been established. So, while the group discussed that day's practice, Bennett instructed, "The line of teaching we have to follow with this team is to go quickly through the drills, to reinforce the techniques we want, and then to move directly into the scrimmage situation, doing away with a lot of the special situations or breakdown drills. That is the only way I can do it. Running drills gets them to play hard and teaches them some techniques, but to get them to play right, they've got to play. That gives me the opportunity to start coaching hard." The assistants did not disagree with him and so the decision was made, and a practice plan prepared, to spend less time on individual breakdown drills and more on team activities.

The importance of that decision cannot be understated. It went to the core of the Bennett coaching style. The team was having difficulty taking care of the ball, scoring on the low post, getting open off screens, and maintaining spacing on the floor. Rather than do breakdown drills that emphasized those techniques, however, he looked more deeply into the problem to find the cause. The players had difficulty transferring the skills they had developed in drills over into scrimmages because they lacked a feel for the game, and a feel for each other. Both the instinct and cohesion would have to be developed as an entire unit. The instinct would develop through repetition. Building team chemistry, however, would not be as easy to develop because of the temperamental psyches of several key players. Nonetheless, something else more personal played on Bennett's mind. He had mostly operated from the position of an underdog, and he was comfortable in that role. A new and different challenge awaited him for the 1996-97 season, though, winning with talent. In a matter of a few months the other Big Ten coaches would know what he already knew. Wisconsin had talent. Bennett began increasing his own internal pressure of developing the team into a legitimate conference contender.

With that in mind, he set out to continue the construction of his team. A week passed and Bennett's strategy had not improved the team. Indeed, by the November 7 practice, their worst of the young season, a foul disposition had settled over the team. The mood went from bad to worse when the scrimmage began. The white team played without purpose or intensity. Even when Bennett inserted Calderwood into the point guard position, play did not improve. Bennett changed his strategy and started to verbally push the team, challenging their effort and intelligence. His criticism did not alter their play positively. Instead, several of the players sulked and mumbled under their breath when they were singled out.

Play deteriorated to the point where turnovers were committed on virtually every possession and bickering between players pushed Bennett to the boiling point. He yelled at the white team to get on the end line for timed sprints. When Daugherty slipped and fell, thus failing to finish in the preallotted amount of time, he made all of them run again. When they finished, though exhausted from the back-to-back sprints, they jumped right back into the scrimmage and dominated the red team for the next two possessions.

Bennett stopped the action, walked into the middle of the players and shook his head. "You guys are prima donnas. You come out here and don't play hard. Then when I get on you, you sulk and mope around. That is simply not good enough! What have you done as a team?" Disgusted with the whole situation, he shook his head again and walked back to the sideline, where he remained silent for the remainder of practice. Bennett called an end to practice soon after his outburst, and after a short meeting at half-court, the players quickly left the floor somber and emotionless. The mood of the coaching staff matched that of the team, which carried over into the next morning's meeting.

Bennett, more optimistic than he was the previous night, pulled out his journal and read. "After yesterday's poor practice, I must learn what I can, to teach what I must. The breakdown was total—no intensity, no team play, no intelligence, no execution. It is a matter of personnel. There are still too many guys who are 'me-first' players. Of the seven players on the white team, there is only one who understands and tries to do what is best for our team every single time, and he is the only new player to the program [Ty Calderwood]. This is what I feared all spring, summer, and fall. At this point we do not have a common dream!"

Bennett flipped the journal closed, raised his eyebrows, and looked silently at each assistant. He then continued, "Some of them are just lousy competitors; they have been spoiled for so long. You always have one or two players like that on a team, but this is my first experience where the nucleus of the team is like that." His frustration broke through his calm demeanor as he became more critical in his assessment. "They are overrated, oversold on their own abilities. I feel like if I come down hard on them they will sulk all that much more. This team has really hamstrung me more than any team I've ever been around. The dynamics of basketball are so interwoven. It is what I have always loved about this sport, but it is why I am so frustrated with this team. Individually they are great kids, but as a group they are the worst I have ever coached. We're talking about a team where the problems of the individuals become the problems of the group. What has not happened, and it concerns me, is that the kids with good attitudes have not stepped up and taken control."

He searched for answers. "I see my colleagues who have gone through this and they handle it by being real positive. I'm torn, I really don't know how to handle it. I still believe we do not have kids that are one hundred percent committed to the team. At least half of our top nine players are more interested in themselves than they are the team. You know what, it probably doesn't matter. When things are going well for those players, then I will play them. When things are going bad, I have to get them out of the game." Bennett explained the rationale of his statement to his assistants. "Players who are committed to the team first will find a way to help when things are going bad, they will do whatever it takes. Kids that are more into themselves will not do that. They will take care of themselves and get more individual when things are tough."

Twenty minutes of discussion produced no new plan of attack for Bennett and his staff. Nonetheless, he had "learned what he must" about the team. The true weakness of his current team, its vulnerability, was the apparent refusal of the individual members to sacrifice their personal egos for the team. In any program this is a problem, but in Dick Bennett's system, this could be catastrophic. For the first time in his life, he had a roster full of individually talented players. What he did not have, however, were the makings of a team whose collective potential was greater than the individual players' talents. The 1995-96 season had been the most difficult for Coach Bennett as a person. Unfortunately, there were early indications that the 1996-97 season would be the most difficult for him as a coach.

Chapter 8

Lessons from Behind the Scenes of a Coaches Clinic

Computers have made certain aspects of coaching easier. Administrative tasks such as mass mailings and data processing have all been greatly enhanced and streamlined. One area that advanced technology has struggled to improve, however, is the ability to enhance the actual instruction, the transferal of thoughts and concepts from one coach to another or from coach to player. Presentation tools are significantly less important than the knowledge of the teacher and the readiness of the student to assimilate the lesson in the learning process. All the bells and whistles can not make up for poor coaching, nor will they necessarily enhance good coaching.

Paul Costanzo, the administrative assistant, had been approached by the owners of a new computer software program. The company offered the UW staff free use of the software to develop computer graphics for their coaches clinic, thus promoting the product. Costanzo presented the idea to the staff, and though Bennett was not sold on the concept, he gave them approval to proceed with the project. Bennett concluded, "Just make sure I have my overhead projector there as well."

Costanzo, with several of the managers, worked hand-in-hand with Bennett and spent considerable time over the next few days programing the software to coincide with his presentation. That weekend, Bennett took his position in front of the five hundred coaches who had squeezed into the Grand Ballroom of the Concourse Hotel in downtown Madison. A large screen had been erected at the head of the room. A liquid crystal projector, connected to Costanzo's laptop computer, sat twenty-five feet in front of it. An old overhead projector, scratched and dented from years of use, stood silently in the shadows of the speakers' stage.

Bennett began his presentation by reviewing the six principles that he had developed for his team to "eliminate failure:" preventing turnovers, taking good shots, not giving up uncontested shots, making free throws, not fouling which negated their pressure, and not giving up offensive rebounds. The coaches around the room pulled out the handout that had been provided for them in their registration packet and followed along.

' The discussion then turned to practice drills, and Bennett was ready to use the new computer-generated graphics for a visual reference. Bennett quipped, "This is way beyond where I have ever been in my life-time," as the crowd joined him in laughter. He stepped back from the screen to get a better perspective and said, "OK, Paul, let's see what you've got." His curious eyes alternated between Paul and the large blank screen, waiting for something to happen. When snickering began to come from the convention hall, he could wait no longer. "Paul, I don't trust your machine." He hastily grabbed the overhead projector and pulled it in front of the screen. The snickers turned to laughter. The comedy continued when Bennett turned on the overhead projector and began to diagram with his pen. Paul finally got the liquid crystal display to work, which projected the graphics onto the screen, all unbeknownst to Bennett who continued to use the same screen for his overhead projector. The simultaneous display continued for another thirty seconds before Paul finally alerted Bennett to the situation.

Bennett had become visibly irritated by that point. He composed him-self and extinguished the lamp on the overhead projector. "OK, Paul, we're going to use your machine now." Five circular objects symboliz-ing players moved around a hypothetical basketball floor. Bennett looked at the screen for several seconds, then turned to the crowd and broke down in laughter. "We're paying five thousand dollars for this. (The actual cost was two hundred dollars.) Some guy is sitting in some office justifying his existence for the next thirty years because he invented a little computer game that coaches are going to go nuts on!" The entire crowd roared with laughter.

Paul, being a computer programmer himself, was eager to use the new graphics and Bennett sensed he had stepped on Paul's toes. He tried in earnest to use the graphics for the remainder of the presentation and the lecture continued uninterrupted for ten minutes, although Bennett became agitated once again by the lack of coordination between his address and the graphics. He attempted to describe the cutting action of the Triangle offense, which the team had been practicing, but the action on the screen was not coinciding with his explanation. He turned to Paul after a few seconds of trying to get it straightened out and exclaimed, "Now you've got even me confused." Laughter again filled the ballroom as Bennett reached out for his trusty overhead projector. There were no more computer graphics on that day.

The events of that morning prefaced comments he was to make to the assembly of coaches at that afternoon's practice. He noted, "I think we must spend a great deal of practice time committed to execution of the fundamentals, the cuts, the screens, the passes, and the shot. I do not believe you are going to win games on cleverness. Concentrate on the execution, not the cleverness." The computerized chalkboard was ingenious, but it was not necessary. Bennett's aversion to the new technology was simple. He just didn't see the need for it. The use of computer graphics was not necessary for him to get his points across to his peers or his players. His method of communicating his thoughts were simple and based on interaction. It was all about coaching.

NCAA regulations governing the recruitment of student-athletes have changed radically over the past half century and recruiting has become an industry in and of itself with professional scouting services, clinics, camps, and all-star tournaments. The computer era has made the whole process significantly more sophisticated. Still, the actual techniques employed by coaching staffs have changed very little. The basic premise stays the same: identify talented potential recruits, contact each individual recruit and start a dialogue in an attempt to entice him to visit campus, and, finally, get him to commit to the school and eventually sign a letter of intent. (A letter of intent is actually a contractual agreement for a scholarship which binds that student to the school.) The campus visit is the best opportunity to impress the recruit with the beauty of the campus, the athletic facilities, and the academic programs. The campus visit is not unlike a first date, because if it goes poorly, there is little chance of seeing the recruit again. Through it all, however, the most nerve-racking time for a coach is waiting for the recruit's final decision on which school he will attend. This is especially true for the most highly talented and sought-after recruits.

Many young men (and women) grow up dreaming of playing for their favorite Division I team. Most of the young players growing up in the state of Wisconsin, outside of the Milwaukee area, dream of playing for the Badgers and are ready to sign their letter of intent on the first official contact. Bennett is fond of this type of athlete, one who is hungry to play for the program. He knows that this will usually mean that the young man will work hard to improve, will buy into his philosophy, and will readily accept his role on the team. The second recruiting class was filled with players who fit that description. Those players had verbally committed to the Badgers in their junior years of high school and simply had to wait for the November 15 signing date of their senior season to make it official. Then there are the blue chippers, the elite high school players who are given superstar treatment by many big-time programs. The academic success of a university, the success of the basketball program and its facilities, as well as the coaches' reputations, all become a blur. Head coaches experience excessive anxiety as they are often forced to wait until the last minute in such cases, hoping that they have won the recruiting war.

That was the dilemma facing Wisconsin. One scholarship remained, and as previously mentioned, that was earmarked for Mark Vershaw, a highly skilled 6'9" blue-chip forward from Peoria, Illinois. Vershaw had narrowed his choices down to Wisconsin, Illinois, and Indiana. Mark had visited Madison in late September, and by all accounts it was a successful visit. However, the Wisconsin visit was only the first in a series of four campus visits. Five is the maximum number of paid visits a recruit is allowed under NCAA rules. Vershaw, over the following month, made trips to Notre Dame, Illinois, and finally Indiana on the weekend of October 26 and 27. On the following Monday, Bennett was anxious to get an update from Shawn Hood, the assistant primarily responsible for recruiting Mark.

Bennett walked into the meeting room, which also happened to be Costanzo's office, later than normal. The assistants, except for Costanzo, who was on the phone, were in place and waiting for him. Bennett looked directly at Hood without a greeting. "Well?" Shawn laughed in his casual way and responded, "Relax coach, the news is as good as it can be." He raised his right hand to stop Shawn while glancing at Paul, indicating that he wanted to wait until they were all together. Bennett jokingly let out an exasperated sigh and covered his face with his hands. Costanzo took the not-so-subtle hint, ended his conversation, and joined the group. Everyone's attention turned back to Shawn.

"I have the best news I could have for now. Mark was excited about Indiana and his visit went very well. In my opinion, we're in a real dog fight." Bennett gave a real sigh of exasperation as he shifted in his chair. Shawn sensed his disappointment. "I think we're in as good a position as we could possibly be in. His mom wants him to go here. His dad wants him to go here. His coach wants him to go here."

The meeting fell silent as the others waited for Bennett to comment on the news. Bennett's body language showed his disappointment; sitting back slouched in his chair, hands folded on his lap, eyes cast downward. He broke his silence after several seconds of staring blankly at the table. "You started out by saying that was the best news. To me, that was the worst news you could have given me. That is what I feared all along. I had hoped that his visit at Indiana wouldn't go as well. My hope was that he would have a lukewarm visit and that would keep us in a prominent position. I would say this dramatically affects us, our chances."

Bennett again fell silent, making eye contact with no one. He pulled himself out of his defeated pose, and when he spoke again, the tone of his voice was full of vigor. "This was a test case, fellas. Remember, I told you that I was going to recruit this kid harder than I had ever recruited before. Do everything we could possibly do as a staff, and we've done that. But it is like a game, sometimes you battle and you battle and somebody just overtakes you. I have lost so many kids that way. We did this at Green Bay countless times. We just did everything right in recruiting a kid, but in the end they went for the whole enchilada, and we lost them. This is following the same format, only on a grander scale."

He paused and looked directly into the eyes of each assistant. "I think the thing we've got here is a basketball player, and a basketball player is going to choose Indiana. That is my first real read on the situation. We have sold him on everything we have to offer at Wisconsin, the education, the city, and the basketball. Indiana doesn't have to sell anything *but* the basketball. That is my fear, that is what scares me." The comments visibly drained the enthusiasm from the room. "I just wanted to say that. If he comes, great. If not, we just gotta go on. But it does tell me something about our recruiting, how we are going about it and who we are going after."

The assistants were not ready to resign themselves to the assumption that they had lost the battle for Vershaw. There was still a chance. More phone calls, more letters. All hope was not lost.

The following week, while discussing the schedule for the upcoming coaches clinic, Hood informed Bennett that Vershaw, his father, and his coach had decided to make one last visit to Wisconsin before making a decision. Bennett was in a jovial mood and mimicked experiencing great exasperation and anxiety at the prospect.

"This is a good thing, coach. This is a good thing!" Brad Soderberg reassured as the others enjoyed a hearty chuckle.

Hood added, "What he is doing is comparing your practice with Bobby's," at which the room broke into loud belly laughter. Bennett played along with the idea that he was in a popularity contest with Knight. "Well, what should I wear?" Then Bennett concluded the discussion with a tongue-in-cheek truth. "You all know what I'll be like the rest of the year if we don't get him. I'll think I screwed it up at that practice."

Vershaw visited on the weekend of the coaching clinic. UW Athletic Director Pat Richter led the young man and his entourage into the Field House with Saturday morning's practice well under way. They all took a seat at center court among the hundreds of educators in attendance. The large gathering motivated the Badger players for practice. They worked extremely hard, executed, and sustained a high level of intensity for more than two hours. It was an impressive display for both the coaches and for Vershaw. Upon completion of practice, each player went over and greeted Vershaw. They, too, understood the importance of signing blue-chippers to the program's future success.

Bennett's anxiety was replaced with confidence. Practice had gone well and he felt reassured that a true basketball player would recognize good basketball, and good coaching, regardless of the style. He had done all he could.

Chapter 9

Just Words on a Plaque?

The final home football game for Barry Alvarez's Badgers took place on November 10. Wisconsin's huge offensive line, averaging more than three hundred pounds per player, manhandled an undersized Minnesota defensive unit. The Badgers dictated the tempo of the game, enabling 260-pound freshman running back Ron Dayne to explode for 297 yards on 51 carries as the Badgers overwhelmed the Gophers 45 to 28. The seniors raised their helmets to the crowd in the traditional home victory salute as they walked off the field for the last time. The 1996 season, however, had been a humbling experience for those seniors, a season that had exposed them to the fragile nature of success and admiration in major college athletics. Many of those same players had been integral members of the 1994 Rose Bowl Championship team. Less than two years later, the same fans that had welcomed them home as Rose Bowl heroes were less enamored of them. The Badgers had dropped four straight games in the month of October. Their fans wanted a prolonged return to the national limelight, so it mattered little that three of the 1996 losses were to top ten programs by a total of ten points.

Badger basketball does not play to crowds in excess of 76,000 fans, as the football team does. Nonetheless, Bennett was experiencing a similar ebb and flow of emotions with his basketball team. Friday, November 9, had started out as the best day of his eighteen month tenure at Wisconsin. Mark Vershaw, his top recruit, had called and informed Bennett that he would be attending Wisconsin in the fall of 1997. Needless to say, the mood in the basketball office that morning was quite jovial. Vershaw's commitment elevated their first full recruiting class from a good class to a potentially great class. Prognosticators ranked the class as the third best among Big Ten schools and one of the top fifteen classes in the country, although the final evaluation of the group would come on the floor. The entire basketball office, including the secretaries, were so excited they put their work aside and joked, laughed, and congratulated one another.

The good news spread quickly throughout the entire athletic department. Assistant Athletic Director Cheryl Marra burst into the office after receiving the news from Pat Richter while in an early morning meeting. She high-fived, hugged, and congratulated each of the coaches.

"I wonder if this gets the monkey off my back," Bennett joked. "Everyone has always said I could coach but couldn't recruit." He continued in jest, "This probably means we will be investigated by the NCAA now." Everyone chuckled at the notion. His diligence to NCAA regulations is legendary.

Bennett had a warning for Marra as she exited. "Just wait until you see this group at parents night." In unison, the assistant coaches broke out in laughter. He explained himself. "We now have an all-parents team as well. I mean they are wild! In all my years of coaching I have never seen a group like this. They are eccentric to say the least." Each assistant took turns recounting his favorite story of the past recruiting season, stories that were all in fun and well intended. They had grown quite fond of the families, as well as of the recruits. They were Bennett's kind of people. The daily meeting eventually began and decorum was restored in the office. Bennett took a moment to congratulate his staff on the tremendous job they had done as a whole, then, as if a switch had been turned, he focused his attention to the task at hand, that evening's exhibition game against Athletes in Action (AIA).

The two exhibition games that precede the season are rarely fan favorites. The Big Ten season provides some very exciting rivalries, not to mention entertaining basketball, and these games pale in comparison. Nonetheless, they are vitally important to the coaching staff. The practice environment is too controlled to get a genuine feel for how individual players will react in an actual game. Therefore, playing against quality opponents is invaluable in these pre-season matchups. Tony Bennett had scrimmaged with the AIA team a few weeks earlier and assured his father that the squad would provide a solid challenge.

Athletes in Action:
Friday, November 8, Madison, Wisconsin

Auriantal and Mason started the game at the guard positions, Okey and Daugherty filled the forward spots, and Grant got the nod at center. The group played sluggishly in the beginning, but after a few minutes they had reacquainted themselves with playing in front of the Field House fans. Still, after five minutes of play, the score was only 12-10 in favor of Wisconsin. The big front line of Okey, Daugherty, and Grant was having difficulty containing the quicker AIA players, especially on the perimeter. Bennett went to a three-guard set, substituting Duany for Daugherty, after an official's timeout. An electrifying follow-up dunk by Grant, a long three-pointer by Duany, and a breakaway dunk by Grant ignited the Badgers and propelled them to a 45-23 halftime lead. The crowd's admiration buzzed throughout the rapidly filling corridors. That optimism, however, quickly subsided as the second half unfolded.

Bennett returned to the big lineup of Okey, Daugherty, and Grant to start the second half, but again the group struggled to defend the smaller, more mobile AIA players. Unlike in the first half, Bennett stayed with Grant, Daugherty, and Okey to determine whether they could fight through the adversity and become effective as a group. The trio found it not only difficult to defend, they also struggled to score against AIA's suspect zone defense. Their opponent exploited those weaknesses and climbed back into the game, though Wisconsin held on for an unconvincing 75-63 win.

The "big" lineup's two weaknesses had been exposed: their inability to play aggressive half-court defense against quicker players, and their ineffectiveness to score against a zone. Yet, Bennett was most concerned about the poor attitudes he had witnessed, both on the floor and on the bench. The forty minutes of exhibition play reaffirmed Bennett's primary concern about this team, that they were individually talented but had selfish attitudes. The Badger basketball staff had scheduled a tailgate party for their families the day after the AIA exhibition game, preceding Badger football, but Bennett was so upset by the poor attitude of the team that he stayed home to contemplate the situation further.

Bennett's decision-making process often resembled a funnel. He isolated himself from the office and the team, pondering all the components that affected the team. It was like pouring all the events of the day into the wide mouth of a large funnel. He then meditated on the issues, wrote about them in his journal, and brought a condensed version of his thoughts to the daily staff meetings, a process similar to the narrowing of the funnel. The staff then collectively decided on exactly what should be brought to the team's attention. Finally, Bennett determined (with the aid of his assistants) an appropriate avenue to transfer that information to the team, which would represent the tip of the funnel.

He followed this exact process for nearly every major issue that faced the team. When I told him of my analogy, he responded, "I was just reading a book by the Pope, in which he says he does much the same thing. I do try to understand the whole thing, but I try to pull out those few things that are teachable and can make a difference. At night, when I am at home, I try to see everything, the interaction of the players and what is happening on the court. From that I try to implement a few things that might help, whether it is personnel adjustments, technical adjustments, or philosophical adjustments. I don't try to change the whole thing. I just address those few areas that I think I can help."

Bennett spoke of the team's disposition with his staff over a glass of orange juice and a bagel, two days removed from the game. "I did an exercise this weekend that I often do with my teams. I call it H and S, for hard and smart. You always start with hard, those players need to be on the floor first. So, I wrote those down. Ty Calderwood plays hard, Hennssy Auriantal plays hard, Mike Kosolcharoen plays hard, Sam Okey plays hard, and Paul Grant plays hard. Next, If you have a kid who plays hard *and* smart all the time, then you have a keeper. From what I can tell, we have two of those kids, Ty Calderwood and Mike Kosolcharoen."

Bennett proceeded to evaluate the top nine players on the team using his H and S criteria. "Sam, Hennssy, and Paul all play hard, but they don't always play smart. On the flip side, I wrote down the players who are smart—Sean Daugherty, Sean Mason, and Duany." He mimicked the exercise on an empty desk and pointed to the phantom list. "They play smart, but for whatever reason, they don't always play hard. Finally, I wrote down Booker, who can be effective, but he doesn't always play hard or smart." Bennett analyzed the results of his exercise. "I looked at that and said I had to get the five hardest guys together—Ty, Mike, Hennssy, Sam and Paul. To reinforce my findings, I went back to the game tape." Pounding his fist with each word he spoke, he professed, "It was that group that had played the best together." The issue was settled in his mind. He had to put that group on the floor to start the next game.

Bennett set his new starting lineup at the first practice following the AIA game and explained the results of the H and S exercise to the team in a pre-practice meeting. Not all the players necessarily liked Bennett's assessment of them as a hard or smart player. His purpose in the exercise, however, was to foster increased self-awareness among the players, not to please them.

The coaches did not break their post-practice huddle until after the players had cleared out of the locker room. Bennett, the last to leave, glanced at the large bronze plaque detailing the five intangible concepts of the program and paused for a moment to reflect. At the very top of the plaque it read:

Humility . . . . know who we are
Passion . . . . do not be lukewarm
Unity . . . . do not divide our house
Servanthood . . . . make teammates better
Thankfulness . . . . learn from each circumstance

He walked out of the locker room, through the Field House, and out into the night air. The climate outside the Field House was no more hospitable than it had been inside. A frigid northwestern wind blew through Madison, single-digit temperatures signaling the onset of winter. Bennett climbed into his white Lexus parked under Camp Randall Stadium, unsure of the impact the exercise had had on the team, and drove home to plan for the next day.

———————

Sub-zero overnight temperatures left a heavy layer of frost on the windshields of unprotected vehicles. A seldom used credit card served as an impromptu ice scraper as I found myself ill prepared for the harsh weather. The engine of my aging Jeep Cherokee hesitated and sputtered when it started. Nostalgic thoughts of countless basketball games watched or participated in over the years filled my mind during that morning's commute to campus. Traffic increased and the pace slowed, crystallized exhaust fumes swirling in the air, when I was struck by the simple thought that pure basketball transcends all levels of competition. Bennett's career, which spanned thirty-two years, epitomized that truth. His approach to the game remained essentially unchanged, but nonetheless effective, since his days as a ninth-grade coach.

My face was partially protected from the frigid wind by the upturned collar of my jacket. I quickened my steps to escape the chill of the morning. The confines of the basketball office provided a warm shelter from the weather, but when I stepped into Bennett's office, his face was pale and fatigued. A flu shot, his deep concern for the team, and the stressful practice had caught up to him. Nonetheless, we proceeded with the topic of the day, the five intangible concepts outlined on the locker room plaque.

"Please explain the five intangible concepts you use as the foundation for your program," I asked.

Bennett rubbed his forehead to alleviate his headache before he spoke. His speech lacked enthusiasm. "It is probably easier for me to deal with them as a whole, especially right now," referring to the problems facing the team. "I concluded some time ago that a major part of success of a team, or of an individual, has a great deal to do with the intangible qualities possessed. The real key is in how a person sees himself [humility], how he feels about what he does [passion], how he works with others [unity], how he makes others better [servanthood], and how he deals with frustration and success, truly learning from each situation [thankfulness]. I believe those concepts are the essence of a good player, team, coach, or individual in any capacity in life." With that, he simply stopped. There was nothing more to say.

"Is that it?" I inquired.

"Yes."

His previous two sentences communicated his underlying philosophy for the functioning of his program.

I was silent for a few moments, deciding on which direction to take the conversation. Finally, I continued, "How did you settle on humility, passion, unity, servanthood, and thankfulness?"

"I have learned from experience, as I analyze any situation, that it is inevitably a result of the presence or absence of these qualities. In victories you see a passion to win, the unity of the team, the players helping each other, and the team learning from previous defeats or mistakes. In losses, however, you see arrogance, or selfishness, a lack of commitment, and finger pointing. It always comes down to these concepts." The conversation concealed his ill health as he spoke firmly. "Assuming we can get kids that are adequately skilled, the battle is to get them to accept the intangibles."

"How do you do that specifically?" I prodded.

"They have to know that these intangibles are important to our program. Therefore, I present it to them daily, but I do not lecture. These intangibles are used every day. They are the foundations of everything I do, and I point it out to them in a subtle fashion. Sometimes, I am not so subtle."

Assistant coach Shawn Hood confirmed Bennett's proclamation when he later expressed, unsolicited, "He [Bennett] *is* the concepts. That is the way he lives his life and coaches the team. The kids see that and learn from his example."

The five intangible concepts speak directly to *how* Badger basketball functions. They do not, however, address *what* the program is working toward. Bennett had discussed his appreciation of the process, but there had to be an ultimate goal. Neither Bennett, his staff, nor his players spoke openly of such a tangible goal, a destination. Nor was one single word written about it. No signs, no posters, and no articles that proclaimed that the Badgers wanted to win X number of games and get into Y post-season tournament. Did that mean that no such goal existed?

Tony Bennett and assistant Brad Soderberg were the first to verbalize this seldom discussed ideal. Tony spoke of a sermon on quality that his father had especially liked and Brad recounted a story he had heard several times of a young Dick Bennett. As a boy of five or six, Bennett would accompany his grandfather on Saturday mornings to a local pub in the Italian neighborhood of Pittsburgh and listen to recordings of opera. The elder Bennett wept at the beauty, the quality, of the music, and that vision had left an indelible impression on the young boy. Could it be that *quality* is the ultimate goal?

"How important is quality to you as a person?" I asked.

Bennett responded emphatically. "Quality is what has kept me in the game for as long as I have been. I am affected by quality basketball, whenever I see it, especially if it is on a team I am responsible for. It affects me very much the same way the opera affected my grandfather. There have been occasions when the ball is so good it brings tears to my eyes. That has driven me even more so than working with the kids."

Bennett further explained, not wanting to misrepresent his position. "I enjoy working with the kids. However, there are more frustrating moments than satisfying moments. So that is not enough. What really keeps me going is my association with quality, and how I can sometimes get a team to perform with quality." Bennett was forthright about his talents as a coach, which was very uncharacteristic of him. "That is the only thing that I do where I have any degree of confidence, experience, and maybe expertise, the only thing where I feel I have something to offer."

Bennett reflected openly on a question that he had obviously been asked before. He reiterated the question, "So what, then, is the big deal about moving up the ladder and working at the University of Wisconsin? Couldn't that [striving for quality] be done at the high school level?

"My logic," he answered in response to his own question, "as screwy as it might be, tells me that the highest level of quality, the highest level of excellence, and the purest form of basketball, is at the highest level of college basketball."

There was the goal, the driving force; pure *quality* basketball. Winning was an indication of, but it did not equate to, quality. Attaining the intangible goal would make the tangible goal not only possible, but even probable.

Chapter 10

Iron Sharpens Iron

Iron sharpens iron,
So one man sharpens another.
—Proverbs 27:17

Australian Select Team:
Wednesday, November 13, Madison, Wisconsin

Bennett's switch to the "hard and smart" small lineup of Auriantal, Calderwood, Kosolcharoen, Okey, and Grant for the second exhibition game against a group of Australian All-Stars produced disappointing results. The unit struggled from the outset of the game and trailed the Aussies at half, 30-26. Even the crowd sensed that the team was playing poorly, with little consistency or confidence. Daugherty and Mason replaced Okey and Auriantal to start the second half and Wisconsin pulled out to a 39-36 lead in the first five minutes. The players' most notable improvement, on both ends of the floor, was in their movement. The stagnant action of the first half quickly gave way to activity and production on offense and intensity on defense. The players who came off the bench, including Okey and Auriantal, matched the second half starters' invigorated effort and the Badgers pulled away for a relatively easy double-digit victory.

Yet something was not right. The two exhibition victories did little to ease the sense of disharmony engulfing the team. Everything seemed normal on the surface, but among the coaching staff an uneasy feeling persisted. The team's offense was still sluggish and the defense lacked consistent intensity. Bennett's lingering doubts about the team were heightened by their inability to function as a cohesive unit. The issue began to consume him. His mood darkened and he withdrew inside himself. His outward appearance was sullen and he avoided interactions with others in the office. He was totally alone with his thoughts, hoping to find the elusive answers.

There were ten days before the season opener against Memphis State in Ottawa, Canada. Bennett hoped that would be enough time to move the team forward. Three practice sessions passed without incident. The players and the coaches were content to get into the gym, work hard for two hours, and then go their separate ways. With five days remaining before the opener, Bennett decided that his starting lineup would consist of Mason, Auriantal, Daugherty, Okey, and Grant (the "big lineup"). He remained committed to this group, as he had been since the end of the previous season. Still, their play as a unit had done little to warrant his confidence in the pre-season. Regardless, Bennett still believed at a gut level that the big lineup was his best bet. He also knew that the experience of Okey, Daugherty, and Grant would be vitally important against an athletic Memphis State team. Bennett also made the decision to force Memphis to play his style of basketball. Memphis was an exceptionally quick, attacking full-court team, and going with a three-guard lineup would be playing into their hands. Bennett wanted the roles reversed. He wanted Memphis to have to make the adjustments and play into his hands. The game would pit the size and strength of Wisconsin's style against the speed and agility of Memphis, a position Bennett's teams had been in many times during his career. He felt confident falling back on his strength.

The move paid immediate dividends in practice. The starting unit dominated practice for two days and optimism was high, as Bennett finally saw the team improve and play as a unit. Still, he was aware of a potential problem facing such a lineup. Six of the top eight players occupied the three perimeter positions, creating an imbalance of talent between the perimeter and the post. The player most affected would be Duany, a sharp-shooting redshirt freshman from Bloomington, Indiana. He was eager to get his chance to play significant minutes, but he realized going with the big lineup was pushing him further down Bennett's substitution rotation.

Practice went well for the remainder of the week and Bennett felt confident going into the Memphis game. "I expect to make Memphis look bad," he told his assistants just before the team departed for Ottawa.

"I know they will come out and pressure us, but our patience will break them down and we will end up getting easy baskets."

Memphis State:
Saturday, November 23, Ottawa, Canada

The game in Ottawa was a promotional event staged as the first major college basketball game ever to be played in the Carel Centre. The new multipurpose arena, home to the Ottawa Senators of the National Hockey League, was quite colorful. A picture of a multi-colored hot-air balloon was painted in the free throw key area. In addition, the area inside the three-point arc was dark blue sprinkled with star bursts. The promotion, unfortunately, was less than a complete success. The crowd was sparse, as few Canadian residents were willing to pay the high ticket prices, (sixty dollars at courtside), to watch a basketball game. The empty seats and flamboyantly painted floor created an unusual atmosphere for a major college basketball game. The surreal surrounding and late morning tip-off time left the Badgers flat in the season opener.

While Bennett chose to start the big lineup, he used the number two offense, a double low-post set that placed Grant and Daugherty on opposite sides of the lane with Mason, Auriantal, and Okey on the perimeter. Grant, using his unusual running jump style, got to the opening tip first and directed the ball to Okey near the center line. Wisconsin showed great patience on their first possession, as they had been instructed to do, but when the shot clock reached five seconds, Mason was stripped of the ball driving to the basket. Thirty seconds later, Paul Grant scored the first basket of the season when his turnaround jump shot found the basket. The Badgers, however, did not register their second field goal for another eight minutes. They missed eight consecutive shots and turned the ball over seven times during the stretch. Bennett went to his bench when the starters fell behind 12-5, replacing Okey with Kosolcharoen, and Mason with Calderwood. Nonetheless, the personnel changes did not turn the momentum of the game around and Memphis continued its domination.

Trailing 19-7, Bennett continued to search for a combination of players who would spark his team. Calderwood stayed at the point, Mason and Okey returned to their wing positions, and Coleman joined Grant on the post. The adjustment worked. Grant converted two baskets and four free throws, Mason added a jump shot, and Coleman had a three-point play of his own, which narrowed the score to 19-18. A minute later, Duany finally got his chance to play. Memphis then regained their composure and pushed the lead back out to eight at the half, 28-20. Wisconsin had made only six of their twenty-eight shots, a dismal 21 percent. Their fourteen turnovers further compounded their offensive woes.

Okey, who had struggled in the first half, came out of the locker room and made his presence known immediately, with a rebound, two assists, and a basket all within the first three minutes of the second half. The game then settled into a defensive struggle and the Memphis lead fluctuated between two and four points for the next ten minutes. In one short burst, however, the Tigers reclaimed their eight-point lead. The teams traded baskets for the next two minutes, pushing the score to 44-36, before Wisconsin turned the ball over on back-to-back possessions. Fortunately for the Badgers, Memphis failed to capitalize on either miscue, committing an offensive goal-tending violation and shooting an airball. Those missed opportunities were the turning point of the contest.

Bennett turned to defense to get his team back into the game. He inserted Calderwood, who teamed with Auriantal and Mason on the perimeter, while Grant and Daugherty protected the post. Grant scored on a turnaround jump shot in the middle of the paint to cut the deficit to six. Then Daugherty stole a post feed, and though Grant's ensuing shot came up short, Mason stripped his man of the ball and drove the length of the floor. His lay-up bounced high off the front of the rim as Grant, who had outrun the pack to the basket, grabbed the ball with his extended right hand and rammed it through the rim. The lead was down to four with 2:15 remaining. Play was stopped momentarily to attend to an injured Memphis player, so Bennett chose to make one final adjustment. He injected Okey back into the lineup, putting him on the post with Grant, rather than playing him on the perimeter.

Memphis State coach Larry Finch also changed his strategy and began to milk the clock. When the Memphis players became hesitant on offense, Calderwood stripped the ball handler for Wisconsin's third consecutive steal. He flipped a long outlet pass to Grant breaking up the right side of the floor. Grant fielded the pass, took one dribble, and spotted Auriantal out in front of the play. He lobbed the ball forward to Auriantal, who completed the play for two more points. Memphis inbounded the ball and took their time looking for a shot. Finally they set up a high screen and roll on the right side of the floor. With time running down, they settled for a long three-point shot which came up short. A fight for the rebound resulted in the ball being tipped out of bounds. The players froze and looked to the official. He pointed toward Wisconsin's basket and hollered, "RED BALL."

Okey hurried down the floor and positioned himself deep on the right block. Mason broke open on the right wing and relayed a pass to Okey. He hooked his player with his right elbow, used his upper-body strength to wheel into the middle of the lane, and muscled up a left-handed jump-hook. The ball fell into the basket and he was fouled. He then calmly stepped to the line and delivered the go-ahead shot with exactly one minute remaining in the game. Wisconsin took only their second lead of the game, 45-44. Okey continued to contribute mightily in the closing seconds, as he forced a turnover at the defensive end of the floor and tipped in a missed free throw attempt. Grant closed out the scoring with a pair of free throws and Wisconsin stole away the win from Memphis, 49-46.

Wisconsin shot a paltry 29 percent from the floor and committed twenty turnovers, but they had their first victory of the 1996-97 season. Grant was the main bright spot for the Badgers and the only player in double figures, with his twenty points. His stat line was impressive for his first game as a Badger: six of 12 field goals, eight of nine free throws, nine rebounds, and two assists. Okey, who had been ineffective for most of the game, did prove invaluable with his major contributions in the last two minutes.

Good teams win even when they play badly. Did that old sports adage apply to the Badgers? They had beaten a potentially good Memphis team. They had played well with the game on the line. Still, Bennett knew that the big team had failed to live up to his expectations, and had really played quite poorly. Experience and instinct told him there needed to be a change. His planning, however, was interrupted by yet another death in the family. His brother-in-law, Carl "Peanuts" Fischer, passed away while the Badgers were on their way back from Ottawa. Bennett joined Anne in Clintonville for the funeral on the following Monday, so no changes were made when the assistants ran practice that afternoon. While deeply sad-dened by the loss of another family member, the extra time away from the team enabled Bennett to consider the fate of his team. He summa-rized his thoughts upon his return to the office.

"We cannot accept in victory what we would not accept in defeat. I am not sure exactly what has to be done, but I do not think we can stay the way we are right now."

Tuesday's practice brought only one adjustment. Calderwood replaced Auriantal on the white team as Bennett searched for leadership and unity. Auriantal, challenged by the demotion, battled Calderwood relentlessly in practice. Auriantal's defensive prowess forced Calderwood to elevate his level of play at the point. Calderwood, on occasion, had shown a propensity to "float" in practice, doing only enough to get by. Auriantal's defense would not provide him such a luxury, and Ty elevated his level of play to match that of Hennssy. The individual battle between the two rose to a feverish pitch and stimulated the members of the red (reserve) team to match the intensity. With the exception of Calderwood, the white (starting) team did not elevate their level of play. Daugherty and Mason went through the motions, stone faced, while Okey forced the action on the perimeter and Grant pleaded for the ball on the low post. Bennett remained silent at half-court and shook his head from side to side each time the group self-destructed on offense. The red team out-hustled, out-rebounded, out-defended, out-scored, out-passed, and totally out-played the white team. Bennett's body language indicated a change was imminent. What could he do that would make a significant difference?

Bennett's assistant hinted at the staff meeting the following morning that they thought he may have been tinkering with the team a little too much. Maybe it would be best to just leave things alone for a while. Bennett disagreed. "I have never felt inadequate because I've changed. When you run a conceptual style of offense, you better be ready to learn and make adjustments." Nonetheless, he did not have a definite plan of action to improve the team's offensive play and that frustrated him. Bennett's decision process was a crapshoot. A solution to the team's ineptitude was based more on pure chance than logical thinking, because many of the players were of the same ability level and mental make-up. To make the dilemma worse, the situation changed daily with the team's inconsistent play. Nonetheless, Bennett's comment had assured his assistants that there would indeed be change.

Tuesday's practice came and went without improvement in either execution or in chemistry. The growing sense of urgency was evident in the Wednesday morning staff meeting. Bennett sat distraught in his customary position and lamented over the team's stagnant personality.

"I have the feeling we are a mediocre team. Our challenge is to figure out how to be the best we can be, but I just don't know exactly what that is." Bennett interrupted his assistants as a few of them started to suggest schematic changes in the offense. "Last year we searched the entire season for an offense that would work with our players. This year we have our offense established, three guards and two posts, and the biggest mistake we can make is to go away from it." The message was clear: the solution was in the personnel, not in the scheme.

Bennett, visibly agitated by the comments, went off on a philosophical tangent. "I know I have been told over a hundred times that our team here is not like my Green Bay teams, or that I coach differently now than when I was at Green Bay. I don't want to be like my Green Bay teams! There are not any teams at this level, that I am aware of, that play the way I want to play."

He dropped the subject as quickly as it came up. He never clearly explained exactly what he meant, perhaps because it was not something that *could* be explained. That style of basketball, quality basketball as he envisioned it, had to be experienced to be understood. (Bennett did later explain, only after being prodded, that his ideal team would have the aggressiveness and confidence of a Kentucky, the high-powered half-court offense of a Kansas, the discipline and intelligence of an Indiana, and finally, the stifling half-court, man-to-man defense of his own teams.)

The harsh tone of Bennett's remarks left the room in silence. He noticed the apprehension of his assistants and shifted the focus of his discussion to a conversation he had had with his daughter, Kathi, the previous night on the telephone. Kathi had been a highly successful coach at the University of Wisconsin-Oshkosh. Her 1995-96 team went undefeated and won the Division III National Championship. She had accomplished all that she had set out to do at Oshkosh, so with the prodding of her father she accepted the head coaching job at the University of Evansville. The transition to a poor Division I program had been traumatic for Kathi. Her roster consisted of six scholarship players and two walk-ons who agreed to be on the team only if Kathi promised not to play them in games. If that were not enough to overcome, her team had to play nine of its first ten games on the road. She made nightly calls to her parents for moral support, and there were many nights when she did not think she could stick it out. One such night occurred when her team played as well as they could, but still got beat by Arizona State 74-64.

She was depressed and distraught as she dialed the phone from the Phoenix airport to speak with her parents. Bennett described the content of the call to his assistants, putting his own team's difficulties in perspective.

"Kathi called me from the airport after their Arizona State game. They got beat by ten, 74-64. She sounded like myself on a hundred different occasions. She said, 'Dad, we are just terrible, we are never going to win any games.' I felt terrible for her, mostly because I encouraged her to take the job, so I let her rattle on. Then I said, and I'll admit it was calculated, 'Kathi, you sound like a loser!' I came down on her hard, maybe as hard as I've ever come down on any of my kids. I felt bad because she started to cry, but she needed to hear that.

"I told her that if she were talking to me about her team like that, she was probably doing the same thing to the team. I also told her that if she continued to do so, she would lose them. I said I know that, because I have done it, and I want to spare her the tremendous heartache of coming down too hard on players, especially when they are playing their hearts out. It made me think of the many times I had jumped on players when it was not the right thing to do. So, I told her to stop feeling sorry for herself and mend some fences."

He further explained that he ended the conversation by reassuring her that the key was patience, much as he had displayed with his own team. Bennett purposely used tough love with Kathi at her lowest point because she needed to hear the hard truth about the situation.

Ironically, Bennett went into that afternoon's practice and did exactly the opposite of what he had instructed Kathi to do. The first hour of practice proceeded without fanfare, even though the intensity level was low, and the white team was being outplayed by the red. Bennett, however, had had enough after an hour. He yelled "stop" after another poor possession and walked slowly to the middle of the floor. He later recounted his thoughts at that moment. "I was contemplating if I really wanted to continue with what I was about to say. However, at that moment, I knew in my heart we couldn't stay the same. Something had to be done."

What had to be done was to firmly and critically express his displeasure with the consistently poor play. Okey was chastised for his individual play. Duany was next, and Bennett berated his moody behavior. He then lambasted Sean Daugherty for his "reactive" and sporadic play, Sean Mason for his refusal to play defense, Mike

Kosolcharoen for losing his humility, and Ty for playing hard only when he wanted to. All of the players, with the exception of one, looked Bennett in the eye when he spoke to them. Finally, he instructed Okey and Daugherty to change over to the red team and replaced them with Coleman and Duany when he had finished his stern reproach.

Bennett was relentless for the remainder of practice, challenging his team harder and longer than he had all year. He was physically and emotionally drained by the time he excused practice. In turn, the players wasted no time exiting the floor as they had heard enough for the day. Bennett, distraught and angry about his inability to motivate the group, slowly walked to the sideline bleachers and took a seat by himself. He remained there with his own thoughts for several minutes, staring at the floor, before joining the other coaches in the locker room.

"A strength of Bennett is his optimism. No matter how devastating the previous day, he is tremendously resilient and comes back the next day with a plan to improve." That assessment came from Brad Soderberg long before the events of the previous day's practice. Bennett's behavior at the next day's meeting, however, supported Soderberg's description. Bennett enthusiastically complimented Soderberg as he started the meeting.

"Brad's head coaching experience really paid off last night. He came up to me during practice and told me that something out there just wasn't right. He could not put his finger on exactly what it was, but he knew it just did not feel right. I agreed with him, so I went home last night and really thought about it, and these are some of my thoughts, for better or worse." Bennett was positive as he started. "I remain convinced we can be a really good team because Paul is really good in the post, and nearly every one of our other players can get better, but I have changed my opinion on how we will be the best. I want to put the players in the best possible position for us to succeed, and I no longer believe that is playing big. Sam is not good enough to play on the perimeter yet. He may be some day, but right now he doesn't have the skill. We have to play small and we have to score more points."

He questioned his assistants, "So, how do we do that?"

The assistants were familiar enough with Bennett's methods to know that he had already arrived at an answer, so they waited patiently for him to continue.

"I am thinking of how best to help Paul. By playing Doc [Duany] and Sean Mason together on the perimeter, we can spread the defense because of their scoring ability." Bennett spoke of Duany's promotion. "I feel you owe your best players the opportunity to show that they are the best. In Doc's case, he is clearly the best long-range shooter and he is also one of our most athletic players. He deserves an opportunity, especially when you consider that we shot 29 percent as a team against Memphis and he hardly even played." He paused and raised his eyebrows, looking for any dissenting opinions. He continued when none was forthcoming. "Also, Sam is very tough on the inside, he scores well and he passes well from the post. If we can get him to rebound and play post defense, I think that is where he can be the most effective. That is where he most helps us as a team. Finally, it is also time to make this Ty's team. He did an outstanding job taking care of the ball against Memphis and he is ready to assume control."

The proposed changes made perfect sense, at least for a day, and that remained Bennett's biggest frustration—finding a unit that can play well on a consistent basis. Bennett rubbed his forehead and leaned his elbows on the conference table. "This may not work, and that is really what scares me. We may change again and not be any more effective. That is the price you pay when you have average players. We have nine players who are basically the same. They do not differentiate themselves on a consistent basis, so we are always searching for the best combination, and it is most likely changing each day. What we can do for certain is to try to get better, and we do that in two ways: We get better as a team and we get better with players who can get better."

Getting better as a team had three components. First, the team could improve by finding the right combination of players and getting them in their correct roles. That would maximize the effectiveness of the team, as well as the individual. Second, developing a selfless attitude on the team, void of individual egos, would allow the Badgers to improve as a team. Finally, developing the individual talents of each player, especially those who *could* improve. The staff had to work with those players who could, and would, show the most improvement throughout the season because not every player had the potential to improve significantly.

That afternoon's practice was a clinic. The confrontational atmosphere and the criticism of the previous day was gone. Bennett taught virtually every moment of practice. Play was crisp, aggressive, and purposeful. The coach repeatedly emphasized the team's philosophy and complimented the players when their behavior reinforced his lessons. The daily scrimmage produced the highest quality of play for the entire season, up to that point. Bennett implored them to play that well consistently, possession after possession, and they did so. Near the end of practice, he challenged the white team of Mason, Calderwood, Duany, Okey, and Grant to put together three defensive "stops" of the red team, in which they prevented them from scoring. They responded magnificently, stringing together three aggressive, intimidating defensive possessions. Not only did the red team not score, they barely got off a shot. Bennett walked off the floor, trailing his team to the locker room, smiling at the team's improvement and effort.

Snow dusted sidewalks outside of Camp Randall the following afternoon as the Badgers repeated the intensity and quality of the previous day's practice. But was it a new beginning, or a brief aberration? Would the game-day environment of the Field House change the attitudes and behavior of the players? Would the individualism of the team return? Would Calderwood, Duany, and Sam excel in their new roles? Would Daugherty and Auriantal play with enthusiasm coming off the bench after being replaced in the starting lineup? Ultimately, would they play as a team? Only time would tell.

UNC-Willmington:
Saturday, November 30, Madison, Wisconsin

The seats of the Field House filled early for the game against Colonial Conference member University of North Carolina-Wilmington. Coach Jerry Wainwright's club was still in search of its first win of the young season, entering the game with an 0-3 mark. The UW pep band created a festive and rousing atmosphere as the Badgers took the floor twenty minutes before tip-off. Bennett's teams are atypical in their preparation prior to the start of a contest. The players arrive at the Field House just over an hour before the game, unlike many teams that arrive two hours early for extra shooting, and then take the floor with precisely twenty minutes remaining before tip-off. In total, the team spends no more than fifteen minutes on the court before introductions. His teams have followed this same blueprint for most of his career because he wants the players fresh and mentally aroused at the start of the game. His method appeared to have worked as the players jogged onto the floor, led by

Calderwood. They looked relaxed and confident as they went through their pregame drills. The intra-squad scrimmage and two exhibition games had eliminated the butterflies and newness of playing in front of a large home crowd.

Grant won his second consecutive tip-off, directing the ball back to a retreating Duany to start the game. Duany took the game's first shot on a driving pull-up jump shot from the right baseline. Even though he missed, he followed his shot to the basket and wrestled for the rebound before losing it to a Seahawk player. The Badgers converted back for their first defensive possession of the game and, thirty-five seconds later, the shot clock horn rang out. Their overmatched opponents could not produce a shot against the Badger defense. The crowd cheered in appreciation. The violation was an appropriate beginning to the second year of Dick Bennett's tenure at the Field House. Next, Grant made an uncharacteristically poor decision and took a three-point shot from the top of the key, turning the cheers to moans, with twenty seconds remaining on the shot clock. He didn't bother looking at Bennett as he retreated to defense. Bennett stared at his seven-footer in disbelief as Paul headed back up the floor.

The game unfolded slowly as both teams struggled to find their rhythm. Wisconsin scored only once in their first five possessions, on a pair of free throws by Okey. On the next possession, Mason threw a pass into the feet of Duany, the ball rolling away from him toward the sideline. Duany's defender dove at his feet in an attempt to tie up the ball, slightly spraining Duany's left ankle in the process. He got up and tried to play on, but he was noticeably limping. Wilmington's first basket, which came on their sixth possession, gave them an improbable 3-2 lead. The crowd had fallen silent. The Badgers held a slim 4-3 lead at the first TV timeout, which came at the 16:00 minute mark. Duany then got his first basket of the season coming out of the break, scoring on a drive to the right baseline.

Bennett went to his bench five minutes into the game. Daugherty replaced Grant on the post. Thirty seconds later, Auriantal subbed for Mason and made his presence known immediately. He met the ball as it crossed over the time line and harassed the ball handler until he fumbled control, at which time Auriantal went airborne, parallel to the floor, and knocked the ball out of bounds off his opponent's leg. That play, as well as Duany's long three on the other end of the floor, lit a fire under the

Badgers. Leading 9-3 at the 11:53 mark of the half, Bennett made whole-sale changes in his personnel. He put the lineup of Calderwood, Auriantal, Kosolcharoen, Coleman, and Daugherty on the floor. The group outscored their opponent 5-0 over the next two minutes. Calder-wood's basket, a jump shot on a two-on-three break, capped the mini-run. UNC-Wilmington called time. Calderwood did not join the Badgers when his team retook the floor. Bennett was teaching him the ever-important lesson of shot selection in his offensive system, whether the ill-advised shot went in or not.

Bennett substituted liberally over the next several minutes as his team blew the game wide open. A back cut by Kosolcharoen bailed out an air-borne Daugherty and resulted in a basket. A three-pointer by Mason, and finally, a thunderous high-flying fast-break dunk by Grant off a Mason feed, punctuated a 17-2 Wisconsin run. Grant swung on the rim, pre-venting him from landing on the hapless defender beneath him, as the once mute crowd went wild.

A Wilmington timeout did not stop the carnage. Moments later, Calderwood dove to the floor for a loose ball and pitched it to Okey from a supine position. Okey broke out of the pack on the dribble and was joined by Duany and Grant for a three-on-two fast break. Okey passed to Grant on the right wing who, though open for another dunk, shuffled the ball back to Sam slicing through the lane. Okey took one dribble, split-ting the two defenders, before elevating for one of his trademark left hand slams. The Field House once again erupted in cheers. The basket extended the Badgers' lead to 27-5 and reflected the progress of the team over the previous four days. Their teamwork and selfless play had begun to bring results on the court.

Kosolcharoen's fifteen-foot baseline jumper with two minutes remaining in the half demoralized the opponent and the lead became a gaudy thirty points, 35-5. Mercifully, the Seahawks hit a few last-minute baskets and limped into their locker room trailing 35-12. The rims at the old barn were much friendlier than they had been at the Carel Centre in Ottawa. Wisconsin shot 54 percent in the half, including four of nine from behind the three-point arc.

Intermission deflated the energy in the Field House. The throng of fans remained quiet, even though the Badgers continued to score at a rapid pace in the second half. The discipline of play on the floor, however, slowly deteriorated and the action became ragged. A "no-look" pass by

Mason on a poorly executed fast break brought Bennett to his feet. He fumed as he walked down the bench and pulled Auriantal up by his shirt sleeve to replace Mason. Bennett was still livid at the first mandatory time-out and chastised the team for their undisciplined play. The players returned to the floor and resurrected the excellence they had shown in the opening half. In doing so, they re-established and maintained a thirty-point margin.

With 6:08 remaining and his team leading 60-29, Bennett summoned the remaining red team members who had not yet played: David Burkemper, Brian Vraney, Troy Schuhmacher, and Matt Quest. He asked who they wanted as their fifth player to join them on the floor. They responded, nearly in unison, "Mike Kosolcharoen." Kosolcharoen spent most of his time in practice working with that unit and treated them as equals. Bennett obliged them. The crowd came alive as they all checked in at the scorer's table together. Moments later, Troy Schuhmacher, a local kid from Sun Prairie who had made the team in the early season open tryouts, took a pass from David Burkemper and drained a three-point shot from in front of the Badger bench. The players jumped to their feet in their excitement as Troy pumped his fist.

Everyone on the roster had scored except for Vraney. Kosolcharoen and Burkemper isolated him on the left block with the last seconds of the clock slipping away. The players, fans, and coaches all watched the unfolding drama. Would Brian crack the scoring column? He got off one shot, which was blocked. Moans rang out from the crowd. He grabbed the rebound and went up for a second shot, but that missed and the good-natured groaning returned as the final horn sounded. Nonetheless, the red team, composed entirely of walk-ons, played as well as their highly recruited teammates and managed to outscore their opponent 8-6 in the final six minutes of the game.

The final score of the game was an impressive 68-35. Sean Mason led the team in scoring, although ten other Badgers hit the score column. Duany added eleven and Okey chipped in ten to go with his game-high six rebounds. In addition, Calderwood distinguished himself as the team's leading point guard with his performance. He scored only six points but dished out seven assists to go along with his four steals and three rebounds. The joyous mood of the game spilled over into the post-game press conference where Bennett praised his team, especially the contributions of the red team. David Burkemper, appointed spokesman for the red clan, joined Bennett at the press table to field questions from reporters. The Badgers were 2-0, happy, and improving.

Brad Soderberg was still jubilant two days later at the morning coaches meeting. "That was a beautiful thing!" he said with a broad smile. The room filled with laughter.

"Did you see Vraney in the time-outs? He looked like he was in the final four," Shawn Hood added between belly laughs.

Soderberg added, arms folded across his chest, "They sure take care of their own. Did you see them playing that two-man game with Brian, trying to get him a shot? The crowd was going nuts each time he shot and got it blocked."

Bennett thoughtfully agreed, "That was beautiful."

Shawn Hood playfully remarked, "When Troy [Schuhmacher] got so open, he had no other choice but to shoot. I bet all he was thinking to himself was 'please God, let this draw iron.' "

Bennett then gave his final evaluation of the game when the good-humored laughter died away. "The thought I had about the red team, and the entire group, was that they played totally selflessly for the first time since I have been with them. Nobody tried to stand out, they preferred to fit in. We may lose that, but we genuinely got to the point where the players were more concerned with what they had to do for the team than what they had to do for themselves." Bennett, always teaching his staff, concluded, "That is what defense will do for you."

Single-game victory celebrations are short-lived (unless the game is for a national championship) because there is always another opponent to prepare for. John Chaney's Temple Owls awaited the arrival of the Badgers in the City of Brotherly Love. The staff turned their attention to that game because the team's new-found unity would surely be severely tested in less than three days. Chaney's hard-nosed, disciplined basketball team, playing in the confines of the 3,900 seat McGonigle Hall, was considered by many to be one of the toughest road environments in the country. Temple would also have redemption on their minds. Wisconsin had beaten them 57-54 in overtime, exactly one year prior, at the Field House. Showing his competitive nature, Bennett spoke of the challenge.

"I am excited about this game! We should get an answer to the question we have about our team, about whether we can continue to improve and play as a team, by playing in such a tough situation. If we do well, then we can feel pretty good about our chances for the rest of the season. This game will say volumes about our future."

The opportunity to play John Chaney, a man similar to Bennett with respect to doing an outstanding job in a difficult situation, however, did not motivate Bennett. When asked about any added incentives, he quickly retorted, "No, there are none. I respect him and the way his team plays. I am excited to play against well-known programs, but it is never a matter of personal pride in beating another coach. I don't think I have ever wanted to be compared to other people. That is mostly self-defeating. Whenever you start to play the comparison game, you are going to lose, you are going to look poor in comparison to someone else. That is an important lesson and I tell our kids not to do that, either."

Brian Hecker inquired about how much time Bennett wanted to set aside for the scouting tape (video) session at that day's practice. Grimacing, knowing his answer would disappoint Brian, he replied, "We are not going to watch any tape before the game." That was nothing new. Bennett had rarely used tape in his preparation, though he had promised Brian he would do more in the future. He justified his decision to Brian. "I get scared when I watch our opponent. I think their coach is better than I am. I think their players are better than ours. I just don't like how it makes me feel."

Bennett followed up this disclosure by citing a favorite story about a Russian high jumper. "I remember watching this guy compete when I was young. I don't remember his name, but he would sit with his back to the bar when his opponents jumped. When he was interviewed as to why he did so, he said that he did not want anything to interfere with who he was and what he was trying to do." Driving his point home, Bennett emphatically recalled, "I remember thinking as a young athlete, 'That is how I feel.' I hated going into a competition with preconceived notions about my opponent. I just wanted to go in there with my instincts and take it from there. Our players do not need to see Temple play. They know they are going to see a very tough zone defense. They will face a pounding low-post offense. They know it is going to be a fight. I don't think they need to know any more than that." Relaxed and confident, Bennett concluded, "All that is left is to take our little show on the road and do the best we can."

Temple University:
Wednesday, December 4, Philadelphia, Pennsylvania

Bennett did not get the best from his team to start the game. Grant did win his third consecutive center jump, once again tipping it to Okey, who had to balance himself on his toes, preventing an over-and-back violation, before handing off to Calderwood. Temple settled immediately into their vaunted 1-3-1 match-up zone. Mason, however, quickly found a soft spot at the right high-elbow (the area between the top of the key and the wing) but missed both of his open threes. Grant was also having no luck on the post. He missed his first shot, which he forced over two defenders, and threw a second ball past half-court when he tried to pass out of a double-team. Calderwood finally got Wisconsin on the board at the seventeen-minute mark when he stepped into the left high elbow gap and sank a three-pointer.

Bennett, unhappy with Okey's movement in the zone, replaced him with Daugherty after only four minutes of play. Temple, in turn, increased the pressure on the wings, sealing the ball handlers to the sideline and, thus, taking away ball reversal to the soft high-elbow. The change in strategy rattled Wisconsin. Duany, who had not taken a shot and looked unsure handling the ball, joined Okey on the sideline. Bennett went on a substitution binge after two more missed shots and two more turnovers. Nearly every dead ball brought the sound of the horn and another Badger substitute. Yet, none of the player combinations were able to handle Temple's zone. Wisconsin looked futile in their attempt to crack Chaney's defense, and when a careless shovel pass by Mason landed in the lap of a hustling Owl, the resulting breakaway dunk stretched the lead to 15-3. Bennett jumped to his feet and called a time-out.

He was angry during the break. He yelled at his team and broke a clipboard for effect, but neither helped when the players returned to the floor. Even when Daugherty and Auriantal managed to score two quick baskets, Wisconsin again went on a turnover spree and lost the ball on four out of five ensuing possessions. Temple reclaimed a commanding lead at 21-9. The half ended with Grant throwing the ball to half-court, right into the hands of a waiting defender, who took one last desperation shot from sixty feet. Counting that turnover, Wisconsin had eighteen turnovers and only seventeen points.

The exceptional defensive play of the Badgers had almost been lost in the offensive debacle. Wisconsin had applied aggressive ball pressure, they had shut down the driving lanes and clogged the post. For the most part, Temple was forced to take highly contested shots. In their own physical and intimidating way, the Badgers relinquished only eight points in the last ten minutes. Temple shot only 28 percent from the floor, and miraculously, UW trailed by just six points at the half, 23-17.

Bennett put the same starters out on the floor to start the second half, and even though they fell back by ten, he stuck with them for the first six minutes. Auriantal and Daugherty then replaced Duany and Okey. Except for a few brief cameo appearances, both of them were done for the rest of the game. Auriantal, meanwhile, hit back-to-back three-point baskets that pulled Wisconsin to within five, 37-32. The Badgers began to hold onto the ball and inch closer to the Owls using a six-man rotation, which consisted of Calderwood, Mason, Auriantal, Kosolcharoen, Daugherty, and Grant. Defense became the battle cry for both teams as they plugged their way toward the closing minutes of the game.

A rare fast-break slam by Grant made the score 46-43 with 4:50 remaining. Then the scoring stopped. Neither team could score for the next two minutes and twenty seconds. Auriantal broke the dual drought with a drive from the top of the key. He stutter-stepped to freeze the defender and then sprinted past him on the right. He split two post defenders with a long lunging hop, reached out past them, and flicked the ball up onto the glass. The official's whistle blew indicating a foul as the ball fell softly through the net. The free throw was nearly as eventful. Auriantal used body language, leaning back at a 45-degree angle after releasing the ball, to help the ball find the rim. His contortion worked and the game was tied at 46-46.

A minute later Temple hit two free throws and was once again up by two. Unfazed by the pressure, or perhaps relishing it, Calderwood calmly stepped back into his favorite zone gap (the left high-elbow), and made his third three-pointer of the game from that spot. Wisconsin led for the first time in thirty-six minutes, 49-48, with less than a minute to go. Temple failed to score on their possession. Mason added a pair of free throws with eighteen seconds to play and the lead was three.

Temple advanced the ball to mid-court and called for a time-out to set up their last play. Rashe Brokenborough cut to the right wing and received a pass. His teammate, Julian Dunkley, moved toward him to set a screen. Brokenborough dribbled hard to his right, but Auriantal cut him off. Brokenborough pump-faked Auriantal and got him to leave his feet. Then, to prevent getting his shot blocked, he jumped backward and sent a twenty-one-foot prayer to the rim. It hit nothing but net and the game was tied at 51 with five seconds to go. Wisconsin, in turn, pushed the ball to half-court and called for time of their own. Bennett set the play. Calderwood was to inbound the ball to Mason breaking from the center circle off a Daugherty screen. Then, Sean was to drive the ball to the basket for a shot if open, or feed Grant waiting on the post. The play went off without a hitch and Mason pulled up for a twenty-five-foot shot. Unfortunately, the ball barely grazed the bottom of the net as the final horn sounded. The Wisconsin-Temple game was going into overtime for the second straight year.

Mason came alive in the extra period and scored his team's first seven points, helping Wisconsin take a two-point lead. His contribution carried over to the defensive end of the floor where he dove diagonally through the air, rebounded a missed shot, and called time-out before hitting the floor. When play resumed, Daugherty set up seventeen feet from the basket on the right baseline, took a pass from Mason, and put Wisconsin up to stay at 60-56.

Wisconsin, shaken badly in the first half, showed great poise in pulling out their second tough road win of the early season. Their record improved to 3-0. The guards had come up big in the comeback. Mason grabbed seven rebounds to go with his game-high eighteen points; Auriantal added twelve, and Calderwood had ten points, seven assists, and four steals. Grant had a quiet but effective game in the post. He scored eight points and grabbed ten rebounds while holding Temple's big man, Marc Jackson, to ten points and five rebounds.

Still, the mood of the team was sour as they made the long late-night trip back to Madison. Bennett, nonetheless, was relieved to see that even though Okey had played poorly and spent most of the last twenty minutes of the game off the floor, he stayed in the game mentally and supported his teammates from the bench. Bennett praised and defended his talented sophomore.

"When I looked at Sam when he was on the bench, he was the cheerleader of the team. He was very much into the game and supporting his teammates. He loves to win and was very happy when we pulled it out. He is more frustrated with himself than anything else. If I didn't know that, I would be much more critical of him. Others perceive his scowl as selfishness, but he is really just upset with himself and I know that."

Despite the late arrival back in Madison, Brad Soderberg was in the office early the following morning sending out recruiting letters. Looking up, tired and weary from the intensity and length of the previous evening, he smiled weakly. "There is only one reason why we won that game—Coach Bennett. I can't really tell you why I feel that way, but I do. It is almost mystical." He chuckled and shook his head as he realized how preposterous his statement sounded.

The mood at practice later that day was subdued. Bennett made his way to the floor earlier than he normally did, before any of the players had arrived. He wanted to evaluate their behavior when they showed up for practice because he sensed that the team had regressed as a unit the previous night. One by one, the individual players slowly made their way onto the court. Most said very little to one another. Bennett was not pleased by the time he gave his pre-practice talk.

"I can understand you guys dragging anchor a little today. You are falling a little behind in the classroom and you have a right to be tired from the road trip. However, you certainly have a choice over your attitude. All we are asking is for a good hard hour from you. Some of you think you have an axe to grind with me. That's OK, because I don't care. I do not try to please all of you. I really do not try."

Bennett's voice grew stern and icy as he proclaimed, "You are not presenting a picture of a team that wants to get better. You are presenting me with a team that is essentially saying, 'Don't bother me.' Fine," he quipped dryly, "I won't. I won't bother you, I'll just tell you what to do." With that, he instructed the team to start a ball handling drill and made his way to mid-court, where he stood emotionless as the team began practice.

The players responded well to Bennett's challenge, quickly elevating their level of intensity. Yet, his method was inconsistent with his personality, his philosophy, and his five intangible guiding concepts. He was not leading the team by truly "serving" them. His indifference was teaching them to be reactionary, a trait he detests, instead of how to take responsibility for themselves and their actions. There was also no "unity" in his approach. Though not directly confrontational, in a passive-aggressive way he had pitted himself against his team. Finally, he was not practicing the concept of "thankfulness." Neither he nor his squad were thankful for the severe test of the Temple game, nor were they seeking the wisdom that the situation had to offer. Bennett knew he had erred in his approach as he stood silently on the sideline. His two recent outbursts had made him unhappy with his leadership.

The office was quiet the following morning. Both Soderberg and Hood were on the road, recruiting. The quiet atmosphere provided an opportunity for Bennett to discuss the events surrounding the Temple game.

"What do you tell your players when they are playing poorly and falling behind in a game, as they did at Temple?" I inquired.

"As you know, the other night I got angry and blew up. That has been a weakness of mine since I started coaching." He was visibly upset as he recounted his actions. "That is so far from what I expect of myself. I think coming down hard on a team actually makes them play tighter, which it did against Temple, as it often does. Thankfully, for the first time in my career, I was able to turn my anger around and be constructive in a short period of time. I had settled down and was more positive by halftime." He paused and laughed at himself. "When my teams have responded to those methods in the past, I think it was in spite of my approach, not because of it." His mood became serious again. "Every time I do that [explode at the team team], I lose myself a little, and I don't like that."

"Would you clarify that last statement?" I asked.

He fumbled through the papers on his desk to find his journal, then thumbed through the pages. "Let me read to you what I am going to share with our players today. I wrote it last night."

He stopped when he came to the passage. "Please understand it is in the form of a prayer," he noted.

"Lord, please help me in this present situation. I notice an increase in my stress level. My team has done better than I expected and I don't really know how to deal with it. During last night's game, I became a raving maniac once again, for the first time this year. It didn't last long and I returned to normal shortly after, but I did blow."

The level of thought he brought to his reflective writing was evidenced in the next passage. "Lord, what place does my behavior have in my obedience to you? If my lack of gentleness is disobedient, please forgive me. I think it is, but I do not seem to be able to change, so will you please help me and show me the way." Bennett stopped reading and explained that he had attended mass that morning. He then returned to his journal and read his concluding thoughts.

"Lord, thank you for sharing your wisdom with me this morning. My outburst on Wednesday night has been bothering me. Many would, and *have* said, that it was needed by the team. That is a good worldly view, but that does not connect properly with God's view. Proverbs suggests restraint rather than harshness. Lord, please help me build people up rather than tear them down. This faith of mine must be solid during the rough times as well as the good. If not, it is not solid faith! I will try to build my team up. I will review that which is proper, excellent, and praiseworthy. I am not going to insult and make people mad. Thank you for these insights."

He closed his journal gently and folded his hands gently on top of it, interlocking his fingers. "I don't want the kids to think my behavior, breaking a clipboard, cussing, or ignoring them was OK. It was not, and it was not in line with my faith. I want to use this as an opportunity to build them up. We have won a couple games that were expected to go the other way. We can still work to improve in several areas, but I think we can use this as a springboard. If we can do that, then we can start to recognize that these are possibly some of the signs of reaching our dream."

Bennett had returned to serving his team.

An evaluation of Bennett's personal struggle to stay faithful to his guiding philosophies was not very different from his approach in handling close games, especially in the closing minutes. The process of improving as a person rarely occurs in a linear fashion. Likewise, the flow of a close basketball game is not linear. Each team experiences peaks and valleys, often in a very short period of time. In those games, as in life, ultimate success is most often achieved by those individuals and teams that stay faithful to their fundamental principles during the good and the bad times. The Wisconsin players need look no further than their own head coach to find a living testimony of this philosophy. Bennett's players are continually exposed to the intense struggle he wages to stay faithful to his beliefs. They can not help but be influenced by Bennett's example, and when they find themselves in a hotly contested game, they understand they must remain consistent with their guiding principles. Thus, his teams have a better than average chance of pulling out those close games when this philosophy is combined with his simple schematic approach.

How simple is his scheme?

Bennett uses only two defenses, half-court man-to-man, and a 3-2 zone for emergencies only. Offensively, he relies on a few basic motion sets he calls "Blocker-mover." A "blocker" is primarily a screener, while a "mover" is essentially a cutter and scorer, though the two are not mutually exclusive. Any of the offensive sets can be used against either a man-to-man or zone defense. The team has only one rule on all out-of-bounds plays: "two small and a big," meaning a guard takes the ball out of bounds, and another guard and a forward work together to get the ball in bounds. Finally, the team runs a very simple press attack (taking only five minutes of practice to learn) which places the responsibility on the individual players in different areas of the floor.

What connection does that simple approach serve in close contests?

There is one primary association. Practices and games are not cluttered with a lot of decision-making. Which offense should be practiced? Which defense should be used? Rather, the primary objective is to identify specific roles for each player that provide him (and the team) the best opportunity to succeed. For example, Ty Calderwood, as the point guard, has the responsibility to take care of the ball. He is free to do whatever he needs to accomplish that goal. In turn, he knows that late in games it is his responsibility to handle the ball and to distribute it to the right people at the right time. That is his specialty and he takes great pride in executing that task. Basically, he takes ownership of the role and is *empowered* to do whatever it takes to succeed. Yet, his acceptance of that obligation does not restrict him in any other aspect of his game, as long as he does not neglect that one responsibility. If he finds himself open late in a game, he has the freedom to take the shot, if indeed it is the best shot his team can get.

Likewise, Hennssy Auriantal is given the assignment of being the defensive stopper on the team. He always defends the opponent's point guard or best perimeter scoring threat. He knows that it is his responsibility to harass the ball handler as far down the floor as he can without getting beat. By doing so, he helps all of his teammates by making it difficult for the opposing team to get into their offense. Late in a game, Auriantal knows that he will be given the mission of disrupting the opponent's offense. Once again, he takes immense pride in this task and is free to do whatever it takes to accomplish his goal.

Every player on the team has a clearly defined role. That includes the players on the red team. Bennett carefully evaluates the players to identify their strengths and weaknesses. In reality, the players are not *placed* into a role by Bennett as much as they *define* it themselves. Bennett simply helps by positively reinforcing those behaviors he desires (strengths) and negatively reinforcing those behaviors he does not favor (weaknesses). This is not a simple or uncomplicated process, as the individual roles are ever-evolving. In addition, Bennett is sensitive to the desires of each player, and allows them the freedom to redefine and expand their contributions to the team.

An eventual outcome of the process, hopefully, is that the players become keenly aware of not only their own roles on the team, but also those of their teammates. In turn, Bennett does not position a player in a situation that calls for him to execute in his area of weakness. Ideally, then, each player is empowered by his own strengths and performs with confidence, regardless of the circumstances.

Bennett's role is that of the team architect. He orchestrates the use of personnel and makes subtle adjustments to his schematic approach, thus maximizing the talents of his players. Bennett calls this process his continual "tinkering with the intricacies of the team." That tinkering, which is really his leadership, is never felt more strongly than in the closing minutes of a close contest. He assesses the situation, puts players on the floor who can succeed in that setting, and empowers them to either win or lose the game of their own accord. To the players' credit, they have won more of those contests than not.

Bennett explained his thoughts on the topic. "It is my philosophy, opinion, and method of coaching to try to develop a style of play and an approach that will keep our team in games, but I believe the kids win the games. I prefer to stay out of the way down the stretch and not over-complicate it. People often ask me what I do in those situations in which we have won close games. The reality is that I do very little. There are no special words or formulas. Most of my work is done by the time the game starts. As I have told the team on many occasions, there is not really much I can do to help them if they can't get the job done at that point. If we have done a good job in practice and prepared well, the players will believe they can win. Then in the game all they have to do is commit themselves to playing great defense and to staying in the game, and something good will eventually happen."

That approach had produced victories over Memphis State and Temple in the early season.

Chapter 11

Be Thankful, Always!

Brown University:
Saturday, December 7, Madison, Wisconsin

The team was struggling to find an offensive identity. Bennett hoped that their next three games against Brown University, the University of Wisconsin-Milwaukee, and St. Bonaventure would solve those problems. Ivy league Brown University, 0-4 on the season and playing their fourth road game in eight nights, was first up. Interestingly, when Okey showed up for the noon shooting practice, his hair, which had been dyed golden since the summer, had returned to its normal dark brown.

Bennett decided to start the unit that had played so well in the overtime period at Temple. Calderwood, Mason, and Kosolcharoen played the three "mover" perimeter positions while Okey and Grant "blocked" along the lane. Grant made it four-for-four on opening tips. He again used his running jump style effectively and tapped the ball to Okey at midcourt. The teams traded turnovers in the first thirty seconds of action. On the Badger's third possession of the game, with the score 0 to 0, Sean Mason took the ball on the left wing, faked a pass to Grant on the low post, and drove hard to his left. He blew past his man, and when Grant's defender did not step out to help, Mason planted both feet hard for a jump shot. His scream could be heard throughout the Field House as his left knee buckled under him. Though he never went to the floor, two of Brown's defenders, Chris White and Paul Krasinski, grabbed him immediately when they saw the pained expression on his face.

The crowd fell silent, recalling similar events just eleven months earlier. He clutched his left knee, however, not his surgically repaired right knee as many in the crowd feared. Okey and Kosolcharoen made a make-shift seat out of their arms and carried him to the bench, where head trainer Andy Winterstein assessed the severity of his injury. Tests later revealed that he would be lost to the team for no less than four weeks due to a strained medial collateral ligament, the ligament on the inside of the knee. Mason was to face a monumental obstacle, playing the remainder of the season on two injured knees.

Only half of the crowd was watching the action on the floor when play resumed. The others were still watching nervously as Winterstein attended to Mason. Offensive fluidity again escaped the Badgers. They turned the ball over for the third time in four possessions. Calderwood finally moved the scoreboard when he penetrated into the middle of the lane and hit a twelve-foot jumper. Seconds later, Okey stripped the ball at the mid-court stripe and tossed it ahead to a streaking Auriantal, who laid it in for a 4-0 lead. Then the offense stalled and could produce only one more basket on a Grant tip-in over the next several minutes. Wisconsin had scored only six points at the fourteen-minute mark, and even though Brown University had committed seven turnovers, a three-pointer by Aaron Butler drew his team to within one at 6-5. Jason Sewer followed that by hitting another three-pointer, his only basket of the night, and Brown led, 8-6.

Bennett went to his "big lineup" for the first time since Memphis State when he found his team still trailing 13-12 after eleven minutes. Brown's tight 1-2-2 zone had packed the lane. Bennett wanted to use his team's superior size of Okey, Grant, and Daugherty to go over the shorter defenders. He also went to the "Triangle" offense to emphasize the height advantage. The Triangle offense places all three post players in a "T" area that extends out to the corners on the baseline and up past the top of the key. The guards, meanwhile, maintain floor balance by staying on opposite wings. The move paid off, as Okey and Grant scored inside, while Auriantal and Calderwood hit open threes on kick-out passes when the defense sagged in to help on the post. Bennett went back to his bench when the score reached 22-15. He substituted freely for the next five minutes, though he did stay with a "big" team. Wisconsin built a 27-18 halftime lead. The offense, however, still toiled in inefficiency. Their eleven turnovers, which came against a passive defense, kept the opponent in the game.

Bennett returned to a three-guard lineup and the double low-post offense to start the half, inserting Auriantal in Mason's spot. The team's poor offensive production, at first a mild concern, became an important fact as the second half unfolded. The poor performances against Memphis State and Temple could be explained away by the quality of opponent and difficult playing environments. When his team's turnovers again matched its offensive output (four in the first seven minutes of the half against an inferior opponent), there was no other conclusion to draw, however. Wisconsin's offense was simply bad! Still, there was a game to win. Bennett called a twenty-second time-out and settled on what he considered his best lineup of the night: Calderwood, Auriantal, Kosolcharoen, Okey, and Daugherty. He jumped back and forth between the number two (double post) and number three (Triangle) offenses, using Kosolcharoen in the "T" area when he went to the Triangle. That group scored six points and held Brown scoreless over the next six minutes to finally put the game away. The Brown players ran out of gas with seven minutes to go, trailing 38-23.

Booker Coleman joined the red team for the final 2:45 of the game. The unit managed only one point, a free throw by Burkemper, but held Brown to only one field goal. That basket was Brown's second of the entire second half, and only their seventh for the entire game. The final score was 52-30. Auriantal led the Badgers in both scoring and rebounding. He had thirteen points and seven rebounds. Defense again bailed out Wisconsin. Brown hit only seven of thirty-eight shots on their way to an 18 percent shooting night, and their thirty points was the second lowest point total by a Wisconsin opponent in the history of the program. Still, no one felt like celebrating. Mason's injury left a big hole in the offense, not to mention the team's psyche. Duany's stat line read DNP (Did Not Play). His lackluster play since injuring his ankle had landed him back on the bench. Though 4-0, all was not well in the Badger camp.

Bennett decided against making an issue of the offensive affliction his team was suffering. Instead, he concentrated on preparing for the University of Wisconsin-Milwaukee. He added only one new wrinkle to the offense, a flare-cut to the wing off a fake dribble penetration by the point guard, the same play that Frank Dobbs' Brown University team had run against him more than a dozen times. Legendary UCLA coach John Wooden once proclaimed that there were no new ideas in basketball. If that is indeed the case, pirating the best ideas of other coaches only makes sense. Frank Dobbs had left his mark on the Badgers, even in defeat.

UW-Milwaukee:
Tuesday, December 10, Madison, Wisconsin

Three days later, on December 10, the Badgers welcomed in-state opponent UW-Milwaukee to the Field House. Bennett decided to return to his "big lineup." Okey, Daugherty, and Grant played the T-area while Auriantal and Calderwood handled the guard spots. Grant made it five for five on opening taps, again going to Okey at mid-court. Okey opened the scoring when he hit his first shot from just inside the top of the key. Unfortunately, the next five minutes produced only missed baskets (four) and turnovers (three). Wisconsin fell behind 4-2. Soon after, Grant picked up his second foul. Bennett called a twenty-second time-out and replaced him with Kosolcharoen. However, he stayed in the Triangle offense with Kosolcharoen working the "T." The Badgers then put together a quick eight-point run and took the lead at 10-4.

Bennett stayed with his starters longer than usual, with the exception of Grant, and nine minutes passed before he subbed. Duany replaced Auriantal on the wing, and Coleman came in for Daugherty on the post. When that crew failed to produce any offense, Bennett went back to Grant. He picked up his third foul less than a minute later, and returned to the bench to resume his spectator duties. Nonetheless, Wisconsin led 16-8 twelve and a half minutes into the game. Then, Okey became a force on both ends of the floor for the remainder of the half. He scored both inside and outside on his way to accumulating fifteen points and eight rebounds. In addition to Okey's performance, there was one other note of interest. David Burkemper played his first "significant" minutes of the season. Bennett had been growing increasingly fond of his style of play in practice and wanted to test him earlier in games. Though not spectacular, he more than held his own.

Bennett went deep into his bench as Wisconsin played much improved basketball in the last ten minutes of the half. Still, the Badgers scored only twenty-nine points, even though they had taken good shots and reduced their turnovers. UW-Milwaukee remained within striking distance at 29-20.

Grant started the second half on the bench. A hustling Mike Kosolcharoen took his place and the Badgers went back to their double low-post offense. Three minutes later, after having sent a message to Grant, Bennett reinserted him along with Duany. The Panthers fought valiantly against their more heralded in-state brethren, but they simply did not have the talent or experience to stay with Wisconsin. The Badgers stretched the lead to fifteen (45-30) with just under ten minutes to play. The stands started to empty with 3:04 left in the game, after another offensive burst had pushed the lead to 59-35. Booker again joined the red team of Burkemper, Schuhmacher, Quest, and Vraney to battle out the final few minutes. Coleman brought the remaining crowd to its feet with a reverse power-slam to punctuate the win.

The 61-41 victory pushed Wisconsin's record to 5-0. More important, however, their offense showed signs of life for the first time since Mason went down with his injury. Wisconsin committed only eleven turnovers for the game, and Okey's thirty points and seventeen rebounds were both career highs. His performance was significant for another, less tangible reason. His impressive performance was not a result of individual play. He played within the context of the team and took only what was available to him. He played hard; he played selflessly; and he played to win. Bennett was glad to have his 1995-96 Big Ten Freshman of the Year back on track.

Bennett's post-game press conference remarks were complimentary to Ric Cobb's UW-Milwaukee crew. "We won the game, but we were clearly outplayed." They hadn't been. Still, Bennett didn't want his team getting satisfied with wins against inferior opponents. He went on to explain that it was no secret that if the team wanted to continue to win, they would have to solve their offensive problems.

St. Bonaventure University:
Saturday, December 14, Olean, New York

Game three of the triad pitted East Coast "style" against Midwest brawn. The contrasting styles—the traditional no-nonsense Badgers and the glitzy showtime of the Bonnies—was evident from the start. The introduction of starters provided the backdrop for the comparison. The Wisconsin players stoically jogged to half-court as their names were called out in a traditional and uneventful manner. Then the dance contest began. Each starting member for St. Bonaventure used their personal introduction as a stage call to slowly dance their way, with a variety of hip-hop and funky moves, to half-court. The crowd cheered wildly in approval. The Badger players stared silently, less than impressed at the display. Their expressions made it clear that they were more concerned with the contest to take place on the basketball floor.

Bennett started the game in a three-guard set, still undecided whether his team played best with three guards or three post players. Calderwood, Auriantal, and Kosolcharoen played on the perimeter of the double post offense, while Grant and Okey again got the nod along the lane. Grant again secured the opening tap to Okey. Grant's turnaround jump shot, Kosolcharoen's back-to-back baskets, Grant's tip-in, and Okey's press-breaking lay-up pushed the score to 10-0. For the first time all season, Wisconsin had a fast start of their own, and the Bonnies' dancing shoes had been put away.

Bennett then chose hard work over talent when Auriantal picked up his second foul early in the action. He looked down the bench and decided to use David Burkemper, the slow-footed, slightly overweight, once-cut walk-on who repeatedly impressed his coach with his intelligence and tenacity. The fast start gave Bennett the freedom to experiment with Burkemper early in the game against a quick athletic team. David initially struggled against the pressure of the Bonnie's David Capers, fumbling the ball off his foot and committing an offensive foul, but he eventually settled down.

Bennett used his bench liberally as his team maintained their lead, thanks to both accurate shooting and aggressive defense. Burkemper's three-point shot extended Wisconsin's lead to 26-10. With under a minute to go in the half, Wisconsin's lead grew to nineteen points on Grant's breakaway dunk. St. Bonaventure hit a three to close out the scoring in the first half, but Wisconsin held a commanding 34-18 lead heading into the locker room. UW's relentless defense, which forced numerous bad shots, held the Bonnies to only 24 percent shooting. The Badgers, meanwhile, rang up the an impressive 64 percent of their first-half attempts. David Burkemper logged fifteen minutes of playing time during the impressive team display.

Auriantal returned for the start of the second half and David watched from his familiar spot on the bench. Wisconsin maintained a double-digit cushion for the majority of the second half. They scored most of their second-half points from the free throw line as the Bonnies repeatedly fouled them with their aggressive, gambling defense. However, the last two minutes of the game became eventful when St. Bonaventure converted four missed Badger free throws into four straight baskets, including three three-point bombs. The score narrowed to 69-64 before Calderwood settled down at the line (having missed four of his last six) and sealed the victory with six straight free throws. Calderwood went to the charity stripe a total of fourteen times in the last ninety seconds of play, converting ten of the fourteen. His efforts were enough to help the Badgers hold on for a 77-68 victory. The point total was their best offensive output of the season.

Grant broke out of his three-game slump by scoring a team-high sixteen points. Oddly, though, he managed only one rebound. Kosolcharoen added fifteen points and Okey had his second double-double in a row with twelve points and twelve boards. The triumph improved their record to 6-0. Bennett and the Badgers finally felt good about their play as they boarded the commuter plane in Olean, New York, and headed back to Madison for a nine-day final exam break.

The players took four days off to prepare for their tests and Bennett was cheerful for the first time in several weeks. The break from practice gave the coaches an opportunity to relax at their morning meetings. Bennett, smiling broadly and swiveling in his chair, commented on David Burkemper's performance.

"I just cannot get over the job David Burkemper did. It should not go unnoticed. Here is a great kid who has mental toughness, tries to do what we want done, and is totally committed to the team over himself. That commitment allows him to do the right thing and to compete. It is what enables him to overcome his fear." Lowering his voice to a soft whisper, as if revealing a long-held secret, he added, "That is why you have to recruit *attitude*! I know that you are not going to win the Big Ten with five David Burkempers on the floor, but if you have guys that have the qualities he has, and are also good players, then you do not have to be as athletic." Bennett shook his head and smiled. "I was absolutely amazed. Did you see me when he made that three-pointer?" Mocking himself, he raised both fists above his head and yelled, "DAVID!" Laughter and smiles returned to the daily staff meeting for the first time in a long time. The coaches enjoyed every moment of it.

The discussion provided a platform for the staff to discuss the behavior and character of their team. At issue was the off-court behavior of the players and how it reflected not only on the individuals, but also on the team. Bennett and his staff were not pleased with that aspect of their team. "I was talking with Jack [his brother and fellow coach] about this just last night. I was telling him that I felt badly about how hard I had been on the kids. He told me, 'Dick, you gotta do it when things are going well, and that includes everything. When it is not going well, then you have a tendency to look at the players and jump on those things that have bothered you all along, but have gone unsaid, blaming those out of frustration.'" Bennett continued, "I have noticed that they are not respecting the people who are helping them out." Several players routinely used profane language, dressed poorly, and treated support personnel such as team managers, waiters, waitresses, and caterers at their training table with little respect. "That has bothered me and we need to sit down and talk about what is right." The team was 6-0 with nothing pressing on their agenda, so Bennett felt it was a good time to address those concerns.

Bennett has very few training rules, unlike many coaches who consider it their professional obligation as the head of the program to set appropriate protocol for their team. Mandating arbitrary standards of behavior and dress, as he had done earlier in his career, had become phony to Bennett. He had become quite willing to let his players set their own standards, as long as it did not infringe on him or disrupt the team. He did not like to "box in" his players with excessive rules on or off the court, a lesson he had learned while coaching his son, Tony. Rather, he preferred to help the players develop an individual understanding of respect for themselves and others. Since that had not occurred, and the behavior of some players could be perceived as disrespectful, he vowed to speak on the issue before the next game. He assured the staff that there would be no mandates and no finger pointing, just advice on earning mutual respect.

"I will gather them and say that they are doing things that are creating a level of discomfort among the staff. I will ask them if they think that treating people with respect and looking presentable is imposing on them in some way? I will ask them why they act and dress that way? We can then explain why it bothers us. But I won't tell them how to act. That is up to them." By doing so, he would demonstrate to them that he had faith in their judgment, that he respected them as adults, and hoped that they would do the same to others.

When finals are complete and most of the Wisconsin students head home to family or friends for the holiday break, there are no winter vacations for the Badger basketball team. The players walked or drove through a deserted campus on their way to practice on Friday, December 20. There was precious little time to prepare for the stretch of five games in the next thirteen days. Still, their attitudes were refreshed with the break from classes as they began to prepare for Providence College, a preseason favorite to win the Big East Conference. Bennett was optimistic that the team could push their record to 7-0 against the tough opponent—optimistic, that is, until Sam Okey's back began to spasm at Sunday's practice. Okey would not play in the game. He had a history of back pain and it made no sense to risk further aggravation at that point in the season. The Big Ten opener against Minnesota was just one week away.

Providence College:
Monday, December 23, Madison, Wisconsin

Paul Grant was late for the pregame meal on game day, December 23, and was pulled from the starting lineup. As was just mentioned, although Bennett has very few "training rules," being on time for team events is at the top of the list. At that point, a dead battery was the last thing Bennett needed, but rules were rules. Coleman would get the starting nod that afternoon. Bennett's makeshift lineup of Calderwood, Auriantal, Kosolcharoen, Daugherty, and Coleman would have to lean heavily on their defense to get the better of a very talented Providence club.

The group did clamp down early, and held Providence to just one of seven shooting, taking an early 7-1 lead. Providence's coach Pete Gillen inserted God Shammgod, a standout guard who was recovering from an injury, into the game. He also changed his strategy and applied more defensive pressure by implementing a 1-2-2 half-court trap to complement the Friars' aggressive man-to-man. Wisconsin could not counter the adjustment and was held scoreless for the next six minutes. During that same stretch, Austin Croshere, a future first-round draft pick of the Indiana Pacers, scored seven of his team's next eight points. Providence moved past Wisconsin, taking a 9-7 lead.

Wisconsin's personnel problems worsened when Calderwood picked up his second foul with ten minutes remaining in the half. The foul sent Corey Wright crashing to the floor and Calderwood to the bench. Bennett chose to go with Duany over Burkemper because he was desperate for scoring, which was Duany's, not Burkemper's, forte. Croshere hit a set of free throws before Duany rewarded Bennett's choice by hitting a three-point basket from the right wing, and Wisconsin regained the lead 12-11.

The scoring came to a standstill for the next two minutes. Auriantal and Kosolcharoen were struggling against the trapping defense, so

Bennett went back to Calderwood. The move, however, did not help Wisconsin's cause. Calderwood missed a quick three which Providence converted into a score. Then, both Kosolcharoen and Duany threw long passes against the press; both were intercepted and converted into fast-break baskets. The 6-0 run had Bennett on his feet signaling for time.

Providence came out of the time-out and went right at Calderwood, who was playing with two fouls. Shammgod isolated him on the left wing and drove hard to the baseline. When Shammgod forced contact between the two, Calderwood had no choice but to let him go past for a lay-up. His caution on defense did not keep him on the floor long. He was whistled for pushing off the pesky Wright for his third foul on the very next offensive possession. Bennett's gamble to play him backfired and his bench reserves dwindled further.

Trailing 20-12, the Badgers regrouped themselves. Auriantal hit a three from the top of the key and Grant followed with his own fifteen-foot jump shot from the free throw line. The Wisconsin fans came to their feet, imploring the Badgers to generate some defense. They did not get their wish. Kosolcharoen lunged for a steal on a pass into the post, leaving his player unguarded at the basket for an easy lay-in. The breakdown did not break the Badgers' spirit. Once again, they surged offensively and closed the gap to only two, 26-24, with just under a minute to play. However, Auriantal missed a driving lay-up that would have tied the game, and Providence converted the miss into another basket to lead at half, 28-24. Wisconsin was still very much in the contest, despite committing eleven turnovers and allowing Providence to shoot 57 percent from the floor.

The second half started with more of the same old, familiar theme—turnovers. Auriantal, Kosolcharoen, Duany, and Calderwood all threw poor passes that resulted in Providence baskets, two on dunks by Croshere. The Friars' lead abruptly vaulted to eight. Providence extended the margin to thirteen, when Shammgod hit Ruben Garces for a spinning reverse lay-up with just over eleven minutes to play. Bennett again called time-out to stop the calamity. Grant came out of the time-out and scored on an up-and-under move. Then Kosolcharoen stole a pass that Daugherty converted into a jump-hook. Just as the crowd grew animated in anticipation of a comeback, Croshere hit a long three to hush their enthusiasm.

Daugherty finally came to life after having been on the short end of the Croshere match-up all night. He dominated the boards on the next five trips up and down the floor, three of which he turned into baskets of his own. His seventeen-foot baseline jump shot narrowed the margin to 46-40. Gillen called a time-out to cool down Daugherty and the Badgers. Croshere came out of the sideline huddle and posted Daugherty up on the left block. However, his spin moves failed to shake Daugherty, and his shot slipped off the front of the rim. Sean gathered up the errant shot for his fifth rebound in a row. Unfortunately, the Badger run was stopped when Kosolcharoen threw away a pass, trying to feed Grant on the ensuing possession. Bennett jumped out of his seat and shook his head angrily, as he saw Kosolcharoen commit yet another turnover. For all his tenacity and toughness on defense, Mike had a terrible time handling the ball on offense, a fact that continually challenged Bennett's patience.

Nonetheless, the Badgers dug in defensively and forced Providence into their fifteenth turnover of the night. Back on offense, Grant's twelve-foot leaping leaner pulled Wisconsin within three at 46-43, with 4:15 remaining in regulation. Amazingly, Daugherty and Grant had scored all nineteen of the team's second-half points up to that juncture.

Providence had again extended their lead to 55-47, thanks to exceptional free throw shooting, and were in complete control of the game with just over forty seconds to play. Calderwood, displaying a flare for the dramatic, summoned up enough energy for one last chaotic push. He took a feed from Duany and hit a long three-pointer as the Friars' Corey Wright sailed past his eyes. The Badgers hastily called time to strategize. Bennett set up a full-court press, but to no avail. Providence advanced the ball easily through Wisconsin's pressure, and Kosolcharoen was forced to foul Croshere, who had made sure he had the ball in his hands. He made both shots.

Trailing 57-50, Calderwood pushed the ball up the left side of the floor, crossed over to his right hand, and pulled up for another three. Wright, however, grabbed his arm before he could get the shot off. Ty calmly cashed in on all three free throws and the margin narrowed to four. Only 19.4 seconds remained when the Friars inbounded the ball. Grant fouled Derrick Brown when, once again, the Badger press failed to produce a turnover. The fans began to stream out of the Field House, believing the game was out of reach. Brown, who converted on both attempts, made it seem that those who had departed early were wise. Still,

Calderwood was not finished. Grant took the ball out of the net and passed it in to Calderwood who raced up the left side of the floor and let another running three fly. It hit all net and the Badgers frantically called their last time-out.

The press failed to produce a trap for the third straight time and Wisconsin had to foul immediately. The ball was, not coincidentally, once again in the hands of Austin Croshere. He stepped to the line with seven clicks left on the clock needing only one free throw to seal the victory, as his team already led 59-56—an easy task considering he had made nine of his ten charity shots in the previous two minutes. The first shot barely drew iron as it skidded under the rim to the delight of the crowd. Those who had departed too early stopped and watched the action unfold on the television monitors located above the concession stands. Croshere overcompensated on the second shot and the ball bounded hard off the back of the rim. Grant grabbed the rebound and shoveled a pass to Calderwood. He drove hard up the left side of the floor, again crossed over to his right hand at the mid-court stripe, and looked for an opening to pull up and shoot. Jason Murdock reached out and grabbed him before he could find an opening. The two-shot foul, a heads-up play by Murdock, sent Calderwood to the line for two free throws. With only 1.1 second remaining, Wisconsin needed three points just to tie! Calderwood made his first attempt. Bennett then put Coleman in the game to join Grant on the blocks, hoping for a desperation tip-in on an intentional missed shot, to send the game into overtime. Ty did his part and the ball bounced high off the front of the rim. Then, as the crowd held their breath and the teams scrambled for the rebound, the ball bounced off Grant's leg and trickled out of bounds. Providence, a team that would win twenty-four games on the season and make it to the elite eight of the NCAA Tournament, had survived the last-second comeback for a hard-fought 59-57 win. The exodus from the Field House then began in earnest.

The team had played well enough to win without Okey, but that was of no consolation. Besides, with only two days to prepare for their next game, there was no time to dwell on the loss. The team practiced on both Christmas Eve and Christmas Day in preparation for their game against Ball State, which would take place on the 26th. Time away from one's family during the holidays is just one of many sacrifices a coach (and player) must make during the season.

Bennett mourned time spent away from family, no matter what time of the year. For this one holiday, however, things would be different. Anne Bennett had organized an early surprise family Christmas following the Providence game. Bennett's brother Bob, a clinical psychologist from Washington D.C., flew in for the special day. Bennett's daughter Amy and her new husband Joe drove down from Green Bay. Tony and Laurel were back in Madison to spend time with the family before heading back to New Zealand. And of course, there was Anne, who had coordinated the whole affair. Bennett was obviously appreciative, as he later commented that it was the first time in his career that he was able to leave a loss behind him at the gym and just enjoy the evening with his family.

Ball State University:
Thursday, December 26, Madison, Wisconsin

Two straight days of powdery snow had blanketed the city in the spirit of the season, and seemed to lighten the moods of everyone. Practices went well on Christmas Eve and Christmas Day. Former UW assistant Ray McCallum made his first appearance back in Madison as a coach, having accepted the head position at Ball State three seasons earlier. McCallum had been a Badger assistant between the years of 1984 and 1993.

Okey's back had healed, Grant made it to the pregame meal on time, and Daugherty was rewarded for his effort against Providence as the "big lineup" once again took the floor to start a game. Calderwood and Auriantal patrolled the guard positions, hoping to make McCallum's homecoming inhospitable.

Grant won his seventh consecutive tip. This time, however, he and Okey had a new twist to their opening ritual. After the tap to half-court, Grant sprinted down the floor for a return pass from Okey and an easy lay-up. The Badgers never looked back. Wisconsin, using their superior size in the Triangle offense, to score the Badgers' first nineteen points, jumped out to an early 19-9 lead.

Bennett went to his reserves and the double low-post at the 13:30 mark, but the unit of Duany, Hennssy, Kosolcharoen, Okey, and Grant struggled. Turnovers and missed shots plagued the group as Ball State narrowed the gap over the next five minutes to 21-17. Bennett went back to starting lineup, as well as to the Triangle offense, and a ten-point lead was immediately reestablished. The Badgers led 36-26 at intermission.

Bennett had lost confidence in his bench, namely in Coleman and Duany, and thus settled into a six-man rotation for the duration of the game. Kosolcharoen was the only other Badger to see the floor, except for the closing seconds when Bennett cleared the bench. In turn, all five starters, Calderwood, Auriantal, Okey, Daugherty, and Grant, scored in double figures and they dismantled a determined but overmatched Ball State team, 74-59. Wisconsin shot the ball exceptionally well, 58 percent for the game. Once again, however, they committed more than twenty turnovers.

Bennett's strategy to use a six-player rotation had been successful against Ball State, but it remained to be seen if he could use so few players over an extended period of time. His new strategy would be tested when his team traveled to Milwaukee's Bradley Center for a New Year's Eve contest against Marquette, and when they traveled afterward to Minneapolis for the Big Ten opener against fifteenth-ranked Minnesota. To cap the holiday spree of games, they were scheduled to return home to face twelfth-ranked Indiana less than thirty-six hours later. That stretch would prove to be a real test for the short rotation, that is, if all remained healthy and were able to play.

"I always feel funny when I go to a place I have never been," noted Bennett as his team readied for their practice at Edgewood College. A high school wrestling tournament in the Field House had forced the Badgers to practice off campus. Edgewood, less than a mile from the Field House on Monroe Street, was their best option. Bennett's premonition proved to be prophetic as Ty Calderwood sprained his right knee, stretching his medial collateral ligament, in an awkward collision diving for a loose ball. Bennett recalled his reaction as he witnessed the injury. "I knew right then and there we were in trouble. That really threw a cloud over everything."

Calderwood's injury, though considered minor, made it doubtful that he could play during the tough three-game stretch. The depth of the team had vanished. Bennett's six-player rotation was down to five. Worse yet, Bennett's hands had become tied as a coach. He could no longer substitute a player who was hurting the team with his play, or make a defensive "stopper" substitution to shut down a hot-shooting opponent. Nor could he protect a player in foul trouble, or rest his players to keep them fresh for the final minutes of the game. Basically, he could no longer position the players into roles that significantly improved the team's chances of winning. Fouls, fatigue, and the opponent would control those decisions, putting him in a powerless situation. The only hope Bennett had was for Mike Kosolcharoen, Duany Duany, Booker Coleman, or David Burkemper to step forward and contribute immediately.

Marquette University:
Tuesday, December 31, Milwaukee, Wisconsin

The 7-1 Badgers and the 7-2 Eagles kicked off their own New Year's Eve party at 7:05 P.M. Bennett was not the only coach that night without the services of one of his top players. Mike Deane would not be able to use Anthony Pieper, a 6'3" senior guard and the Golden Eagles' third leading scorer, because of a dislocated left shoulder.

Auriantal assumed the point guard responsibilities in Ty's absence, while Duany slid into the vacated guard position. Grant lost his first tap of the year when Marquette's Faisal Abraham outleaped him to start the game. A pre-designed allyoop dunk failed for the Eagles. Using their Triangle offense, the Badgers went to work, hitting ten of their first thirteen shots. Wisconsin built a 25-14 lead in the first eight and a half minutes of play. Bennett finally went to the bench at the 11:00 mark and replaced Okey with Coleman and Duany with Kosolcharoen.

Wisconsin gave the ball away on their next three possessions, and Bennett began to substitute freely, trying to find a substitution lineup that could maintain the lead. He finally settled on Burkemper, Duany, Kosolcharoen, Okey, and Coleman. The group stemmed the flow for a few minutes, but when Burkemper had difficulty controlling the talented Aaron Hutchins, he was replaced by Auriantal. Bennett was steadfast in staying with the unit of Duany, Hennssy, Mike, Sam, and Booker, (though he did alternate Sam and Sean), so that he could keep Paul out of foul trouble and keep Sam and Sean fresh for the second half. The unit, however, played poorly down the stretch. They produced only one basket for the remainder of the half and were outscored 20-7. Wisconsin trailed 34-32 at the break.

Daugherty scored the Badgers' first nine points of the second half as the team reclaimed the lead at 41-38. Duany's three with just under fourteen minutes to play pushed the lead to 44-38. Marquette then held Wisconsin scoreless on their next three possessions, and pulled even with nine minutes to go. Moments later, Hutchins hit another three-point basket to put his team back on top. Sensing Wisconsin was at the breaking point, Deane began trapping the Badger guards, a strategy that had worked well in the first half. When Okey drove through the trap for an easy lay-up, however, Deane went back to his man-to-man defense. That would be the last highlight for Wisconsin.

Bennett stayed with the six-player rotation of Duany, Mike, Hennssy, Sam, Sean, and Paul for the entire second half. Unfortunately, whether as a result of fatigue or a lack of hustle by the Badgers, Marquette got every loose ball and every rebound in the final four minutes of the game to pull out a 59-52 win. Wisconsin produced only seven baskets in the last thirty-one-plus minutes of the game, going seven for thirty-two, a mere 21 percent. Duany did register a career high fourteen points in thirty-three minutes of play. That, however, was little consolation for Bennett.

"That loss hit us harder than any loss since I have been here. Everybody is bothered by it. Not that Marquette is not a good team, they may even be a better team than us, but it is the way we lost. That one hurt! Even though we had obstacles to overcome, I thought we were too willing to let Marquette take the game away from us. We didn't *fight* for the win."

Bennett considered his next course of action on the team's late-night flight to Minneapolis immediately following the game. There was nothing he could do about his personnel. Injuries had dictated which players would have to be on the floor. There were no technical adjustments to be made for the Minnesota game, so his best recourse was to get the team mentally prepared to compete in a hostile environment against an athletic, deep, and talented Minnesota team. Therefore, Bennett settled on reinforcing the idea of competing. A team meeting was called when the team reached their hotel in downtown Minneapolis. At 1:30 A.M., on New Year's Day, Bennett lectured his team well into the night. He was especially displeased that they had shown a propensity for going soft in practices and in games when things became tough. That was inexcusable in his eyes, and had become the primary limitation of the team, next to their sporadic offense. They had not yet competed, played hard, and refused to lose for forty minutes in any of their games. An exhausted team and coaching staff crawled into their beds at 3 A.M. Their New Year's celebrations would have to wait.

University of Minnesota:
Thursday, January 2, Minneapolis, Minnesota

Bennett was pleased with his team's response to his message over the next two days. He noted before that evening's game, "They understood what I meant and took it to heart. I can sense the commitment to not let that happen against Minnesota, or any other game. I can sense it in their attitude since that meeting. They are much more purposeful in our meetings, practices, or whatever little thing we are doing." His team would need every ounce of competitive spirit they had to battle the Gophers. In the hostile Williams arena, optimism was high for Clem Haskins' team, as it entered the game on a nine-game winning streak. Their 11-1 overall record had Haskins outwardly proclaiming his team's intentions of winning the Big Ten championship.

Williams Arena, a legendary basketball venue, has one of the purest traditional basketball environments in the entire country. The university had wisely decided to renovate the old building instead of tearing it down and replacing it. The dark maroon bleachers cascade down to a four-foot elevated floor, where the players are literally "on stage." The cavernous building and the brick walls hold in every sound of the frenzied crowd, creating a deafening and unnerving setting for the visitors.

Wisconsin opened the game with the same starting unit of Auriantal, Duany, Okey, Daugherty, and Grant. Grant lost the tip to the quick-jumping and powerful John Thomas, a 6'9" 275-pound center from Minneapolis. Minnesota wasted no time in attacking their opponent in their Big Ten home opener. Their aggressive play and the ever-increasing decibel levels inside the "old barn" rattled the Badgers. Wisconsin missed their first six shots and committed three turnovers while falling behind 11-0 in the first five minutes of the contest. A furious Bennett called his second timeout and berated the team for failing to do any of the things they had spent two days talking about. They were not competing in the face of adversity. Bennett admitted after the game, "I compounded the problem with my behavior. I should have tried to settle them down instead."

Nonetheless, he inserted a limping Calderwood into the game after a second time out. Ty's presence, even at three-quarter speed, settled the team down. Kosolcharoen and Grant executed a perfect two-on-one fast break against the Gopher press, ending in a Grant slam, to crack the goose egg. The next time down the floor, however, Auriantal committed his third turnover of the game. Bennett, standing above his team on the elevated floor, hastily walked to the end of the bench and sternly beckoned Burkemper to replace him. David truly got his first taste of a difficult situation, which he handled admirably. He moved cautiously and carefully with his dribble, avoiding Gopher traps and getting Wisconsin into their offense. Bennett used a variety of player combinations throughout the half, and Wisconsin inched their way back in the game, again due primarily to outstanding half-court defense. Okey's free throws, with 3:49 remaining in the half, pulled them within one, but the Gophers made a final push of their own to go into the locker room leading 22-18.

Bennett's rhetoric during the intermission again emphasized competing. He shuffled his lineup to start the second half, unwilling to risk another slow start. Calderwood and Kosolcharoen replaced Duany and Auriantal. It was Wisconsin's big men, however, that got them off to a good start. Okey hit two three-point shots, and Grant added a basket and two free throws, as the Badgers grabbed their first lead of the game, 28-26. Minnesota never blinked. Bobby Jackson and Eric Harris both hit threes to reclaim a four-point lead. The game settled into a classic Big Ten matchup, with physical, pounding play in front of a chaotic midwinter crowd.

Minnesota's lead fluctuated between two and four points for the next six and a half minutes. Haskins tried to break the game open by again extending his defense to the full-court, but for the most part the Badgers handled it well. Indeed, Shawn Daugherty's double-clutch reverse layup, with 6:40 remaining, tied the game at 42-42. Then, however, the Badgers finally buckled under the relentless pressure. The Golden Gophers went on a 13-2 run helped in part by Wisconsin's deteriorating shot selection. The depth of Wisconsin's effort was conceded by their ragged and disheartened play, as Minnesota posted a 65-48 victory.

Wisconsin's season record fell to 7-3. For the third game in a row, Bennett had settled into a short substitution rotation, choosing to stay with his second-half starting unit (Calderwood, Kosolcharoen, Okey, Daugherty, and Grant), using Auriantal and Burkemper only sparingly. Although Bennett did not view this loss in the same harsh light as the Marquette defeat, they were similar in the fact that the Badgers had again committed more than twenty turnovers and faded late in the game. Despite that, Bennett had his eyes focused ahead.

"In all of my years in basketball, I have never been in an environment like that. What an incredibly aggressive atmosphere, with the crowd noise, the physical play, it was just unbelievable! So, even though we lost for the second straight time, I am encouraged by what I saw as far as our ability to play hard in a tough environment and compete," he stated.

Beaten and bruised, the team headed back to Madison. Sleet and fog, however, prevented the plane from landing at Madison's Dane County Regional Airport and it was diverted to Milwaukee. The long exhausting road trip was extended another three hours. They had to wait for a bus in Milwaukee before finally boarding and making the ninety-minute trip back to Madison. They did not arrive until well after midnight.

What now? After all, Indiana waited just around the corner. The Badgers had demonstrated that they could commit themselves to playing hard, but that alone was not enough to win. Bennett lectured his staff on their only day off between games, "If you are going to beat the good ones, like Minnesota [or Indiana], you have to combine competing with execution of a smart, sound offense." Indeed, that was the lesson to be learned from the Minnesota game. In addition to playing hard, they also had to combine great intelligence and soundness into the mix. That combination for success had to be put together in a relatively short period of time, however, as the 14-1, twelfth-ranked Hoosiers would arrive at the Field House less than thirty-six hours later. Bennett, well aware of the physical beating his team had taken in the previous three days, kept practice short that afternoon. The entire session consisted of a team stretch, twenty minutes of easy shooting, and a few half-speed defensive drills. The majority of their preparation time was spent in the locker room studying film of the Hoosier's fabled passing game offense.

Game-day shooting practice was scheduled for 8:30 A.M. An unseasonable January rain cleansed Madison, as the Badgers casually made their way onto the floor. Bennett followed the players onto the court and inspected two Creative Sports Network crew members as they installed a microphone behind the north basket. Shooting practice was actually a misnomer for the game-day ritual. Bennett used the opportunity to simply get the players out of bed, stretch their legs, and feed them a good breakfast. As noted before, he did not want to diminish the players' energy, but rather to focus on the forty minutes that really mattered on that day. There was no authoritarian message, no strict organized practice, no micro-management of insignificant details, no stifling rules to be understood and followed.

Bennett relaxed in a lounge chair in the small coaches room adjacent to the players locker room after "practice" was over. We had a conversation about that night's game, and I couldn't help but notice that his attitude and mannerisms were surprisingly relaxed as he spoke.

"We have not played well. We have played hard, but we have never played well on offense; taking care of the ball, taking good shots, and being patient. I will never be comfortable as a coach until that happens." The stress of the past week and the impending afternoon game only became apparent when he added, "If that never happens, I just won't be here as the coach."

"Do you look forward to coaching against Knight?" I asked.

Bennett's response reflected his current struggles with his own team. "I do. I have even more respect for him now than before I coached against him. I see how hard it is to maintain quality at this level. He has good players, not great players, and he continually gets them to play well together. That is really an amazing thing. Seeing someone who does it consistently, game after game, is very impressive to me."

He discussed the lessons of the past week for the better part of a half hour; his handling of the players, the injuries. Bennett concluded the conversation by explaining the role that his personal foundation, his faith and philosophy, played over the past four days.

"I lean on my faith when things are not going well or when we are losing. I pray that I can handle defeat and frustration appropriately, as Jesus would. So far I have." He rushed to qualify his last remark, "Not during games! I still go off, but as soon as the game is over I am able to compose myself."

A puzzled look had come over his face, which was pressed against the index finger of his left hand, as he spoke. "My faith has very gently and subtly taken control of my life. Hardly a moment goes by that I am not aware of, or praying for, the presence of the Spirit in me. I have concluded that without my faith, my life would be hollow. In spite of my limitations, in spite of my weaknesses, I return very quickly to a feeling state of having the Lord with me. I try to do what the Lord wants me to do, directs me to do. I think through studying significant scripture and through prayer you give openings to the Lord, to the wisdom of the Bible, and that takes seed in your heart. It is the things that you dwell on that become important to you. Most people think I dwell on basketball, but I don't. I dwell on the concepts. I think about what is right, proper, and pure in each case."

Bennett rocked his head back and forth, wondering how such a transformation had taken hold in him. "I think it is an answer to a prayer that I started praying twenty-five years ago. *Let me dwell on what is noble, excellent, and trustworthy. Do not let me dwell on what others, the world, say is proper. But let me dwell on what is right and proper in your eyes, Lord.*" He ended our conversation on that note and joined his team at the training table for the pregame meal.

Indiana University:
Saturday, January 4, Madison, Wisconsin

Rain in January? That was almost as unthinkable as, well, a victory over Indiana. Wisconsin last defeated the Hoosiers on February 5, 1980, an almost inconceivable thirty-one straight losses! Yet, the bizarre weather indicated that things were not "life as normal" in Wisconsin that day. The Field House crowd was not only late in arriving, but they were also unusually dressed. Many of the Badger faithful had forsaken their red-and-white attire in favor of green and gold. As it turned out, the game just so happened to overlap the second half of the Packers-49ers NFL playoff game. However, the Field House was filled to capacity as Knight and Bennett walked onto the floor just before the game, due in large part to the Pack's commanding 21-0 halftime lead. Knight passed casually by the Wisconsin bench in an ambling relaxed gait, then paused momentarily to greet Bennett, and finally strolled to the IU end of the court. Bennett, by contrast, paced pensively with his arms folded tightly in front of him. No matter how vehemently he chose to deny it, his behavior made it obvious that the Indiana game was monumental to him personally. He wanted to beat his mentor. A deep competitive drive stoked that desire, regardless of how he wanted to approach the matchup.

Bennett was able to start the game with a lineup of his choosing for the first time in four games. Calderwood and Auriantal started at the guards, while Grant, Okey, and Daugherty again got the nod as the Badgers continued to use the "big lineup" and the Triangle offense. Indiana's passing game had made Bennett's defense look helpless the year before. He was nervous that they would do it again, but not even Bennett could have hoped for the kind of start the Badgers put together. Indiana was paralyzed offensively by Wisconsin's man-to-man defense, failing to score in the first seven and a half minutes of play, as Wisconsin built a 17-0 lead! Bennett, determined to use more players in his substitution rotation, went to the bench and inserted Duany, Coleman, and Burkemper. But the bench again came up short, giving up six points and failing to score in the next four minutes. Bennett went back to his starters as the crowd settled back into their seats after their opening minutes of celebratory hysteria. Grant immediately hit a jump shot from the block and the Badgers offense, as well as the crowd, again came alive.

Then, Indiana's Robbie Eggers mishandled a pass in the post, and when he picked it up and dribbled out of traffic, the crowd and Bennett went nuts screaming for a double-dribble. Bennett was still screaming at the official when Michael Lewis drained a three-point shot off a pass from Eggers. Bennett became incensed and raced up the sideline after official Tom Rucker, who quickly whistled Bennett for a technical, in response to his tirade. With the crowd and Bennett still livid at Rucker, Lewis buried both free throws to draw Indiana within six at 17-11.

In defense of Rucker, he had made the correct call. A "muffed ball" is not considered a dribble, so Eggers had not committed a violation when he put the ball down before passing. Regardless, Bennett's outburst forced him to regroup both himself and his team. He called a time-out, and after leaving the huddle, the Badgers once again took command of the game. The starters stretched the lead back to 25-11, at which time Bennett again went to his reserves. Coleman, Duany, Kosolcharoen, and Burkemper all saw action over the next four minutes. But the second group again failed to maintain the point margin, as they were out-scored by Indiana 8-2, narrowing the lead to eight. Forced into a yo-yo substitution rotation, Bennett reinserted his starters, who restored the lead to double figures. Wisconsin led 35-23, as they jogged off the floor to the standing ovation of the appreciative Badger fans.

Could they hold on to win? Could they finally defeat the fabled Indiana Hoosiers, even though the Badgers were 1-3 in their last four games? Those thoughts may have been on the minds of the fans, but they were not the thoughts of the coaches and players. The team took the floor for the second half filled with a purpose: play hard, play smart, and wrap up the win. The opening possession gave an indication of which team was hungrier for the victory. Indiana's Andrae Paterson fumbled the ball in the low post, and as it trickled toward the key area, he was joined on the floor by three Badgers, Calderwood, Auriantal, and Grant, in a fracas for the ball. Indiana, however, was not 14-1 by accident. Knight had his post defenders actively switching the Triangle screens and clogging the offense. Nonetheless, Okey's free throws and a two-handed follow-up dunk allowed Wisconsin to maintain their advantage. Jason Collier's play-acting flop, however, sent Okey to the bench on the next possession with his fourth foul. Indiana scored the next nine points to close within five, 39-34, with 14:30 remaining. The crowd, and Bennett, grew restless. Undaunted by their first-half performances, he turned to the bench to swing the momentum back in Wisconsin's favor. Duany and Kosolcharoen joined Calderwood, Grant, and Daugherty on the floor as Bennett went to a smaller lineup, though he stayed primarily with the Triangle offense. Duany didn't waste any time getting into the mix of things. He took a pass on the right wing, hesitated twice, and then rose over his defender to score his first basket against his hometown Hoosiers. Kosolcharoen then hit a three on the very next possession, and the crowd roared in jubilation.

Indiana never seriously threatened again. Calderwood took charge of the team, keeping the ball in his hands as much as possible, eating up the clock, and passing off to teammates for open jump shots. By the time Okey reentered the game with six minutes to go, Wisconsin held a comfortable 56-48 lead. Indiana's young team did not have the experience to come back on the road while facing a rapidly improving Badger defense. The crowd became euphoric when the reality set in that the thirty-one game losing streak was finally going to end! Their growing cheers motivated the Badgers to make one final push. Auriantal and Calderwood hit back-to-back threes. Auriantal then stole the ball and drove the length of the floor for an uncontested lay-in, and Duany scored the Badgers' final points of the game with a break-away dunk. The 71-58 victory removed the albatross from around Wisconsin's neck, and gave Bennett his first victory over his most respected mentor.

Thirteen turned out to be Wisconsin's lucky number as three Badgers, Okey, Grant, and Daugherty, each matched that number in the scoring column. The most rewarding statistic for the game, however, had to do with turnovers. The *team* had committed only five turnovers for the entire game! The victory was sweet reward for their commitment to concentrate on what truly mattered during the tough five-day stretch; to be thankful for each experience, good or bad, and move ahead. Playing tough, playing smart, and competing for forty minutes had finally all come together for the Badgers to accentuate that intangible concept.

The crowd lingered in the stands as the two teams and the coaches exchanged handshakes at center court. Knight complimented Bennett on his team's performance, before Bennett walked off the floor emotionless and exhausted. He did not hear the loud roar that went up for him as he stepped off the court and made his way to the locker room, as he was already deep within his own thoughts. Nonetheless, the applause was a fitting tribute.

"Everything leads to something," Bennett told a local radio telecaster immediately following the game. "At no time during the previous four games did we fail to take the lesson that was available to us and learn from it. So that prepared us as well as it could for today, and it showed."

Ironically, the difficulty in his personal life in the previous year had led him to something as well, the ability to appreciate the significance of the victory. The last contest his father attended had been Wisconsin vs Indiana in Madison, one year earlier. The powerful memory moved Bennett to tears in the locker room.

Chapter 12

To Look Within

. . . But suffering directs a man to look within. If it succeeds, then there, within him, is the beginning of learning.

Soren Kierkegaard, Philosopher

Sean Mason, sidelined since the Brown game, finally rejoined his team on the floor. Mason, an icy-cool kid from just outside Chicago, had endured a great deal over the past year and a half. Recruited into the up-tempo systems of former Badger coaches Stu Jackson and Stan Van Gundy, he often found himself at odds with Bennett's patient, defensive approach to the game. A graduate of Rich Central High School in Olympia Fields, Illinois, he hoped to follow in the footsteps of fellow Central star Kendall Gill, a University of Illinois standout and member of the NBA New Jersey Nets. Mason had surpassed Gill's career scoring record while in high school with 1,254 points. He came to Wisconsin to play up-tempo basketball, score, and prepare himself for an NBA career. Less than two years later, he struggled to play at all on two injured knees.

Mason, with the cool demeanor that had originally caused Bennett to question his passion for the game, made his way onto the floor and began to shoot with the other players. He still limped noticeably as he went through the warm-ups. He had been given medical clearance to practice at full speed, despite still feeling tenderness in the knee. Nonetheless, his presence added to the optimistic mood at practice. The team had apparently survived the rash of injuries, and in retrospect, set the stage for a successful season, going 8-3 in their first eleven games. Calderwood's performance in the Indiana game proved that he was back to full strength and in control of the team's offense. Mason's return was sure to help the offensive production of the team, and most importantly for Bennett, he would once again have a full arsenal of weapons at his disposal to make coaching decisions.

Bennett instructed the team to move to the south end of the floor and get into the three-on-three help drill, a defensive routine. Mason stepped to the front of the line, anxious to prove that he was fully recovered and ready to go for the next game. The casual pace of the warm-up drills quickly gave way to game conditions, which included aggressive full-speed cuts. Mason sprinted hard across the lane to the right side of the court without any problem, but when he planted his leg hard to stop his momentum and make a cut, his knee gave out and sent him crashing to the floor screaming in agony. His teammates froze where they stood, deathly silent, in disbelief. Bennett and trainer Andy Winterstein rushed to Sean, as he writhed in pain. His teammates hesitantly gathered around, but Bennett dejectedly waved them to the other end of the floor. Sean repeatedly called out in an anguished voice, "I'm sorry, I'm sorry," as Bennett tried to comfort him, and Winterstein assessed the damage.

The assistant coaches attempted to resume the drill at the north basket, but the attempt was futile, as no one's attention could be pulled away from the disheartening scene playing out on the other end of the floor. Brad Soderberg stepped in, stopped the drill, and let the players move back down the court and gather around Mason. Practice had just started, but in the players' minds, it was over. Mason was carefully moved to the training room after the pain and shock of the injury subsided sufficiently. The players tried to call out words of encouragement as he was helped past them, but their words were forced and awkward, as they knew there was nothing they could say at that moment to help. When he was out of sight, a subdued practice resumed.

Michigan State University:
Thursday, January 9, Madison, Wisconsin

"Now we will see if we can handle success or if the Indiana game was a fluke." Bennett was ill at ease with his team on the eve of the Michigan State game, and was befuddled with his team's lack of purpose during the week. The team had not practiced well in the four days they had to prepare for the Spartans. Bennett would have no part of any possible excuses; Sean's season-ending anterior cruciate tear, overconfidence from the Indiana win, or too much time on their hands over the holiday break. A win against Michigan State, a game he counted on, was crucial to the continued development of the team. A home victory against a team predicted to finish in the second division of the Big Ten was a must. There was one other motivating factor that went undiscussed. The game was to be nationally televised by ESPN.

Grant and Okey executed their tip play perfectly to start the game. Grant raced up the floor after tapping the ball to Okey for a return pass and a two-handed slam. The Badgers led 2-0 five seconds into the game. Michigan State's prized freshman recruit, Mateen Cleaves, tested Auriantal with a hard drive to the left baseline, but Okey left his man to help on the play and went airborne with Cleaves. He reached out from behind the play and grabbed the ball away from Cleaves with his big right hand. Okey headed up the floor on the dribble as Cleaves looked around curious as to where the ball went. Nonetheless, on the very next possession, the talented Cleaves continued to play with a confidence beyond his years, when he threaded a "highlight" pass to Jon Garavaglia on a fast-break to tie the game at two.

The first five minutes of the game, however, belonged to Okey and Grant. Grant had three baskets to match Okey's three blocks and the Badgers took an early 6-2 lead. When the pesky MSU freshman countered with a three-pointer, the Badger coaches realized that Cleaves was going to live up to his lofty prep reputation. The crowd meanwhile, was as quiet as they had been all season, seemingly lacking their normal energy. The storied Field House mystique had been neutralized, not by Michigan State's exceptional play, but apparently from plain old apathy. Michigan State played loose in the impersonal environment and claimed their first lead of the game, 11-10, with just over ten minutes gone in the half. The Badger Triangle offense bogged down and the visitors went on a 16-4 run, which silenced the crowd even more. Bennett switched his team to the double low-post offense, and the Badgers went on a 9-0 run of their own to close out the final 3:15 of the half, narrowing the deficit to 26-24. The crowd, like the Badgers, showed signs of life heading into the break.

Kosolcharoen started the second half in place of Grant, who had gone quiet after his opening flurry. Bennett also made the move so that he could have three guards on the floor to run the perimeter-oriented double low-post offense. Okey and Calderwood scored early as the Badgers retook the lead 29-26, before the game settled into a nail-biter. Grant came off the bench on a mission. Wisconsin rode his back over the next eight minutes, a span of time in which the game experienced five momentum swings and lead changes. The Badgers finally sustained a slim lead between the eleven and five minute marks. Then, Wisconsin made a costly mistake when they went away from Grant. Bennett called time-out after the Spartans had capitalized on several poor shots by the Badgers, tying the game at 47-47. Bennett sternly reminded the players that Grant was to touch the ball in the low-post, and coming out of the time-out, he did just that. Unfortunately, he missed the shot badly. The Badger players had broken a cardinal rule in basketball: do not let a "hot" shooter go too long without touching the ball, otherwise he/she will cool off. The error proved to be costly.

Thomas Kelly converted two free throws with 4:04 to go to give Michigan State the lead. The Spartans maintained the lead as the last minutes counted down. The turning point of the game came with one minute to play. Wisconsin, down by two points, needed to get the ball back without giving up any points. Mateen Cleaves prolonged his dribble at the point, while the rest of his team ran a set play. Taking matters into his own hands, he blew by Auriantal with an explosive first step. Calderwood was the only Badger in position to help. He faked at Cleaves as if he was going to step in front of him, but then retreated back to his own player on the wing. Cleaves never broke his stride as he sailed in uncontested for a lay-up. His basket gave the Spartans a four-point lead. Wisconsin failed to answer the basket at the offensive end of the floor and was forced to start fouling. Michigan State converted all of their free throws in the last minute to lock up the 58-50 victory. Tom Izzo's Spartans became the second visiting team in four games to leave Madison with a win.

Bennett was troubled by the loss. Their defensive intensity was fine, but the team shot only 33 percent from the floor in the defeat, and the guards were a dismal 3-17 from the floor, something their Big Ten opponents were sure to recognize and try to exploit. Bennett nonetheless tried to remain optimistic in the post-game press conference. "This team has surprised me before with their ability to bounce back. We'll see if they can do it again." To "do it again," they would have to do it to the Iowa Hawkeyes in Carver-Hawkeye Arena, which would be no small task.

University of Iowa:
Saturday, January 11, Iowa City, Iowa

Frigid temperatures returned to Madison as the Badgers boarded their chartered bus at 10:00 A.M. for the three-hour ride to Iowa City. Bennett knew that his team was in for a tough night, despite his hopeful comments the previous night. "I'm concerned because experience has taught me that when you lose an emotional home game and then have to go on the road, that is a real tough trip." Iowa was a difficult team for the Badgers to play. Dr. Tom Davis' system employed an aggressive full-court press and multiple zone defenses, which had built the team to a perfect 3-0 Big Ten mark and an impressive 12-3 overall record to date. That was not good news for the Badgers, as they had struggled against those defenses all season.

Okey opened up the game with a three-point shot from the right wing, but the Hawkeyes quickly countered with a patented "jump shot pass" lob basket, before adding a three-pointer. Okey again scored for the Badgers and the score was tied at five. Then, without warning, the mood of the game changed. Grant failed to connect on a lay-up and was called for a reaching foul going after the rebound, which was a bad turn of events. He further compounded the problem by verbally expressing his displeasure about the call, and was quickly hit with a technical. Instead of leading 7-5, Bennett found his team trailing 7-5 and without their center, as Grant headed to the bench with two fouls, three minutes into the game.

Wisconsin failed to connect on their next three shots, all of which Iowa pushed down the floor and converted into baskets, so Bennett jumped to his feet and called a time-out, hoping to stop the mounting Hawkeye momentum. Duany entered the game and gave the Badgers instant offense, scoring four points to keep the Badgers within striking distance at 16-9. His contributions, however, were not enough. Two consecutive turnovers by Coleman and Calderwood sparked a 13-0 Iowa run. Meanwhile, Wisconsin could not solve either of Iowa's two defenses, the 1-2-2 half-court zone or their full-court press. They turned the ball over four times against the press before reaching half-court, and when they did manage to advance the ball to the front-court, they missed all four of their shots against the zone. In turn, the Hawkeyes built a 29-9 lead after only eleven minutes of play. Bennett had no choice but to go back to Grant. He scored eight points in the next six minutes without picking up his third foul, but he got very little help from his teammates as the Hawkeyes raced to a 43-24 halftime lead.

Bennett was exasperated and angry about the Badgers' horrific performance. Yet, there was not one area of their play that he could turn to as a foundation to get his team back in the game. Even their fabled defense had disappeared in the wreckage. Grant also fell into Bennett's doghouse at the start of the second half, when he allowed his man to get two open shots in the low-post. Bennett was not going to let the defensive lapses go unnoticed even during a blowout. Therefore, despite having to bench the only player able to crack Iowa's defense, he pulled Grant from the game. Wisconsin's execution remained sloppy and ineffective, except for a pair of Daugherty threes and a dunk. After five minutes, Grant reentered the game and played inspired defense, though his singular efforts were like putting a finger in a leak of the collapsing dike. Bennett finally pulled out the white flag with 2:51 remaining and went deep into his bench. The final damage was 78-53, but the game was not even as close as the score indicated.

Bennett's worst fears about this team had come to fruition: the Indiana game was a fluke and his team was in a deep tailspin. Despite their 8-5 overall record, they were 2-5 over their last seven games and 1-3 in the Big Ten. Bennett was at a complete loss after the Iowa game and was disappointed in his team's effort, but he was equally disappointed in his own performance.

"I think I might have outsmarted myself to counter the letdown following the Michigan State loss. I tried to come up with some strategic changes to counteract what Iowa would do, which we covered in a chalk session and a walk-thru. I think I distracted our kids. When game time came, and we got off to such a bad start, all that strategizing was gone. We would have been better just hammering away. In my efforts to make it better, I made it worse.

"I was also very hard on the players during and after the game, very critical and negative. I took the poor performance personally and my pride got in the way. The combination of feeling that it reflected badly on me, and the fact that we stunk up the floor, caused me to just unload on those guys. We played miserably and after the game I proceeded to tell them what I thought, and I think that an attempt to be honest and somewhat objective turned out to be much too critical and subjective."

For Bennett, a moment of truth had arrived. Wisconsin basketball was not well, and the Badgers were smack in the middle of bad times. His team could not continue down the same path they were on, but what could be done at mid-season? A coach's true character, his ability to lead, is never more important than during such times. Fortunately, Bennett had seven days to prepare for Penn State; seven days for his leadership to surface. Each day of that week was an education in itself, and signified a new step in Bennett's own personal recovery from the losing streak. A challenge was the first step. A meeting was called in the locker room immediately after the players got off the bus in Madison. Bennett challenged every person in the program, staff included, to work harder, find areas that could be improved, and commit time and energy toward that improvement. Everyone then departed and took the rest of the weekend to deliberate on what that meant to them personally.

Monday, January 13: Anger!

The assistants arrived at the office earlier than normal and went directly to work. Soderberg and Hood worked diligently on their recruiting efforts, writing letters, making phone calls, anything to take the sting out of the past weekend. Hecker reclined in his chair and replayed the Iowa game, searching for sections that he thought Bennett would want to review and share with the team, while Costanzo, as the administrative assistant, organized the events of the day for the staff. The activity, though productive and necessary, also camouflaged anxiety among the staff. They were still learning the methods of their boss, and, having never experienced a losing streak under him, were not sure what to expect that morning.

Bennett emerged from the stairwell leading to the third floor basketball office. His eyes were bright and his walk brisk. He greeted Sally Huegel and Barb Winterstein, the basketball secretaries, as he made his way toward his office. Life-size action photos of the Wisconsin players lined the hall behind Bennett, who had paused at the door to Costanzo's office. He instructed Paul to get the other coaches for the meeting. All the staff members had taken their familiar seats around the table in under a minute. Bennett sat at the head of the table, nearest to his office, Costanzo sat in the first chair to his left, and Soderberg in the second. Hood sat immediately to his right, I sat to the right of Hood, and Hecker occupied the seat at the other end of the table in front of the video station. Bennett opened his journal, which sat in front of him, and began the meeting.

"First of all, let me apologize to you guys again. I said some things during the game that were uncalled for. You guys are just doing your job. I was disappointed in myself. It was just such a frustrating evening." His apology was genuine, but he did not dwell on the topic of bench proto-col. He instead turned his attention to the thoughts he had put in writing.

"I believe we have to make some physical changes, and these are the ones I have come up with." He referenced his journal as he continued, "Number one, we have to begin doubling the post big-on-big [use the opposite post defender to come across the lane and double-team the low post]. Our post defense is a major part of our weakness, and we are not going to invent a great post defender, so, we just have to start doubling it.

"Number two, we have to start trapping the ball screens because we are consistently being hurt by that. Number three, I'm thinking of play-ing some 1-2-2, but that is third on the defensive totem pole, because we need to work on the others. Number four, we are going to run the three offense [triple post]. We have to get good at one thing on offense, and that is the Triangle offense."

Bennett's proposed changes were both consistent, yet at the same time inconsistent, with his own philosophy. The general consensus, at least among the armchair quarterbacks, was that Wisconsin's biggest problem was in their offense; not enough diversity, not enough scoring opportu-nities. Yet, *consistent* with his philosophy, Bennett turned to defense for answers, as three of the four "physical" changes were defensive adjust-ments. Indeed, two of his favorite one-line anecdotes address just that situation: "Sometimes your best shot is no shot," and, "If you can't score, then you better not let your opponent score."

Defense had defined Dick Bennett as a coach for his entire career. It was his foundation, and it is what he leaned on when faced with adver-sity. The *inconsistency,* however, was the proposed traps. His defensive principles did not, nor had they ever, emphasized trapping the ball. The two radical changes from his established foundation indicated the level of concern he had about his team.

The one offensive adjustment, however, was very consistent with his plans going into the season, to play deliberate power basketball with Okey, Daugherty, and Grant on the post. His suggestions, or rather his delivery of these ideas, revealed something else that Bennett was trying hard to disguise. He was angry! His face was flush with color and his eye contact strong and direct. He was animated and passionate, and sat on the edge of his chair. The tone of his speech was strong and unwavering. The adversity of the past three weeks had simmered inside him to the point where he took it as a personal affront.

"I find this frustration I am experiencing to be a challenge to me. This brings out the best in me, not the worst. I have been an underdog all my life and now I feel like an underdog. So now you'll get my best!"

The meeting was not for the faint of heart. He critically assessed the performance of himself, the team, the coaching staff, and even the Big Ten officials for the better part of two hours. He first turned his attention to the limitations of the team. "The first prediction I made about this team, even publicly, was that the key to our season had nothing to do with technique or ability. It had to do with what we do from the neck up, the concepts, and this team is obviously very weak in that area. When you have a steady diet of good teams, your weaknesses show. Our weakness is from the neck up. It is a selfish team, lacking passion and unity. Almost every kid thinks of himself first. All you have to do is watch the game tape to see that. They are just so into themselves."

The assistants sat motionless and quiet as he vented in the confines of the office. "It is the most dysfunctional team that I have been a part of. Those are the facts! This team has taken away what last year's team gave us. Last year's team gave us a year of grace. This team robbed us of that! This group doesn't appear to have gained a thing from last year. Not a thing! We have stuck with these kids for two years. We could have chosen to go out and recruit to fill the gaps, but we didn't. There is *nothing* that has kept our scholarship players from getting better. They have wasted that opportunity."

An internal voice sounded inside Bennett's head, alerting him to the severity of the rebuke he had just delivered. He then accepted his behavior for what it was. "So, at the bottom of all my blaming, there is great anger."

His displeasure was apparent, but he was not finished. His assistants were also subject to his wrath. "So what? We have to work to change that. We owe it professionally to the players to keep working hard. Each of us has to work. I think as a staff we do a less than adequate job on the floor. I thought about what the difference was between my old staff and you guys. I think the staff at Green Bay worked much harder on the court than we do. From the moment my assistants at Green Bay hit the floor they were coaching. They didn't wait for me to tell them to do it. They just did it. They knew it was important to work with the players individually. It was *every single day*, come hell or high water! It was never skipped. Here we do it when we feel like it. I think you guys act a little too much like head coaches, and that is not your job. You have a tendency to talk and visit too much before practice. I don't think we work with the kids enough. I think that is the major difference."

His words cut deeply. The experience was new to them, except for Brad Soderberg, who had played for Bennett, and it hurt them personally to hear those words. Whether his assessment was correct or not, and his assistants had varying opinions on that, the reality was that Bennett found the situation intolerable and he was lashing out. Still, his castigation had created an awkward silence in the room. The honeymoon was over. His abrasive comments gave his assistants a taste of what it was like to be on the biting end of his disapproving tongue. Understanding the sensitivity of his comments, he went on to reassure the group, although he made no apologies for his assessment.

"I promised you guys that as long as I coached here you would have a job. You know that! You guys are knowledgeable and active recruiters. You do a great job during games. I think you are terrific with the press and the families. I'm not dissatisfied! I just think we do a less than adequate job on the floor." He paused a few moments to gather his thoughts. "That is as candid as I can be, but it is an honest observation. I'm just telling you that when you are deficient, you can either sit back or you can work to change it. Isn't that what we are asking the players to do? If we do not identify our mistakes and learn from them, how are we different from these kids?"

Bennett took a deep breath, sighed audibly, and finally leaned back in his chair. The anger had momentarily subsided in the wake of his brutal assessment. Hidden behind the aggressiveness of his approach was the fact that he knew, more than anyone else, that he was ultimately responsible for the success and failure of this team. Therefore, he was most disappointed in himself.

"I blame myself because I have not been passionate."

No one other than Bennett had spoken for the entire meeting. He looked at his watch, sat back up in his chair, and delivered the daily mandate to the staff. "It is our job to work, work, work, at whatever it is they need. Our time from one-thirty to three-thirty is the most valuable time we have. We have to go back to the factory, to the assembly line. The answer is in the fundamentals and work ethic."

Bennett had reverted to the behaviors that he professed were his greatest curse—pride, anger, confrontation, harsh criticism, and a lack of empathy. Would his venting do more than provide an outlet for his own displeasure? Would his comments motivate or alienate the staff? Or both? Bennett had not concerned himself with those questions, because he was damned mad. His last concern was stepping on toes with his team 2-5 in their past seven games. Needless to say, that afternoon's practice was full of energy, leadership, and coaching. It had been a critical and anxious day, but by all accounts it had also been productive.

Tuesday, January 14: Rationalizing

Jane Albright-Dieterle's Wisconsin women's basketball team, "Badgerball," rolled to victory after victory on their way to a top-twenty national ranking. Albright-Dieterle glowed in Madison's spotlight while Bennett fielded questions about his unraveling team. Callers into "The Sports Review," a local talk show on radio station 1310 WIBA, became increasingly critical of Bennett and his style of play. "Boring" and "ineffective" were the two most common words used to describe his team's efforts, which were contrasted and compared to Badgerball's entertaining full-court style. It was inevitable that Bennett would hear the criticism in a city the size of Madison. The comparisons and the relentless probing questions from the media had the coach making excuses for his team's predicament.

The mood in Tuesday's meeting was less stressful for the assistants, but more stressful for Bennett. He could not rid his mind of the question local sports reporters were sure to ask him after that day's practice. "What ails the team?" Bennett again turned to his journal to find the pages that contained the previous night's deliberations.

"What events led up to the recent struggles of the team? I would like to list the things that are causing our difficulties right now. I am sure to field that question and I want to have answers." Bennett was not asking for his assistants' input, as they were well aware, and thus he proceeded uninterrupted. "Number one, I think injuries have really drained us to the point where we have never really recovered. They started at the end of last year with Mosezell [Peterson], and I think they have taken their toll.

Our junior class has been depleted, and we have had to put players in roles they shouldn't be in."

There was little doubt that he was correct. Injuries had devastated the team's depth, which had dwindled down to only seven healthy recruited players. The injuries were felt most acutely on offense where both Mason and Peterson's scoring abilities were sorely missed. Still, the rationalizations and the excuses did not fit with Bennett's reputation, and were not the answers to what was wrong with his faltering team.

"Number two, we have no senior recruiting class left in the program. As you look back, there have been three lost years of recruiting for one reason or another. Not one player out of those classes has made it through a four-year career. I am not pointing fingers at anyone. [He was.] But it is just impossible to compete when you lose three classes in a row."

While his assessment was correct again, these were more excuses and rationalizations. The list grew.

"Number three, the Big Ten is an improved league. We are facing better competition." He looked around the table. "Don't you agree?"

The assistants all nodded in agreement with varying degrees of conviction. "Not only that," added Paul Costanzo, "the other teams no longer look past us. We are not sneaking up on our opponents."

Were the other teams improved? Possibly. Yet other leading Big Ten teams also had injuries and graduations to overcome.

Overlooked? Doubtful, as it was even unlikely that anyone overlooked Wisconsin during Bennett's first season because of his reputation for fielding solid teams, not to mention their upset victory over Michigan in the conference opener. Bennett resumed his countdown.

"Number four, I have to say the decision we made to wait on recruiting may have been a mistake." Second-guessing that decision, at least in hindsight, was a mute point.

No problems were solved and no course of action had been agreed upon. The events of the day were unproductive and unflattering to Bennett. The first two days of the week were spent in anger, rationalizing the genuine possibility that his second year at Wisconsin would prove to be a flop, especially when compared to the first. His pride was getting in the way of his coaching. A more positive spin on the day, however, would suggest that the meeting had been an exercise in self-awareness. Still, when those four factors appeared on the nightly sports broadcasts, they sounded more like excuses.

The long delay between games was giving Bennett too much time to internalize the losses, and a week of booster events did not allow him to isolate himself from the fans. For that reason alone, the day's activities provided a somewhat productive exercise, to help clarify the picture for less informed supporters. That evening Bennett and his staff were the "main course" at a fund-raising dinner for 150 faithful boosters at the Avenue Bar. Bennett's anger had yet to fully subside, though he covered it well. He and his staff informally replied to questions throughout the cocktail hour, and then Bennett took center stage after dinner. He answered any and all questions, regardless of their level of absurdity, concerning the plight of his team. He even gave some of the supporters an opportunity to offer advice, giving no outward indication of how distasteful he found the grilling. He was committed to *outlast* them, just as he had taught his players to do.

Wednesday, January 15: Rejection

The anxiety and events of the week had made it a long haul, and it was only Wednesday morning. The assistants were as weary as Bennett, but were relaxed and casual as they recounted their tales of the previous evening. Stories centered around fan inquisitions and suggestions. Bennett listened quietly for a time before he joined in with a frustrated proclamation.

"Fans are fans. They are the same everywhere in America. Badger fans are no different. That is why I wanted you there. I wanted you to see that fans will desert you in a minute. Less than ten days ago they watched one of the biggest basketball victories in years at this school. It just shows they are going to pick out every little thing, win or lose. That is why you don't have to please anybody! You have to do what you have to do, because the fans are going to criticize you either way."

Bennett knew that fan criticism comes with the territory of a basketball coach, so once again he assumed the responsibility. "I have been reeling a bit this week because that Iowa game really hurt. I have been dragging it with me all week. They [the boosters] are all good people and you have to let them sound off. They spend a lot of time and money on this program, and after all, they are just trying to be helpful."

A meeting of only a few short minutes followed. A practice plan that emphasized defense and the Triangle offense was set before the staff returned to their daily routines.

That afternoon's practice did not go well. The double teams on the low-post and ball screens did not work. The offense repeatedly found open shots when the ball was passed out of the traps. Bennett did not like what he saw and stopped practice to address the team. He directed them to forget about the double-teams and return to their basic man-to-man principles. The adjustment, however, did not stop the offenses from getting open shots. Bennett looked on expressionless from half-court as the intensity of practice waned.

Finally, as a last resort, Bennett turned to the 1-2-2 half-court zone. He took a few minutes to align the players and explain the rules. Calderwood played on the point and was responsible for the top of the key. Auriantal and Okey were positioned on opposite wings and told to defend from the free throw lane to the sideline. Finally, Grant and Daugherty were positioned on the blocks and told to protect the low post and baseline. Bennett further explained to his team that he preferred the 1-2-2 over other configurations because it was the only zone that had all five players responsible for defending the perimeter. In Bennett's eyes, the vulnerability of the zone, defending the deep corners with post players, was an acceptable weakness.

The "big lineup" took to the defense like a duck to water, neutralizing the quickness advantage of the red team. With each defensive stop, the white team's confidence grew and they proceeded to put together their best practice in nearly a month. Their mental approach to their play, invigorated by the success of the 1-2-2, became concentrated and intense as communication and purpose returned to their execution. Bennett finally left practice with a reason to be optimistic about the upcoming game against Penn State.

Thursday, January 16: Acceptance

Bennett had finally put the Iowa loss behind him and focused on Penn State. His mood was lighter than it had been all week as he detailed a four-prong strategy.

"I have formulated the plan that I think we need to follow. One, we need some zone to make us tougher defensively. When we have Paul, Sean, and Sam on the floor, we will play the 1-2-2 zone. Two, on offense, we need to go inside first. Three, we will start Duany, and play him more, because he has potential for improvement. And four, when I sub I will do so for defensive purposes. I'd like to sub Booker for Paul, Mike for

Sean, and Hennssy for Duany. That is our best defensive team, so we will then go man-to-man and really turn up the defensive intensity."

Everything was back to normal. The emphasis was back on what was important, getting the team ready to win the game. In addition, the seven-day layoff allowed several key players time to heal nagging minor injuries. Auriantal rested a strained hip, Calderwood's knee returned to normal strength, and Duany's sore ankle, injured early in the season against Temple, was finally given time to heal.

That afternoon's practice was once again productive. The starting unit of Calderwood, Duany, Okey, Grant, and Daugherty played well in the zone, and, in addition, found a renewed fluidity in the Triangle offense. In fact, it was the best they had played as a unit all year. Paul dominated on the block, Sam played effectively both inside and out, and Sean shot the ball with uncanny accuracy. The crew dominated the red team for the entire practice, and even when they struggled to execute, their aggressiveness and hustle controlled the action.

There were two other subtle differences apparent during the scrimmage. First, Calderwood and Auriantal pushed the ball up the floor after making baskets, instead of taking their time, as they had done all season. Bennett hoped the increased pace would give his team a few more seconds to search for open shots. Secondly, the interaction between the players and the assistant coaches had noticeably changed. The extra one-on-one work had fostered a more unified and supportive atmosphere, which resulted in increased communication between players and coaches on the court. The adversity of the past seven games began to forge a bond that had, up to that point, been absent on the team. The harmony, however, was precarious. If the team did not win soon, that chemistry would surely vanish amid shattered egos.

Friday, January 17: Paradox

Though the team was well-prepared, the preceeding four days had been an exhaustive mental search for Bennett. And now his apprehension about his solution was readily apparent when he opened the morning's staff meeting.

"I sat up late last night and talked to Tony. I told him that for probably the first time in my coaching career, I am not sure about what we are doing."

Bennett revealed a truth about the entire process when he explained, "I told him that when things get real tough, I am doing what I've always done. I go to a real conservative approach, and if I am going to change something, it is not going to be real extravagant."

His assistants were not enlightened by his remarks. They were well aware that he would not digress from his fundamental beliefs, regardless of his self-proclaimed doubts. His commitment to his philosophy, his style, had been his greatest strength during his entire career. This exhaustive process, which embodies the following elements, had repeated itself many times: (1) coach from an established philosophy, but (2) question that philosophy during times of difficulty, which (3) increases self-awareness, while (4) questioning whether or not there is a more effective strategy, nonetheless, (5) resisting the temptation to change for change sake, and thus, (6) maintaining the original principles, thereby (7) delivering the team back to success because of consistent leadership, to ultimately (8) increase Bennett's *self-reliance* on his own judgment.

Bennett's quiet confidence had been forged through years of continually struggling through those tumultuous steps. In his essay *Self-Reliance*, Ralph Waldo Emerson wrote, "No law can be sacred to me but that of my nature." Bennett's behavior certainly supported that proclamation. At the lowest point during the week, he returned to that which he knew to be true, regardless of the outcome. Emerson explained such a personal revelation, "To believe your own thought, to believe that what is true for you in your private heart is true for all men—that is genius." True for all men, maybe not, but true for Dick Bennett, absolutely!

Bennett's self-reliance, hidden earlier in the week, is a surprising paradox of his personality. *One truth* is that Bennett did experience a deep and genuine anxiety as to whether his system was adequate for his team. His search for improvement, for changes, was real. He gathered information from every source imaginable. He even opened himself up in a public forum, despite his innate reluctance to do so, and this made it difficult for him to be second-guessed. He took to heart all the criticism about his style of play and searched for hidden wisdom. Finally, he withdrew into his own thoughts for a thorough and critical analysis of what was best. That process inevitably led him back to the *second truth*, that he ultimately remained unwavering in his commitment to both his offensive and defensive philosophies.

That day's practice assured that Penn State would not leave Madison with a victory. The team spent more than an hour recommitting themselves to the techniques and effort required to play "Bennett-style-defense." Bennett put the players through a long and grueling workout to ensure that no rust had accumulated during the layoff. He concluded the session with "the zone game," a half-court scrimmage in which the white and red teams square off and play up to 21 points. The defense plays the 1-2-2 zone, while the offense counters with the Triangle offense. The game is played "make-it-take-it" style. If a team scores on their possession, they get the ball back. The white team demolished the red team in less than ten minutes, 21-4.

They were ready!

Penn State University:
Saturday, January 18, Madison, Wisconsin

The Nittany Lions, 0-4 in Big Ten play, were just what Wisconsin needed to get back on the winning track. Anger and frustration had been converted into hard work and determination and the only question that remained was not if they would win, but rather, by how much? The largest crowd of the year literally packed the Field House to the rafters. (In the Field House, the rafters virtually meet the upper row of balcony seats.) The cheerleaders and band, who were back in full force after the semester break, created a great college basketball atmosphere.

Wisconsin started the game in a crushing man-to-man defense and forced Penn State to turn the ball over six times in their first eight possessions. The Badgers spurted to a 9-0 lead. Unfortunately, the Triangle offense was less than artistic and produced only two points over the next six minutes. Inspiring little confidence in either Bennett or the fans, the Badgers clung to an 11-8 lead deep into the first half. Then, at the nine-minute mark, the crowd pinched themselves as they witnessed Bennett's team fall back into a zone. Penn State was equally shocked and proceeded to throw their first two passes out of bounds. Bennett stayed in the 1-2-2 zone for seven and a half minutes and his team allowed only six points, two bombs by Pete Lisicky, over that stretch. Wisconsin used an eight-man rotation that included Auriantal, Kosolcharoen, and Coleman off the bench, as Bennett had planned, and took a 31-18 lead into the break. The crowd cheered for the Badgers as they departed for the locker room and the Fargo-Moorhead Acro team took the floor. Few people left their seats as the group of gymnasts set up their springboard runways and crash pads. I was well aware of the treat the Madison crowd was in for, as I had first seen this unit's forerunner perform twenty years earlier during the Minnesota District 23 basketball tournament in Moorhead, Minnesota. The nimble gymnasts whipped the crowd into an appreciative frenzy with their athletic tumbling runs and intricate high-flying mini-trampoline routines. While the F-M Acro team had changed their routine very little in more than twenty years of performing, they still received standing ovations at every performance. They, too, practiced what Bennett had rediscovered during the week. They had been doing it right all along, so why change.

The Badgers returned for the start of the second half as the crowd buzzed with chatter about the halftime performance. Bennett started the same lineup, but he replaced Grant less than two minutes later, and used the opportunity of the double-digit lead to give Booker Coleman extended minutes. The same eight-man rotation added to the lead until it finally reached twenty-four points with 3:05 to go. Only then did David Burkemper see the floor. He no longer saw action when the outcome of the game was still in question. He was, by most accounts, just another red team practice player. Be that as it may, Wisconsin won the game 64-45. They had done so, or so it seemed, the Dick Bennett way—with defense, discipline, intensity, unity, and purpose. Truth be told, however, they had also met the right opponent at the right time. Penn State was a weak team with little depth and even less confidence. Regardless, the two-game losing-streak had come to a halt and Wisconsin's Big Ten record improved to 2-3, while their overall record reached 9-5.

Chapter 13

One Coach's Living Legacy

Regardless of the level of competition, Bennett's teams have consistently been among the elite defensive units in the country, and have excelled in the two areas which most accurately measure defensive efficiency: *points allowed per game* and *opponent field-goal percentage*. He has done so using aggressive man-to-man defense, although he has used two slightly different styles of that defense.

At UW-Stevens Point, he taught an extremely aggressive, overplaying, man-to-man defense which came to be known as Bennett's "up-the-line/on-the-line" or "push" defense. Bennett's early teams were so successful that he made an instructional video, "Pressure Defense—A System," which outlined the basic principles of his system. That video (which is still widely-circulated among today's coaches) introduced Dick Bennett to the national coaching fraternity. In the push defense, the defenders funnel the ball to outside of the floor, toward the baseline. Ball reversal back to the point area is denied, and when successful, the offense is forced to play on a quarter of a court, in an outnumbered situation. The goal is to create havoc and force turnovers.

Interest in Bennett's push defense grew during his last three seasons at UW-Stevens Point (1982-85) when his teams made three straight NAIA National Tournament appearances. Over the years, many coaches have used Bennett's system, though few have replicated his success. That suggests that there are other factors that are not, or cannot, be transferred by an instructional tape. In addition, there is one other clue which suggests that Bennett's defensive success cannot be explained entirely through a description of techniques.

Bennett stopped using the push defense during his early days at UW-Green Bay. He found that his Phoenix teams consistently faced teams with superior athletic ability and quickness. Those teams exploited the aggressiveness of his slower players, by penetrating the overextended defenders with the dribble. The push morphed into the "pack," the same defense Bennett currently employs with the Badgers. He describes the pack as "a man-to-man defense with zone principles." The players on the ball side of the floor position themselves in a triangle between their man and the ball. Bennett calls this the ball-you-man relationship. Playing in the "gap" between the two players takes away the driving lanes and forces the ball to the perimeter. The objective of the defense is to force the opponent to take a contested jump shot. The advent of the shot clock allows Bennett to make the philosophical change, because the clock places the pressure on the offense as it counts down. Thus, the shot clock eliminates the necessity to "overplay" on defense.

The 1996-97 Badger team would not be one of the better defensive teams he had coached. Bennett knew that it would take four to five years to build a program based on great defense, as it had at Stevens Point and at Green Bay. Still, these Badger players were good and getting better. Only the team's lack of overall quickness and, at times, passion to play defense, prevented them from being the absolute best. Nonetheless, Bennett strove to instill the intangible keys to great defense, many of which were based not on technique but on teamwork. Like so many other elements of the program, he taught defense with the five concepts of humility, servanthood, passion, thankfulness, and unity, as his foundation. The following is a brief analysis of the components he continually emphasizes.

Solid Philosophical Foundation and Confidence in the System

Bennett had developed an unshakable philosophy in his defensive system, which was the product of thirty years of extensive, exhaustive study and thought on what was the best method for his teams. He had become unyielding in this doctrine because he simply knew it worked! He had long been self-reliant about that fact. Numerous successful campaigns over his career had built a quiet, strong confidence in the system and in his ability to teach it to his players. Ironically, it is that incredible confidence in the system that allows him to question it so thoroughly.

As pointed out in the previous chapter, that is a part of the process which builds his confidence in the defense. Still, his defense system is a work in progress, changing ever so slightly over time, due to the contemplation and questioning. The basic teaching principles, however, have remained unchanged.

The solid philosophical foundation provides the basis for all of his defensive decisions, whether the team is winning or losing, and enables him to overcome the temptation to change in the face of adversity.

Defense is the Top Priority. Nothing is More Important.

Great defense is expected!

"Every team must have one thing that it tries to be great at," Bennett said at his 1996 clinic. That one thing will always be man-to-man defense for him and his teams—no switching, no trapping, just relentless, aggressive defense. In turn, Bennett's role is vitally important in leading his team to that end.

"A team will do what you emphasize, not what you teach."

That phrase, often spoken by Bennett, is not a compilation of hollow words. Defense is emphasized in every imaginable phase of the program. Defense is daily emphasized in practice, and when the team plays poorly on offense and loses a close game, it is defense that is emphasized at the next practice. As already noted, when the team faltered, and lost five of seven games, Bennett used the off week to concentrate almost entirely on defense. Offense was an afterthought, even though nearly everyone else in Madison, and the team for that matter, believed that offense was the team's problem. The message was unmistakable to his players. Defense Matters! They had to accept that fact if they were going to play for Dick Bennett.

Results Matter More Than Methods

Bennett does teach specific defensive techniques, especially when a player first joins the program. Yet the players are empowered to "get the job done" in any way they can. This was actually the first observation I made while I watched him teach his defensive system to his new UW team in the fall of 1995. He first explained the guiding principles of the defense to the players, and as part of that explanation, he clearly identified the desired outcome, the goal. The players were then given the freedom to accomplish that goal in a method that best suited them. For example, he instructed the players that they were not to allow any penetration toward the baseline. He did not, however, instruct the players where to position their feet, or where to position their bodies, to accomplish that task. He did not "over-coach" the technique. His only concern was with the results of their efforts. The players, therefore, were freed to develop individual methods that best suited them. Their minds were not so cluttered with details that they lost sight of the goal—"NO OUTSIDE!"

Alone, With Others

The first principle of the defense is to stop the ball, which means to prevent it from penetrating toward the basket on the dribble. That responsibility falls squarely on the player guarding the ball; *alone*. He must pressure the ball, guard his offensive man closely, and thus create a level of discomfort in the ball handler. The pressure must be sufficient to make it difficult to shoot, pass, or dribble the ball. Failure to do this gives the offensive player the advantage, as he can see the floor clearly and has time to anticipate the action on the floor. This tight defensive position, however, is a vulnerable spot for the defender, especially when defending a quicker player. Therefore, the strength of the defense is also based on the level of confidence the defender "on the ball" has, in knowing that he will get help from his teammates "off the ball" if his man gets past him; *with others*. This confidence in his teammates, in turn, allows him to concentrate entirely on the principle of *stopping the ball!* The players simply would not be effective in stopping the ball without this unity on defense. They would have to back off on their pressure, and the defense would be rendered ineffective.

There is a second important element of the defense that is best described by the *alone, with others* symbolic terminology. That fundamental is the action of defending screens, whether on or off the ball. A screening situation consists of a cutter and a screener. The cutter is the offensive player, cutting off the screen, in an attempt to get open for a shot. The screener is the player who tries to obstruct the path of the defender, who is guarding the cutter. Most cutters move toward the ball or the basket in an attempt to get a shot. The moment when the cutter breaks off the screener, the defender on the cutter is completely *alone*. He has no responsibility at that moment other than to get through the screen. Bennett explained the concept to Ty Calderwood at one of his earliest practices. "When you are being screened, you are no longer a team defender." There was a very practical reason for this principle. No matter how good a defensive player is, he simply cannot fight through a screen and worry about helping his teammates at the same time. Therefore, he turns his attention solely to his own man. But even then, he will invariably get separated from the cutter, if the offense team is skilled at screening. During those few moments of separation, he must defend *with others*, getting help from his teammate who is defending the screener. That defender momentarily jumps into the path of the cutter, and jams the cut. The offensive player then has only one option, to move away from the basket. Successful execution of this principle is difficult, but when done correctly it approaches artful expression and separates the pretenders from the contenders.

Trust and Servanthood

There are two intangible concepts that make the latter maneuver possible. The player defending the screener must give total and complete help to his teammate, to get through the screen. Any hesitation on his part will cripple the defense and give the offensive cutter the opportunity to catch the ball and shoot a rhythm jump shot. At that moment, he must *serve* his teammate and stop the cutter. Thus, his priority of helping his teammate becomes greater than that of defending his own man. There is also a component of *trust* which must be present when the two defenders properly execute this technique. The screen defender jumps out and stops the cutter, yet he cannot stay too long. He has to return soon to his own player, the screener, before that player becomes a scoring threat himself. He *trusts* that his teammate will get through the screen and recover to his own man, the cutter. Therefore, he actually leaves the cutter open for a split second while both defenders return to their original players. At that point of transition, both the screener and the cutter are left open, but for such a short period of time that neither of them can take advantage of the opening.

This movement can be accomplished only when the players work together and trust each other. The instant one player fails to serve or trust his teammate while defending the screen, the artistic timing of the maneuver breaks down and the defense becomes porous.

Communication

Defense is one situation where talk is not cheap. A team must communicate to be effective on defense. This is never more important than when defending a screener or when in the "gap" off the ball. The easiest way to explain this concept is to examine a poor defensive player and a great defensive player. A great defender communicates well with his teammates, while the poor defender rarely talks. The contrast is obvious, and the reason is quite simple. The poor defender has a difficult time communicating on defense because he does not have a sense of what is about to happen next. He lacks the ability to anticipate the movement of the offense. As a result, he is always one step behind the offense and in a perpetual state of catch-up. This makes it impossible for him to have the presence of mind to communicate with his teammates. A player with this limitation may be a great one-on-one defender, but he simply cannot be a great team defender.

A great team defender has a feel for what the offense is about to do. He can anticipate the action, and thus communicate to his teammates what is going to happen next, before it actually happens. He is not always correct, but he is rarely caught off guard by the offense. The most obvious physical characteristic of a great team defensive player, one who communicates well, is that he is rarely out of position to help his teammates. His awareness allows him to maintain the ball-you-man relationship that is so important in help defense. Moreover, when in the ball-you-man relationship, he has better "vision" of the offense.

Continually Right Your Course

Bennett teaches, "The rule of ball-you-man is constantly being broken, therefore the repositioning off the ball is absolutely essential." Bennett is often heard imploring his team to constantly battle to reestablish their ball-you-man position. In fact, Bennett considers this principle to be the backbone of his defense. Offenses rarely stand stationary. Therefore, when the ball moves, or when the players move on the floor, the defense must continually adjust to the ever-changing environment. The reality in basketball is that the defender will constantly get knocked off track in the course of a defensive possession. That is why it is imperative that each player perpetually works to regain the correct defensive position. Failure to do so by any of the five defensive players will create a breakdown in the team defense, and, moreover, a potentially good scoring opportunity for the offense. Essentially, getting "broken down" on defense does not guarantee failure, but giving up at that point does!

It is not a coincidence that this intangible principle has significant implications for life beyond the basketball court.

Every Wheel Must Have a Hub

The hub on defense is defending the low-post. Great post defense may be even more important than playing great defense on the ball. Furthermore, post defense is more about toughness, determination, aggression, and relentless effort than it is about technique. On the first day of practice Bennett reinforced this idea, when he reprimanded Grant, Okey, Daugherty, and Coleman for their apathetic approach to a low-post screening drill.

"You guys have no idea how hard it is to play great post defense. There is no glamour in this. All it is, is hard work, banging and pounding, relentless effort!" He pointed to the other end of the floor where the guards were doing the same drill. "Just look! They are working their asses off and they don't even have to do this in a game. This is your number-one responsibility, but you don't care enough to even do more than just go through the motions. This is not something you just turn on in a game!" He stomped away toward the sideline without looking back. "We will never be any good defensively because you guys don't have what it takes to play tough post defense!" Bennett's orchestrated tirade made it clear to everyone involved that the defense started on the block and worked its way out. Needless to say, the quartet resumed the drill with renewed vigor.

Bennett is so concerned about post defense that he routinely instructs his team, "When the ball gets into the post we must treat it as a disaster! We have to do everything we can to get it out of there." He understood that even though there are few guarantees in basketball, soft post defense against a good team almost always guarantees failure.

The above is obviously not an inclusive list, and is heavily laden with esoteric basketball terms. Nonetheless, each of these components is critical to the overall effectiveness of Bennett's defensive system. Even the casual observer can identify the distinguishable characteristics of Bennett's teams by watching closely.

Chapter 14

Ideology Versus Reality

Purdue University:
Wednesday, January 22, West Lafayette, Indiana

Bennett was not overly optimistic after the Penn State game. Wisconsin had not looked fluid enough in the win to totally eliminate the memories of the Michigan State and Iowa defeats. Bennett's anxiety continued to build as the team headed into West Lafayette, Indiana, to face Gene Keady's underrated Purdue Boilermakers. Keady's "rebuilding" team played well in the opening three weeks of the Big Ten season and had just blown out in-state rival Indiana University four days earlier. Nonetheless, the Badgers had practiced well and continued to improve following the Penn State victory, so Bennett was cautiously optimistic heading into the game.

Bennett started Duany, Calderwood, Okey, Daugherty, and Grant for the second straight game. The unit settled into their familiar Triangle offense and man-to-man defense, and proceeded to jump out to a 10-4 lead at Mackey Arena. Purdue closed the gap over the next two minutes, as the teams settled into a grueling, well-played basketball game. Grant picked up his second foul seven minutes into the game and joined his teammates on the sideline. Bennett, for the third straight game, used an eight-player rotation in the first half. Kosolcharoen and Auriantal were the first off the bench, six minutes into the game, and Coleman followed two minutes later.

Grant rejoined the game with the score at 20-20. He took a feed from Okey and hit a six-foot turn-around jump shot from the left block. Thirty seconds later, however, he picked up his third foul while going for a block and returned to the bench. Play wore on without either team gaining an advantage. Duany had a chance to put his team ahead by four heading into the half, but his bonus free throw bounced off the back of the rim. Purdue's Alan Eldridge took the outlet pass and pushed the ball up the floor, pulled up over three Badger defenders, and banked in a thirty-footer as the horn sounded. The crowd jumped to their feet cheering Eldridge as he pumped his fist and ran off the floor. Purdue led 31-30.

West Lafayette, Indiana is rarely a friendly stop for visiting teams. Yet the Badgers had positioned themselves to challenge Purdue for the win. All they had to do was stay intense, smart, and unified in the second half.

The teams exchanged turnovers to start the half before Okey scored his only basket of the game on a three-point shot from the top of the key. Moments later Grant, who had still not learned his lesson about playing with fouls, missed a short jump shot and then climbed on Brad Miller's back going for the rebound. The whistle blew and he had his fourth foul. His lack of discipline irritated Bennett, who clenched his jaw and cast Grant an annoyed stare before replacing him with Kosolcharoen.

The game turned into a "hack-and-grab feast," which made it difficult for either team to score. With his team trailing 40-38, Bennett went back to the double low-post offense to generate more movement and scoring opportunities. Calderwood immediately drove hard into the lane for a seven-foot pull-up jump shot, to get the scoring restarted. Grant, who had re-entered the game at the seven-minute mark, scored two quick baskets to help give Wisconsin the lead at 46-44. The Badgers soon lost their offensive discipline, however, as Calderwood, Kosolcharoen, and Duany all missed tough floating jump shots. Purdue took advantage of the misfires and reclaimed the lead at 53-50, with under two minutes to play. A minute later, Calderwood's open three-pointer clanged hard off the back of the rim and Grant picked up his fifth foul going for the rebound. Two more desperation threes missed, while Purdue went four-for-four from the free throw line, and the final score ballooned to 60-52 in the Boilermakers' favor. Grant had ten points and six rebounds in only twenty-two minutes of play, but the team's nineteen turnovers and the last-minute shot selections made their conference record plummet to 2-4.

Just when Bennett thought his team was moving forward, breaking the cycle of last-second defeats, they regressed to their old habits. There were no longer any doubts that this team was inconsistent. They played like two different teams, one good and one bad. Bennett had become introverted and impatient with both his team and staff, as the stress of coaching such a group began to take its toll. His facial expression changed little, and he became terse in his interactions, making it difficult to converse with him on either a personal or professional level. The Purdue loss was the final straw for Bennett. He blew up at the team in the post-game locker room. His competitive nature had taken over and his reproach was hardly consistent with his Christian values. Bennett's frame of mind remained agitated over the next two days as the team prepared for their game against the Fighting Illini in Champaign, Illinois.

Providence, Marquette, Minnesota, Michigan State, and Purdue; five out of their last seven games had ended in late, second-half defeats. That fact more than anything, dumbfounded Bennett, who was used to his teams pulling out such games. When asked about his expectations late in those games, his response indicated his frustration.

"The ball should be in the hands of our best ball handler and he should be running our offense! We should not be doing anything but that! We should be doing the same things we did earlier. Now we break down mentally and everybody stops moving. Then one guy takes the ball and panics, throwing up a poor shot."

Wisconsin had forgotten Bennett's early-season lesson which emphasized the six keys to preventing defeat, which are never more important than in the last minutes of a close game.

1. Take care of the ball, prevent turnovers.
2. Great shot selection, shoot to our strength.
3. Make our free throws.
4. Affect our opponent's shots, no rhythm shots.
5. Do not give up offensive rebounds.
6. Keep fouls down, don't give up free throws.

University of Illinois:
Saturday, January 25, Champaign, Illinois

How would the team respond to Bennett's locker room tongue-lashing? That was impossible to say, but their pregame attitude just before tip-off in Assembly Hall had Bennett frustrated and dismayed. He waited in the locker room for his team to return after their fifteen minute warm-up, before he heard an energized and enthusiastic Fighting Illini club return to their locker room just down the corridor. The Badgers, in contrast, were so quiet and stoic as they entered the locker room that they caught Bennett by surprise. His calm review of the game plan, however, stopped mid-sentence. The lethargy of his team unnerved him as he looked into their emotionless faces, further setting off his already short fuse.

"You guys still do not believe in what we are doing! It is obvious in the way you act; it is obvious in the way you prepare; and it is obvious in the way you play! You don't believe in the system and you don't believe we can get this done!"

The game plan written on the chalkboard went unnoticed as the team retook the floor after the national anthem. Bennett's rebuke was unrehearsed and he wondered how the timing of the message would affect the team. Mike Kosolcharoen replaced Sean Daugherty in the starting lineup as Bennett decided to stay with the three-guard lineup, primarily because he thought that Daugherty had taken the Purdue loss "a bit too well." Strategically, the move also allowed Bennett to start the game in the double low-post offense instead of the Triangle, which had become ineffective. Duany hit a long three less than fifteen seconds after the tip-off for the game's first score. On the next possession, Kosolcharoen injured his wrist when he crashed to the floor on a drive to the basket, and was replaced by Auriantal. Bennett's irritation with the team was evident as he used nine different players in the first five minutes of the game. A mistake by any of the players bought them a ticket to the sideline. Adam Shafer didn't mind the quick hook, as he finally saw his first action in a Badger uniform since his transfer. Soon after, both Bennett and the Badgers settled into a less sporadic pattern and built a comfortable 31-20 halftime lead, thanks in large part to exceptional defense and four three-point bombs by Duany.

Illinois tried to turn the game into a full-court melee at the start of the second half. However, Wisconsin maintained their double-digit lead with their own brand of destructive defense. Wisconsin eventually took a 54-40 lead when Duany and Grant's dunks punctuated two fast breaks against the press. With eight minutes remaining in the game, Bennett reached into his bag of tricks and pulled out the 1-2-2 zone, which he used for the remainder of the game. He also went back to his big lineup and ran the Triangle offense to eat up clock and control the glass. Ironically, for a stretch of two minutes he had a lineup on the floor that Badger fans would soon become familiar with—Calderwood, Burkemper, Okey,

Daugherty, and Grant. Wisconsin went on to win the game 73-56 in their most impressive road display of the year. They did not collapse in the second half.

Kosolcharoen's wrist injury and Bennett's ire turned out to be blessings in disguise. David Burkemper was released from his tomb at the end of the bench, and reminded his coach why he thought so highly of this (re)walk-on. Also, Duany, with a game- and career-high twenty points, and Okey, who collected sixteen rebounds, both came back to life after several uninspired performances. Wisconsin held Illinois to 28 percent shooting from the floor and only three of thirty-three from the three-point line. That nine percent three-point statistic was impressive, considering that the Illini had shot 50 percent in their previous two games. Bennett's nature took on a significantly improved demeanor as his Badgers left Champaign with a victory for the second straight year, a feat that had not been accomplished since the 1913 and 1914 campaigns. The win had all the earmarks of a turning point.

Bennett's attitude had unequivocally changed by Monday morning as he addressed his staff. Relaxed and upbeat, he joked about getting lost for the third straight week on his way to the TV station for his weekend program. He explained that Tony had asked him upon his arrival home, "Dad, are you really that stupid?" The staff joined him in the merriment that accompanied the big road win. Bennett continued to entertain the staff. "Anne, God bless her, stuck up for me. She said to Tony, 'Well, he's gotten lost differently each time.' And that is the fact! I have gotten lost three different ways, which means I don't know where I am." Laughter filled the room before everyone settled down to the business at hand, Wednesday's game against Northwestern.

The unconstrained climate of the morning's discourse carried over into practice. The team spent just over an hour in defensive breakdown drills, which had become the norm following the Iowa defeat, and the players executed with rejuvenated verve. As practice progressed, Bennett became more vocal than he had been during the entire season. As his intensity increased, however, so did the frequency of his critical comments. Inexplicably, especially in light of his earlier temperament, the rift between his Christian values and his intense competitive nature widened. That dichotomy, I decided, needed to be explored.

Bennett arrived in the office late on Tuesday, and although his external appearance remained calm, it became obvious that his agitation remained, as our conversation unfolded.

"I notice you became very intense and introverted when the team was going through the losing streak. Just how does losing affect you as a person?" I inquired.

"I do get quieter and keep more to myself. It is not like death, but it has some of the same symptoms."

His reference to death confused me. I had *roughly* based the stages Bennett went through after the Iowa loss on the grieving process, but even in that context his remark seemed peculiar.

"I never realized how competitive you were, how badly you hate to lose. Where did that competitive nature come from?" I asked.

Bennett sat back listlessly in his office chair as he answered in a monotone voice. "I have never thought about how far my competitiveness goes; however, I know I am extremely competitive in the areas that I am concerned about, and obviously that includes coaching."

He began to speak with interest about the subject and became deliberate in his speech. "By the same token, I've had to be [competitive] to achieve anything. I have never felt that I have been gifted with excessive intelligence and I did not come from a background where opportunities came my way. I did not come out of somebody else's program where I had a bunch of contacts. So, from the beginning, I had to do well to get the next job and to have an opportunity at the next level. Most of the places I have gone, with the exception of Madison, I had to earn my spurs."

His wife Anne had echoed the same sentiments several weeks earlier. "It is funny that people think Dick could have any job in the country. That is simply not true. Marquette never really wanted him. Madison never really wanted him. And a few other jobs he looked into never really wanted him. I felt badly when he went after certain jobs and they did not even want to interview him."

Bennett's admiration of hard work and "paying the price" carried over to his players as well. "I really had to earn everything I got, and rightfully so, and that's affected my dealings with players. I am hard on them until they prove they can play and earn my respect. If a guy is highly touted, I am not real quick to share that opinion until I see it."

Most of the players on his current team had not "earned their spurs" in his eyes. That bothered him, and the losing made it difficult to hide that fact. When would the team earn the victories through hard work and commitment on a consistent basis and stop playing like a bunch of individuals? With over half of the schedule played, and sitting 3-5 in Big Ten play, Bennett strongly doubted that it would happen during that season. The season, the team, which started out with so much potential, was on the verge of a major bust. Potential, Bennett was learning, is sometimes simply a polite word for underachievement. He had rarely experienced that phenomenon during his career, and it perplexed him. He knew of only one way to succeed; through a combination of hard work, singleness of purpose, and a relentless competitive spirit. He knew that. He lived it. But how could he instill that competitive drive in his team? Bennett's face grew stern and his eyes piercing. He shifted from his reclined position in his chair, sat erect at the edge of his chair, and searched the source of his own competitive spirit for answers.

"Much of those instincts go back to my childhood and the way I was raised. My father always wanted me to do well and I wanted to please him. When I was an athlete, I had to do more with hustle than natural ability. I think that has something to do with it. As a coach, my competitive nature is tied up in the sheer desire to raise the level of performance with whatever means I have available. And finally, some of it, the weakest aspect, is pride. I do not want to look bad and I personalize the failure."

The combination of the losses, his occasional lack of respect for his team's preparation and competitiveness, and his own pride, exposed the latent dichotomy between his Christian ideals and his competitive nature. Bennett's frustration grew as he explained the bipolar motivations.

"Again, my competitiveness is both a blessing and a curse. Our society is so competitive and we are conditioned that if we do not win, then we are not good enough. I detest that kind of thinking and I talk against it, yet I am conditioned by it. My competitive spirit has developed over all these years of coaching by always having to scratch to get ahead. That is the blessing."

"How is it a curse?" I asked.

"It is a curse when it goes beyond doing what is appropriate. I have been known to chastise kids on a personal level when they do not measure up. I don't think that's right. People who are real competitive have a real down side, and that is dealing with their competitive drive when things do not go well."

But what was the best method to motivate his current team? Which approach best prepared the team to succeed in the Big Ten and, hopefully, the post-season? I asked if he thought his team got better as a whole when he was tough on them all the time.

"Probably," he responded. "Unfortunately, I think I have observed that to get this team ready, there has to be that toughness. They seem to respond better when they think there is a little crisis."

His mind battled the conflicting methods even as he spoke. "I think I was a better coach for the first twenty five years of coaching because I was tough all the time. I have mellowed now, but I still go back to being tough when I am confronted with losing and poor play. However, I think the best way would be to stay consistent with who you are and just keep working. Now I go back and forth and I do not know what is best."

The inconsistent play of the team did not help matters. There just did not seem to be any rhyme or reason to their level of play. Bennett's comments reiterated the dilemma.

"I was real tough on them for the Illinois game and they responded. I wonder if that is how I have to be all the time, and I am wrestling with that now. The game is a very intense atmosphere for two hours and you have to prepare your players for that. It is much like a drill sergeant in boot camp. He is preparing those people for a time when there is no other way to perform than a hard, focused way." Still, Bennett lamented those tactics. "I feel I have slipped. I show the human side so much that maybe the players get mixed messages." With that, he stopped his homily and waited patiently for my next question.

"Is one of the down sides of your competitiveness that you just spoke of the skewing of the priorities in your life; God first, family second, and basketball third?" I probed.

He once again sat back and sighed heavily. "I am working very hard to keep the Lord first in my life. That has been a lifetime struggle, but it has become more dramatic in the last five to ten years. I battle that constantly and it is never far from my consciousness. My faith is real to me and I want to keep my priorities straight, but I have been so conditioned to this competitive world, that I have terrible conflicts. I have let my competitive nature overrun my Christianity way too much. I know it is improper to swear, nag players, get after referees, or worse, lose my temper. In my desire to be competitive I step over the line. That is the battle. I have lost the battle numerous times, but I am still determined to win the war."

Success in his profession often demanded that he be highly competitive, desiring intensely to win. It is unreasonable to think that he could be successful at the highest level of college basketball without that competitive drive. The internal conflict between his Christian ideals and competitive behavior, therefore, are inevitable. Some psychologists even suggest that such an ongoing conflict may contribute to the lowering of an individual's self-esteem and the onset of mild depression. The theory seemed credible to me as I witnessed Bennett struggle with the ever-increasing chasm between his Christian idyllic beliefs and his competitive behavior. Therefore I asked, "How happy are you during the season?"

"Not very," he replied. "The feeling after a win is the best feeling, especially the morning after a home-court victory. That is a powerful emotion. I get up early, make a cup of coffee, and just enjoy the moment. Actually, I am always comfortable at home, but beyond that I am not very comfortable. Right now I am having a hard time. For some reason I woke up with this hard feeling inside of me and I do not have a good feeling about anything. I mean personally." Bennett clarified his previous statement. "I like our kids. I like the way they are playing and I feel we are in reasonably good shape as a team. But on the 31st, it will be one year since my brother Tom passed away and I am having a hard time with that and I'm struggling with the demands of having to be 'up' everyday. I just want to back off. This week I would just like to be somewhere else, just be a Green Bay Packer fan."

"Does any of this have to do with your own mortality?" I asked, recalling his earlier comment about death. Only when Bennett answered that follow-up question did the depth of his despair that morning become fully evident.

"Not really," he calmly responded, "To tell you the truth, I sometimes look forward to the end." I frantically searched his face for clues as to whether or not he was serious. He finally broke the awkward tension of the moment. "I just think I'm tired. It is coming on to February and it has been a long haul this year. We have faced this challenge without a lot of new faces, and sometimes I wonder if we will ever get to the next level." He hesitated, then admitted, "If I were perfectly honest, part of this feeling is that I am afraid of losing to Northwestern. We lost twice to them last year and I am afraid of losing to them again."

Late January and early February are the dog days of a college basketball season. The entire staff and players have worked virtually non-stop for the better part of four months, only occasionally getting a day off to relax and unwind. Even then, there are the non-stop recruiting calls, game plans, promotional events, and the ever-present pressure of the next game. Therefore, I asked, "Coach, is this cyclical? Do you go through it every year?"

"Yes," he replied stoically.

"How have you gotten through it in the past?"

"I tough it out," he quipped.

"When does it start to turn around?"

With much more empathy in his voice, he finally explained, "Eric, I really do not know, but this is what I predict will happen. My faith, the Lord himself will step in here and take me through this. You will see me at some point, at practice today or at the game tomorrow, at peace. That is what my prayer is, because I won't get through this on my own. I think I am better this year than I have been in the past, all things considered. I am better with the kids; I handle the pregame anxiety better; and I handle losses better. But the draining is always there."

The weight of the struggle showed clearly on his face as he continued to speak. "It is a daily process and I cannot win the battle myself. That is why, if my faith is real as a Christian, I have to say that God is Lord *and* Savior of my life. He is more than my Savior who died on the cross so man's sins would be forgiven and all could enter heaven. He is also *Lord* of my life, and that means every moment! When I remember that, things fall into place."

With that insight, I knew there was nothing else I needed to talk about on that day. So, I thanked Bennett for his time, and left him to his thoughts.

Bennett began the day's practice with a chalk talk on the court instead of in the locker room. It was the first time all season that he had done so. He pulled the mobile dry erase board over to the end line bleachers and instructed the players to join him. After a few minutes of instruction, the team went through their pre-practice warm-up ritual. At first, Bennett appeared to have moved beyond the morning's tumult, but as practice moved into the second half hour, his demeanor showed that he had not.

Paul Grant had become a weak link in the team's post defense. The team's overall defense simply could not improve unless Grant played significantly better. Bennett verbally rode him relentlessly on every possession. Grant became determined to show Bennett up and totally committed himself to stopping his man, Booker Coleman. Predictably, he concentrated so heavily on Coleman that he let Auriantal drive right past him for an uncontested lay-up, thus breaking the defensive rule of vision. Bennett slowly walked across center court, head down and cheeks flush. "Paul, in our system there is never an excuse for not seeing the ball, NEVER, EVER!"

Play resumed and Bennett stewed on the sideline. The red team scored at will against the starters and Bennett's criticism quickly spread to the entire team. Unable to stand still, he walked across the baseline and shook his head quickly from side to side. "You inspire very little confidence! Why do we even waste our time talking about this?"

The next possession resulted in another missed defensive assignment on the low post and a basket for the red team. "STOP!" Bennett screamed, as everyone became motionless on the court. He stepped out from the baseline and pointed at the right block. "If they get the ball in the post they will beat you! Do you understand that? Do you believe that? They will beat you!" He hesitated momentarily, sternly looked into the eyes of all the post players, and then slowly turned and shuffled off the court with his head down.

Bennett had clearly chosen to remain intense and to ride the team hard in preparation for Northwestern. Though not the method he pre-ferred, the style had proven successful in the past, and he could not leave anything to chance. His team *had* to beat Northwestern! Whether or not his approach was calculated, his intensity remained at a fever pitch for the better part of an hour. On one occasion, he stopped practice right in the middle of a drill, something he never does, and challenged the team.

"I don't know what to make of you! There are times when you are very sound and you can play with anyone. But there are also times when you are so unsound you can't play with anybody! You guys are victims of whatever happens to you. If things are going well, then you play well. If things are going bad, then you play bad. You must play through it and make your own opportunities. If they are not there, you must create your own opportunities!"

The team finally responded, as if a switch had been flipped, and they became purposeful in their play. Yet there was still one problem. The white team began to emulate Bennett's confrontational temperament. Players barked angrily back and forth at each other, blaming each other for mistakes. Once again Bennett slowly strolled onto to the court to lecture the team.

"You guys know what you are? Right now you are just perfect assholes. You do not make it easier for one another. My Lord in heaven, don't you get that yet? You need to come together!" He pointed his finger at Grant and then Daugherty. "You get mad at him and then he gets mad at someone else." He turned and addressed Okey. "You get mad at everyone and then I get mad at you! We need to come together! We need to believe in each other and in what we are doing." He hesitated at the free throw line to let his words sink in, before he walked off the floor to the baseline.

He had pushed the team to their limits and he knew it. The tearing down was complete. The faces that stared back at him were no longer angry, they were blank. The time had come to build them back up, and though he remained intense for the remainder of practice, his comments became far more positive. He even turned the atmosphere playful when he concluded practice with a series of "fun" shooting competitions.

Practice had lasted two hours and was the most emotionally charged of the season, for both Bennett and the players. Bennett's behavior made it clear to the players that the Northwestern game was a must win. A loss would simply be catastrophic. There would be nothing left to play for and the season would be a total loss in his eyes. The ferocity of that day's practice would surely become commonplace if such a thing happened. Even Northwestern's poor record, only one win in the conference, did not calm Bennett. That victory had come earlier in the week when the Wildcats blew out Ohio State by thirty-one points.

Northwestern University:
Wednesday, January 29, Madison, Wisconsin

The usual rush-hour traffic in downtown Madison was further congested by the flow of Badger fans driving in for the game. Wednesday's early 6 P.M. start time accommodated ESPN regional television coverage.

The Field House was barely three-quarters full at tip-off. Bennett stayed with the three-guard set and opened up with Calderwood, Auriantal, Duany, Okey, and Grant. Thousands of fans hurried to their seats as the starters built a 13-3 lead. Bennett again went deep into his bench, as Auriantal, Kosolcharoen, Coleman, and Daugherty all saw early minutes. Wisconsin's stifling defense, especially against standout Evan Eschmeyer, did not give up its second basket until the nine-minute mark. Unfortunately, the Badgers' offense slowed to a crawl and Wildcat freshman Joe Harmsen came off the bench to score ten points, narrowing the lead to 21-18. A seventeen-foot jumper by Daugherty and a put-back by Coleman, however, gave Wisconsin breathing room as they headed into halftime, leading 25-18.

Northwestern made another comeback in the second half due in large part to Wisconsin's anemic foul shooting. The Badgers were 3 of 13 from the line after the first four minutes of play. Harmsen's fifteenth point of the night pulled the Wildcats to within two, 31-29, two minutes later. Fortunately, the Badgers answered the threat with six baskets in the next four minutes, which included two by Okey, who hit all six of his shot attempts in the game. Northwestern never challenged again, and with four minutes remaining in the game, Bennett repeated the strategy he had used at Illinois. He went to the Triangle offense to burn the clock and control the boards. Defensively, he went to the 1-2-2 to prevent open threes and fouls.

The 65-53 victory evened Wisconsin's conference mark at 4-4. Okey led the team in scoring and rebounding, with seventeen and seven respectively. Grant chipped in sixteen, and five other players contributed four or more points. Wisconsin also shot forty-eight percent from the floor and turned the ball over only eight times for the game. Bennett, for the first time in a long time, had reason to be optimistic about the remainder of the season. They had vaulted to the top of the Big Ten defensively, they had improved offensively, and they had won three of their last four games. Bennett's encouraged outlook, however, turned out to be short-lived.

Chapter 15

Collapse . . . into Grace

Ohio State University:
Saturday, February 1, Columbus, Ohio

Bennett traveled to the Buckeye state wanting more than another tally in the win column. He wanted to erase the memory of the last time he was there. His team played poorly and was beaten badly on January 31, 1996, at OSU's St. John Arena. That was also the night his brother died in Boston. However, in order to erase the memory, he had to face Randy Ayers' unpredictable and erratic Ohio State squad, who (like the Badgers) were playing well, despite their 3-5 conference record.

The atmosphere in St. John's Arena was surreal as the small Big Ten crowd sat quietly in apparent disbelief of the game that unfolded in front of them. Ohio State started the game in a sagging 2-3 zone, making Wisconsin prove they could score from the perimeter. The Badgers missed their first five shots, which increased the Buckeyes' confidence. Their defense grew more aggressive on each successive misfire by the Badgers. Ohio State turned up the pressure on Wisconsin, and applied a 2-2-1 full court press after their own baskets. Randy Ayers' strategy held Wisconsin scoreless on their first thirteen possessions of the game, which resulted in eight missed shots and five turnovers. Ayers, apparently unhappy with those results, changed to a man-to-man defense. Grant immediately got open on the low post and was fouled on his shot. He made one of two, and with 11:58 on the game clock, the score was an unbelievably low 6-1. Ayers went right back to the zone.

Ohio State's zealous defense forced four consecutive turnovers before the Badgers could get off another shot, but even that was laughable. Duany air-balled a baseline drive, which Okey rebounded, but then stuffed himself on the rim going back up for the uncontested dunk. Even then, after he regained possession of the ball and was fouled, he went to the line and missed both free throws. Sean Daugherty finally made a basket with eight minutes to go in the half and Wisconsin trailed 13-4. Their offensive production up to that point showed nine turnovers, one for nine from the field, and one for four from the line!

Remarkably, the Badgers were not out of the game. Daugherty hit another three-point shot, while Okey and Auriantal added two free throws apiece. The deficit had narrowed to 16-11. Yet the fire went out as quickly as it started, when the Badgers could not manage another point for the rest of the half. The return of Wisconsin's offensive ineptitude crushed their competitive spirit, and even their exulted defense failed them in the closing minutes of the half. The game was essentially over before the halftime horn ended their feeble play: fourteen turnovers, ten percent shooting, and a numbing 26-11 score.

Wisconsin fought and scrapped to start the second half, showing a character that was absent in the first twenty minutes, but Ohio State had an answer for everything they tried. Every shot, every rebound, every loose ball, and every break went the Buckeyes' way. Then the Badgers broke down mentally. Thirty seconds of tough defense became a turnover on a careless, ill-advised half-court outlet, and a three-on-two break was nullified by an inexcusable over-and-back violation. In addition, the players were less discriminate in their shot selection as the deficit grew. Their defense, for the most part, was solid enough to win, yet offensively they were nothing short of disastrous. Bennett raised the white flag with three minutes to go in the game and removed his starters. They trailed 58-34. The red team closed out the final four minutes of play by scoring eight points, reducing the margin of defeat to eighteen, 60-42. The mental collapse had been total. Wisconsin had been beaten badly, but what troubled Bennett most was that his players had given up long before the end of the game. He was so upset that he thought it best not to address his team after the game. Bennett later explained his disenchantment.

"I was caught totally by surprise because we had been playing well and we simply fell apart. Our performance was nothing short of dreadful! I knew if I said anything, I wouldn't stop, so I had enough sense to keep my mouth shut."

Bennett, however, was not as reserved in the post-game interview.

"It was a real embarrassment! I had hoped Badger basketball would not sink as low as it did today. I have coached a lot of teams, but this is the most embarrassed I have been in thirty-two years of coaching!"

Was that the truth? The answer really didn't matter; he believed it. The team he put on the floor had once again failed to play consistent quality basketball and, for the second time in the Big Ten season, they had folded offensively in the face of adversity. The totality of the breakdown at Ohio State literally shook Bennett to his foundation.

He sat in the airport after the game and wrote in his journal, still unable to discuss the game with his staff. "We were beaten badly and we looked pathetic. No heart, no smarts, no ability. This game was as bad as it gets for us. We could do absolutely nothing on offense. I know that I have said before that I really don't know where to turn, but this time I don't. The real question is where do we go from here. I think we really need to shake up the personnel. Certain guys must come out of the lineup."

He could find no distractions upon his return to Madison. Sunday was filled with unrest and reflection. "I couldn't even look at the tape. I watched the first ten minutes of the tape and I actually got physically sick. I got nauseous. It bothered me so much I had to put it away. It wasn't until later, after I went to bed, that I finally got back up and watched the whole thing." That viewing prompted one final entry in his journal. "After watching the tape, I am even less impressed with the effort!" The frustration level had peaked for Bennett with ten games left in the regular season. The timing and the situation were ripe for change. Faced with relentless self-doubt on finding a way out of his dilemma, Bennett once again returned to his core beliefs in search of an answer.

He stood up and grabbed a marker at Monday's meeting. "What I would first like to do is list all the reasons why we think we play so poorly so much of the time. I want to hear what you have to say."

There was a moment of contemplative thought before the assistants shared their own insights. Bennett scribbled each response down on the wall board as they were called out. Brad Soderberg first noted, "We are poor shooters." Shawn Hood followed that up with, "We fail to get the ball into the lane enough, either on drives or by feeding the post." Brad spoke up again, "We do not have enough quality players with a feel for the game." Brian Hecker sat forward in his chair and added, "We have bad chemistry." Paul Costanzo added one final comment, "We are poor passers."

Bennett replaced the cap on the red marker, placed it carefully in the aluminum lip of the board, and took his seat at the head of the table. "That is even more than I was looking for, but they are all important points." He turned his chair and studied the board for a moment. "I agree with Paul. I also think the poor passing affects us a great deal. This is the poorest passing team I have coached, which is primarily a product of our guards. I think we are starting to see how bad our guards are. Last night Tony said to me, 'Dad, you have no chance of winning until you get some guards.'"

Paul, with his ever-present statistics, added, "Two of our three starting guards are shooting under 30 percent."

"O.K., enough bad-mouthing," Bennett said when he realized that the ground was fertile enough to receive his next comments. "What I am leading up to is that we have to make some changes. The question is what do we do?" It was a rhetorical question and he did not wait for a response. "My first reaction on the plane ride home was to go with Ty, David, and Mike at the guards, with Sean and Sam at the forwards. We would get a team that would make good decisions, but I have backed off that idea a bit." That group was simply not big and athletic enough to match up with Big Ten competition. In addition, Kosolcharoen was one of the poorest passers on the team and had become unreliable as an offensive threat. "The last thought I had last night, after watching the entire tape, was to go with a big lineup that included Booker. That lineup would be Ty, Mike, Sean, Sam, and Booker. That lineup would help minimize the effect of the guards by having only two on the floor at a time."

Bennett turned his attention toward his post player when he continued. "As I have said before, big players either win you titles or they get you fired. Everyone thinks a big man should be playing and contributing, but the reality is that sometimes they simply are not that productive and their contributions are minimal. That describes Paul right now. If he is not scoring, he just is not giving us anything." Bennett then enthusiastically proclaimed, "Booker, however, excites me a bit and I haven't been excited about him before. As I watch Booker, I see that he is really trying to play defense the way we want it played. He is defending the post, helping on screens, really going after shots and, overall, doing a very good job. I also think he has a knack for keeping the ball alive on the offensive glass, which might be the catalyst Sam and Sean need to get their hands on the ball."

He slid his chair back and bent forward. His elbows resting on his knees, he let his head droop low in thought. After a long pause, he slowly lifted his head and spoke defiantly. "I had one worthwhile thought yesterday. I have placed all of the standards that I have lived by professionally on the back shelf." His face was blank as he murmured his next words out of frustration. "That is depressing me. I want to shout out to our fans, to everyone, 'You guys haven't seen good basketball here!' I then thought to myself, I am trying to get kids who are incapable of playing good basketball to play it."

Was Bennett simply venting, or was his assessment genuine? Coming so close on the heels of the Ohio State loss, it was difficult to differentiate. Nonetheless, Bennett expounded on his own insights. "It comes down to this. You play good basketball in one of two ways. One, you have very good players who go out and play very hard. Or two, you have guys who are limited but are very smart. Of course there is a lot of crossover and players are on a continuum between the two extremes. But the fact is we are not getting any better, so we have to get smarter. That is our problem. We can't get any smarter with the kids we are currently playing. Some of them are just never going to be smart players, it is not in them, they aren't going to change. Once you start thinking for your players, it is the beginning of the end. That is the one thing that I know and I have put that on the back shelf. Therefore, I have reached a conclusion that we cannot get better until we get smarter. I don't think we have any choices.

"Which way do you want to go?" Bennett asked his assistants. "Do you think I'm crazy to put David Burkemper and Booker Coleman in the starting lineup?" Again, he allowed for no response time. His posture straightened and his voice became enriched with emotion. "In my heart of hearts, I know it is the right choice. Once before the end of the season I want to try 'my formula'! That team would resemble my Green Bay teams more than anything else I can put out there."

Soderberg, Hood, Hecker, and Costanzo were not about to contest Bennett's impassioned decree. They understood their head coach's rhetoric was about more than just one game. His address was about the ideals and vision he held for the game of basketball. Such a drastic change in the lineup would be an emphatic statement of what he believed to be "right and proper." Still, such a bold move was easy to discuss behind closed doors, but just days before facing the vaunted Michigan Wolverines? That was a different story. Was the timing right? This was to be, after all, a nationally televised game against an opponent ranked thirteenth in the nation. Was that the correct platform on which to make such a stand? Bennett would look downright foolish if the move led to a disastrous performance. On the other hand, if his plan worked, there could be no more powerful endorsement of his philosophical foundation. The same strength of personality and wisdom had brought him to Madison in the first place. Thus, Bennett knew there was much more at stake than a basketball game. He had internalized the struggles of the season and made them intensely personal. In doing so, he brought his own professional integrity into the mix. His firm announcement made that point obvious.

"There comes a time when you have to say it is time to move ahead. I am not going to continue to play this kind of basketball. You all need to know this because it directly affects you. If this is the kind of basketball I have to coach, I will not do it. I will quit!" He pounded his fist on the table and squinted his eyes. "This is not just my work, it is half of my life! I don't care if they give me an insurance policy. I don't care if they add years to my contract. I don't care if they build a new building. I don't care about any of that stuff! I care about good basketball! I go home every night and I want to vomit because I have gone through another night of watching Big Ten players throw the ball into the bleachers and shoot air-balls! There comes a time when you have to move ahead. I want to get to a style of play that we can replicate. If we are going to get to a level of play here that we can carry over to the future, we have to establish smart play and we have to establish it now!"

Bennett's compelling sermon continued for two hours, though there were lighter moments as well. At one point, he joked about the audacity of one of his reserve players who refused to go into the Ohio State game. The player claimed he couldn't because he had not been taped. Bennett recalled those events, then dropped his chin to his chest in playful exasperation. He chuckled and shook his head from side to side. "Boys, you've got to laugh at times like this. Believe me, I have!"

Bennett still wrestled with his radical lineup change as the team took the floor for Monday's practice. Therefore, he put off a decision, and instead emphasized shooting and offense. The idea needed more analytical thought. As it turned out, the players themselves ultimately made the decision for Bennett. Tuesday's practice, like Monday's, lacked productivity and inspiration by the players. All of the players "on the bubble" had bad practices or did not practice at all. Hennssy and Doc did not practice because of lingering injuries. Mike repeatedly turned the ball over and missed open shots. Paul, meanwhile, was rendered harmless by Booker's vastly improved defense. Bennett was disappointed in their lack of mental toughness in preparation for such an important game. Their performances had not inspired confidence in their coach.

Bennett informed his staff at Wednesday's meeting, "I have decided to start tomorrow's game with a lineup of Calderwood, Daugherty, and Okey; augmented with Burkemper and Coleman." With his hands in front of his face as if praying, he glanced around the room to get the initial reaction of his assistants. When there was none, he continued, "I tried it out on my wife this morning, and she usually supports me in anything I do, but when I asked her she just said, 'Oh?'" Laughter broke out around the table as Bennett imitated his wife's quizzical reaction. "I know it sounds crazy, but in my heart of hearts, I believe this is the best lineup for us, to play the way I want our team to play."

Shawn Hood sensed that Bennett was seeking confirmation for his decision. "I saw that group work together yesterday and I'm not surprised you are going that way. They played well." Brad Soderberg also definitively agreed. "I am totally comfortable with that lineup. You have a firm yes vote from me." Paul and Brian also nodded their heads in support as Bennett spoke.

"Well, then, if you guys aren't at all shocked by this, then that tells me it has happened." He looked around the table one more time and pointed out the obvious worse-case scenario. "This could be a disaster waiting to happen, coming out of the chute with this team, but if it is going to be a disaster, I would prefer it be at the start of the game, since we have now proven we can come back from a slow start." Muffled laughter emanated from the staff.

When informed of the decision at that afternoon's practice, Booker and Dave were like children with a new toy. Doc, Hennssy, Mike, and Paul, to their credit, accepted their new roles with maturity. They worked hard, kept a positive attitude, and helped prepare the starters to face Michigan. I sat in the stands amused by the human drama that would unfold (or flop) in just over twenty-four hours. Bennett would pit his formula for success against one of the premier programs in the country. This time, however, he would be doing so with a seldom-used post player and with a walk-on guard who had been cut during open tryouts! Was he crazy? Maybe. Or maybe just crazy like a fox.

University of Michigan:
Thursday, February 6, Madison, Wisconsin

> *. . . 'Tis grace that brought me safe thus far,*
> *and grace will lead me home . . .*

Those words originate from the evangelical hymn, "Amazing Grace." Though difficult to define exactly what grace is, a metaphysical definition might suggest that grace is a powerful force that originates outside of the human realm and touches our lives in innumerable and incomprehensible ways. Should that definition be true, there was definitely a touch of grace present in the Field House on the night of February 6.

The arena seats filled more quickly than normal. An aura of excitement filled the air by the time the teams took the floor to warm up in front of an already near-capacity crowd. Burkemper's nervousness showed when, on his first shot attempt during warm-ups, he threw up an air-ball. True to his nature, however, he shook his head and laughed at himself as he jogged to the end of the rebounding line. His shaky hands were understandable. The idea that this once-cut walk-on was about to start for the Wisconsin Badgers, on national television, against the highly touted Michigan Wolverines was preposterous. It was amazing that he could even tie his shoes! Booker, well, was Booker; calm and collected, regardless of the situation. If he had any anxiety about his move into the starting lineup, he wasn't showing it. And then there were the Michigan players, swaggering around the court with their cool and confident disposition, a demeanor that often accompanies great physical ability and skill.

The Wisconsin fans were more raucous than usual, as it became obvious that this was not to be just another Big Ten game. Cheers and taunts echoed down from the furthest reaches of the Field House as the players were introduced. Daugherty, Okey, and Calderwood joined Coleman and Burkemper to start the game. David and Booker both made their presence felt early in front of the capacity crowd. Burkemper turned down an uncontested shot only seconds into the game, following Bennett's instructions, and deferred to his teammates. On the defensive end of the floor, Booker forced a turnover when Michigan tried to feed the ball to

Maurice Taylor, whom Bennett considered the best player in the Big Ten. Though the future NBA first-round draft pick did get an early basket on Coleman, he was then effectively denied the ball on nearly every possession. Meanwhile, two baskets by Daugherty and another by Okey, all out of the Triangle offense, gave Wisconsin an early 6-5 lead.

Bennett went to his bench six and a half minutes into the game and replaced Burkemper with Auriantal, and Coleman with Grant. The two had performed admirably and helped give the Badgers a one point lead, 9-8. In turn, an appreciative crowd gave the pair a rousing round of applause as they trotted off the floor. Just one minute later, Michigan suffered a big blow. Maurice Taylor took an inadvertent elbow to the face from Grant as he pressured the ball at the top of the key. The impact sent him crashing to the floor. Grant, meanwhile, drove in for an open fifteen-foot jump shot. As the ball swished through the net, an official's whistle stopped the action. A pool of blood quickly formed beneath Taylor's badly broken nose. The impact, which also caused a minor concussion, prevented him from returning to the game that night.

The trainers attended to Taylor and the managers carefully removed the blood from the playing surface. When action resumed, the Wolverines played inspired basketball while the Badgers managed only two points in the next six minutes of play. Bennett interjected Booker and Dave back into the lineup at the eight-minute mark, with his team trailing 16-13. The unit of Dave, Booker, Ty, Duany, and Sam stayed together for only two minutes, but in that time, played exceptional defense and converted on all three of their offensive possessions to take a 19-16 lead. Bennett again used his bench liberally, and alternated back and forth between the Triangle and double low-post offense, as both teams played exceptionally hard and limited each other to only a few good looks at the basket. The Badgers maintained the slimmest of margins, 23-22, as the half ended.

Bennett's experiment, the return to his formula, was working. David played his role to perfection. He was a settling influence on offense with his intelligent passing and ball handling; and on defense he used his tireless work ethic to continually harass the much quicker opponents. He was not great, but then again, he was not supposed to be. Bennett had told ESPN commentators before the game that he was playing David because of "what he will *not* do, not for what he will do." In that light, he was "not" doing exactly what Bennett wanted. Booker's first-half review was also encouraging. He was doing an outstanding job of keeping the ball out of the low post and away from Michigan's front-line players. Booker was a non-factor on offense, but Bennett knew that going in. More importantly than any individual performances, however, was the play of the team as a unit. They were playing selflessly with sureness and purpose. Even UWGB fans would have recognized this familiar trait of a Bennett-coached team, in which "the whole was greater than the sum of the parts."

Bennett went with the same starters after the break. However, Coleman committed two quick turnovers and a foul, and was replaced by Grant after four minutes. David, all the while, scrapped and clawed to stay up with a red-hot Louis Bullock. Grant's tip-in with twelve minutes to play help Wisconsin inch out to a three point lead, 34-31, but the game remained mostly a one-point contest for the next six minutes. Michigan clamped down on their perimeter defense and Wisconsin's scoring options dwindled. Nonetheless, Wisconsin stayed extremely disciplined on offense. Ty Calderwood finally gave Wisconsin a hint of a lead when he took a pass on the left wing and drilled a three-point shot to put the Badgers up by four, at 42-38.

Then they got a break. Michigan's Robert "Tractor" Trailer was surrounded in the paint and threw the ball out of bounds. The Michigan players protested the call, and thus were slow getting back on defense. The official handed the ball to Okey on the end line and he threw a full-court baseball pass to Grant, who ran down the floor, well ahead of everyone. His uncontested dunk increased the lead to six.

Michigan steadied themselves and climbed back into the game, trailing by two with 2:30 to play. Calderwood then took control of the situation on offense. He curled off a Daugherty screen, took one dribble to clear the defense, and hit a twelve-foot jump shot. However, the unstoppable Bullock was not to be outdone. He retreated to the opposite end of the floor, took a pass on the left wing, and drove Burkemper hard to the baseline. Just as Burkemper cut him off, Bullock elevated and dropped a difficult twelve-foot shot, as he faded out of bounds. The Badgers led by two, with 1:15 to go.

Daugherty then drew a foul as he wrestled for an offensive rebound. At the line, he converted his first free throw, pushing the lead to three. He missed the second, but Grant tipped the ball out to the perimeter, where Burkemper sprinted in from half-court and scooped it up. Wisconsin had the ball and a three-point lead with one minute to play. Fifteen seconds later, Grant took a perfect feed from Calderwood, spun away from his defense, and dropped the ball through the hoop for a 53-48 lead with only forty-seven seconds remaining. Wisconsin extended the lead to six over the next thirty seconds, but Louis Bullock was not finished yet. He drove to his left around the arc, shook Burkemper on a screen, and rose up for yet another three. The Badger lead was once again down to three.

Daugherty instinctively grabbed the ball, jumped out of bounds, and threw it to Burkemper who was fouled immediately by Bullock. David had yet to take a single shot during the game. If he made the free throws, the game was over. If he missed, Michigan would have one final chance to send the game into overtime. The Field House crowd rose to their feet as the national audience looked on. David Burkemper, a recycled walk-on, a cast-off, walked calmly to the line and swished both shots. The crowd erupted, and nine seconds later David had defeated Goliath.

Bennett relished the success of his formula which produced quality basketball, while the team and fans just celebrated a big win! But was the win attributable to grace? The game marked Bennett's 600th career victory. He had returned to *that which had brought him safe thus far*. He trusted what he saw deep inside a young man's heart. He believed that David Burkemper was the improbable impetus to return his team to quality basketball.

    . . . and grace will lead me home.

Sam Okey's final stat line read triple sevens—seven points, seven rebounds, and seven assists. Bennett's gamble had indeed hit the jackpot.

Chapter 16

Just Win!

Northwestern University:
Saturday, February 8, Evanston, Illinois

Wisconsin traveled two hours southeast on Interstate 90 to Evanston, Illinois, to take on Northwestern for the second time in less than two weeks. Grant returned to the starting unit and joined Burkemper, Calderwood, Okey, and Daugherty. Bennett finally settled on the five starters that he would stay with for the remainder of the season, and it had taken only seventeen games! Okey started quickly with a three-pointer from the left corner, but Northwestern retaliated with three quick baskets of their own. Close observation of Wisconsin's offense revealed a few changes. Bennett no longer felt the Triangle or the double low-post offenses were effective by themselves. Therefore, he tinkered with the double-post offense, moving Okey back out to the perimeter and allowing the post players to move away from the lane. Actually, he encouraged Daugherty and Grant to "loosen" off the lane to provide more opportunities for low-post isolations. Bennett also encouraged Okey to seek out opportunities along the lane, not just to settle for perimeter jump shots.

Northwestern held a lead for the first eleven minutes of the game, while the Badgers got a feel for their new offense. Still, the Michigan win had given Wisconsin the mental toughness Bennett longed for, and there were no apparent signs of their self-destructing on the road, as they had done in the past. Duany came off the bench and nailed his first two three-pointers for his first major contribution since the Illinois game. Burkemper, who was more aggressive on offense with a game under his belt, tied the score at fifteen with a back-door lay-up. On the very next possession, Calderwood put Wisconsin back on top when he hit from beyond the arc. He followed up the three-pointer with a steal and break-away lay-up, to turn the tide in Wisconsin's favor for the remainder of the game. Other than their 35 percent shooting, Bennett was pleased that the Badgers had executed their game plan. The score at the half favored the Badgers 27-20.

Wisconsin's big three, Okey, Grant, and Daugherty, dominated the backboard in the second half, as the Badgers played just well enough to maintain a comfortable lead in front of the five thousand nonchalant Wild-cat fans. Wisconsin held Northwestern to only forty-four points on their home court, eight of which were scored in the last ninety seconds, for a sound 56-44 triumph. Bennett had guided his team back from the verge of Big Ten obscurity to a 6-5 conference record. Ricky Byrdsong, in contrast, experienced the opposite end of the competitive spectrum. The following day, Northwestern officials announced that he would not be back on the sidelines as their head coach for the 1997-98 season. Unlike four years earlier, Dick Bennett would not be an applicant for the vacancy, when his letter of interest went virtually unnoticed.

The victory prompted local sports reporters to prognosticate about the Badgers' chances of advancing to the NCAA tournament for only the second time in fifty years. Bennett immediately dismissed their comments, yet he too realized that his team had rekindled their chances of an at-large bid—but only if they kept winning! That was no small task, considering that their next two games were against the twentieth-ranked Illini and the always tough Purdue Boilermakers.

Preparation for the upcoming games was put on hold as the new week started. Bennett preferred to spend a few moments in praise of his new starting guard at Monday's meeting.

"David Burkemper is like a hundred other players I have coached who only do one thing, they just win!"

David was, for the moment at least, the catalyst Bennett had looked for all season, one who could transform the team into a cohesive unit. Although his contribution could not be substantiated by his stats line, his influence on the team's chemistry was undeniable. Bennett was under-standably dismayed when an assistant pointed out David's minimal sta-tistics. "Statistics are the least important part of this whole discussion! Everything is smoother with Dave in so many little ways. I've been down this road too many times and the statistics just do not tell the story! I can't stand stats that interfere with what is right!" What was right was how the team's play finally began to move toward Bennett's vision of quality basketball. In defense of his assistant, there was a "catch 22" in the comprehension of Bennett's quality basketball ideal. While that vision was clear in Bennett's mind, it was difficult to discern without fully experiencing it first-hand. He had experienced it a hundred times over, but his assistants had not.

Still, David's positive influence was readily evident on the team, even in practice. He was, by all accounts, still a member of the red team, a distinction he wore proudly. However, his new role as a starter gave him a platform to influence the white team as well. His infectious enthusiasm and broad grin lightened the solemn personality of the group. The only lingering doubt Bennett had about the move was how long his influence would last. Presumably, that would be at least as long as the team continued to win.

David's impact on the team overshadowed Booker's development, who, though moved back to the bench, played with confidence for the first time in his college career. Even after being relegated back to the bench after his Michigan performance (great defense, poor offense), he played with conviction at Northwestern. Bennett turned to him early when Grant's post defense became porous. His presence immediately stopped the Wildcats' post offense cold. In addition, his athleticism allowed him to guard quicker players when he was pulled out onto the perimeter. Booker had, in a few short games, become the defensive "stopper" Bennett longed for on the low post.

Possibly the most significant result of the grand experiment, however, was the behavior of Duany, Hennssy, and Paul. They handled the shake-up with maturity and humility. They worked hard in practice and played more precisely defined roles. Basically, that meant playing smart and to their strengths 100 percent of the time, which had been Bennett's major complaint of the trio.

Sometimes it is not what you say, but what you do not say that is important. Again, Bennett heeded his own advice. Some of the players had turned a deaf ear to Bennett's repetitive instruction, either because they did not comprehend his ideal, or did not accept it. Therefore, the root of the problem rested in Bennett's inability to get the players to conceptualize, and/or accept, his vision for their play. That is why the addition of David and, to a lesser extent, Booker, were so important in the transformation of the team. More rhetoric would not solve the problem. The combination of David and Booker, however, eliminated the need for words. They reinforced what Bennett wanted, because they put his ideal into action on the floor—motion on offense, commitment to defensive excellence, selfless dedication to teammates, passion, and unity to attain a common goal. With the two of them heavily involved in the mix of the action, things began to happen quickly for Bennett and his team.

A win would move them into the top half of the Big Ten standings and position them to make a run at the NCAA tournament. A loss, on the other hand, would confirm that this team was just too inconsistent to salvage that goal. During Monday's practice, two days prior to the contest, Bennett was heavily involved and vocal throughout the session. Initially, he moved non-stop around the floor as the drills progressed and provided incessant commentary on both effort and technique, something he had not done all season. About an hour into practice, when it was evident that his intensity was not being matched by the players, his comments became more personal. "Burkemper, I don't even know you are out here! If you do not start doing something, you are going to find yourself back on the end of the bench!" The starting unit continued to struggle, and then Daugherty became the target. "Sean, you have become invisible on the floor; you might as well be extinct." Daugherty provoked Bennett's ire when he looked back at him with an emotionless, deadpan expression. "Sean, you are the most uncoachable kid on this team. In your mind, no one has anything to say that can make you better. Your arrogance won't let you listen to anyone."

Daugherty turned and walked away, slightly shaking his head, but his response did not concern Bennett. He was only concerned that his message got across, and it had. Daugherty drove the baseline aggressively and tried to dunk over Coleman. He missed, then yelled out a few expletives as he hung on the rim. That was fine with Bennett, that was the fire he needed to see in Sean, and not another word needed to be said to him for the remainder of practice.

Bennett pushed the team hard, verbally and physically. When his team refused to respond to his assertive demeanor, he "went over the edge," as he describes it. His intense desire to beat Illinois superseded his Christian ideals once again. He walked to half-court, away from his team, and loudly chided, "I know you guys are all saying to yourself, 'Who cares, the old guy is just riding us again today.' If that is what you are thinking, that is just horseshit. I'm not! You just don't get it. Whenever you get a chance to make some ground as a team, you die! You just die!" He could not tolerate their apathetic approach to the game any longer and, moments later, dismissed them unceremoniously.

University of Illinois:
Wednesday, February 12, Madison, Wisconsin

The intensity at practice waned little over the next two days before the Illini rolled into Madison for a Wednesday night showdown. As the game started, Wisconsin's movement on the floor was the best it had been all season. Each player settled into his role and performed well. In addition, there was an aura of confidence surrounding the crew. The Badgers jumped out to a 5-0 lead, and then Paul Grant pulled out a new weapon from his arsenal of offensive moves, a running hook shot across the free throw lane, putting his team up seven. By the fourteen-minute mark, back-to-back jump shots by Daugherty stretched the lead to 12-4. The Badgers then cooled off from the field, while Kiwane Garris and Matt Heldman hit long threes to pull the Fighting Illini within two. The Badgers then regained the poise with which they started the game, and built the lead back to eight on a long ball by Auriantal and free throws by Daugherty and Duany.

Illinois' zone defense then clogged the middle and forced Wisconsin to shoot from long range. Again the Badgers went cold, and when the long shots banged hard off the rim, the Illini pushed the ball up the floor for transition three-point shots. Illinois took their first lead of the game, 20-18, with just under six minutes to play in the half. The Badgers stayed close when Calderwood found a few gaps in the Illini's zone. Despite his effort, another long three by Heldman sent the Badgers into the locker room trailing 32-29. Lon Krueger's team had an answer for Wisconsin's vaunted defense: run the ball up the floor, penetrate the lane before the defense could set, and then kick the ball out for open threes when the defense collapsed to stop the ball. Bennett went into halftime with the sole purpose of rectifying those breakdowns.

There were no technical adjustments made at half. Bennett simply reviewed and reinforced the principles that had made his team one of the best defensive units in the country. First, they had to get back quickly in transition. Second, they had to prevent Kiwane Garris from penetrating into the lane area. And third, they had to close out quickly and take away the rhythm three-point shots. The Badgers did not return to the floor until the final horn sounded to indicate the end of intermission. The team hurried out of the locker room, led by Calderwood, just in time to resume the game.

Kiwane Garris scored the first basket of the second half and the lead grew to 34-29. Then Wisconsin finally began to crack Illinois' 2-1-2 defense. Both Daugherty and Okey found a seam at the top of the key and hit back-to-back shots to regain the lead at 36-35. On the very next defensive possession, Calderwood stole the ball and advanced it to Daugherty for a five-foot bank shot. The lead was three and the crowd chanted for another defensive stop. The uproar continued for the entirety of the Illini possession, which ultimately ended in an offensive foul, thus triggering a further explosion from the crowd. Twenty seconds later, "Doc" Duany dropped in a rainbow three from the deep wing and the rout was on, the Field House crowd frenzied with excitement. The "fight" left Lon Krueger's Fighting Illini. They could not regroup against the Badgers' smothering defense. Less than two minutes later, after an Okey three and a tip-in by Daugherty, Krueger finally called time-out with his team trailing 46-35.

Booker Coleman erased the Illinis' best opportunity to end the run. Garris fed Chris Gandy on the left block; he spun away from Okey and drop-stepped hard to the basket. Gandy elevated for a jam but was met by Coleman, who had released his man on the other side of the basket. Coleman exploded into the air and snuffed out Gandy's attempt. Gandy fell back, reeling from the confrontation. Coleman retreated to the offensive end of the floor, took a pay off pass from Okey, then wheeled to his left for his own thunderous dunk to accentuate Wisconsin's 21-0 second half run. Garris finally put the fans back in their seats when he ended the free-fall with a fifteen-foot jumper. At that point, Wisconsin had built an insurmountable 52-37 lead with just over six minutes remaining. Coleman wasn't through, however. Playing his best basketball of the season, he added a tip-in and two free throws to push the lead to 57-39.

Illinois scored six meaningless points in the final two minutes, bringing their total for the half to thirteen, for a final score of 62-45. The Badgers held their opponent to only 19 percent shooting in the crucial second half. In the process, they made a good basketball team look helpless. Even Bennett, void of the anxiety he had felt for the previous seventy-two hours, was so pleased in the post-game press conference that he told reporters, "That kind of play makes me want to stick around a lot longer." Daugherty, whom Bennett had confronted on Monday because of his passive play, led the assault with a double-double, scoring twelve points and grabbing ten rebounds. He also led the team in floor burns, sprawling his 6'10" body on the floor for loose balls no less than four times. The win was a genuine team effort and in the Burkemper (and Coleman) era, the Badgers were a perfect 3-0. The elusive vision of quality basketball was getting clearer!

My removed perspective on the process of the past two weeks, or even the entire season up to that point, revealed a hidden truth about Dick Bennett. His *Dharma* was to coach basketball. *Dharma* is a Sanskrit word that the ancient Indianic Hindus used to describe one's divine "purpose in life." Bennett's focus and singleness of purpose could only be a product of such a phenomenon. Later that day, when we sat down to discuss that subject, his insights were revealing.

"Sometimes my singleness of purpose is really a curse. The Illinois game is a perfect example. After the Northwestern game, I realized that we had worked ourselves into a position to make a move in the conference and I was terribly nervous and anxious. In my focus to make that happen, I went beyond what was normal. I was never really able to back off and settle down, so I thought my focus was too much."

Bennett, much more relaxed than he had been in weeks, swiveled in his chair as he philosophized. "My greatest struggle is a very basic one: When is it too much? When does it take you away from your true calling? As a Christian I am called to develop a relationship with Christ. I, like other Christians, am called to be in the world, but not of the world. That is what happens to me when I go over the line, and I have gone over the line a lot."

"Why do you go over the line? Is it winning?"

The chair suddenly stopped rotating. Bennett raised his eyebrows and looked at me out of the corner of his eye, his mouth curled up at the edges as he tried to hide a smile. "Oh yes, definitely. I talk a good game about quality basketball. I try to teach it and get our team to play it, but it is about the winning."

Bennett used the past to support his point, as the smile disappeared from his face and he resumed the pivoting motion in his chair. "The fear and anxiety that overwhelmed me on Sunday, Monday, and Tuesday before the Illinois game was generated by the thought that we would not win. I looked at that game and told myself, 'you gotta win,' and that really ate me up inside. The only way I have been able to buffer that type of thinking is through prayer. I pray that I can get the upper hand and not cross over the line, not being so preoccupied, and that has helped me. Ideally, I do what I can do to prepare, do what I feel called to do, but not let the anxiety to win eat me up."

Terms and phrases such as *anxiety, excessive focus,* and *eat me up inside* do not conjure up pictures of perfect health. Indeed, the inordinate demands of coaching, and the anxieties it produces, have come at a cost to Dick Bennett. At fifty-four years of age, his body shows the effects of a half-century of intensity. He has had both hips replaced, suffered a bleeding ulcer, and undergone emergency diverticulitis surgery. The effects of his lifelong love affair with sports was particularly noticeable that afternoon when he replaced Paul Grant in a 5-on-0 drill to demonstrate how he wanted the post players to screen. Though he did so for only about twenty seconds, even that short demonstration came at a cost. He limped and breathed heavily as he walked away from the drill, his face grimaced in pain when his back was turned to the team. The time when he moved on the basketball floor with an athlete's effortless grace was thirty years past. His body, unfortunately, continued to pay the price. Life costs!

"What is the price you have had to pay for success in coaching?" I asked.

He gathered his thoughts while firmly rubbing his forehead with the palms of his hands. "Well," he slowly responded, "I think with the focus I have, which is singular in purpose during the season, I have forsaken most outside activities; social, recreational, or otherwise. I have pretty much confined my activities to whatever Anne and I do. We take walks, occasionally go out to eat, or just order in a movie. That is really about it. With the summer leagues, camps, and other basketball commitments, we have never even really taken a vacation. Our life has always centered around our team." His use of the word "our" instead of "my" team was a thoughtful testimony to Anne's role in his career.

"Also, I personally didn't get involved with the activities of our two oldest daughters. I could say it was because of a time management problem, but it was more of an emotional issue. I was so drained from my job, that I wouldn't have the energy to go to their activities. I have always regretted that because they were such great kids." He rationalized his absenteeism, "The flip side, however, was that they were able to be a part of my life because of the high school and college basketball games. They were fun for them. So that brought us together, even if it was in an unusual way." With a warm chuckle, he added, "Instead of the parents following the kids, it was the kids following the dad.

"I really think my focus and my intensity early in my career kept people away from me. I got along well with everybody, but I was not very close to many people. I didn't develop deep relationships probably because they could see that I was so focused. My relationship was with basketball." Bennett is, if nothing else, a bit of an introvert. He prefers to spend much of his time either at home or in his office. Nevertheless, he has developed deep friendships over the years.

"How do people get close to you, develop an intimate relationship?" I continued.

He shook his head as he answered. "They don't, I guess. I'm of the opinion that you develop many acquaintances, but in reality, it is your family and a few people whom you have known forever that you remain really close to. I don't have the need to seek intimate relationships, because I have my wife, my family, dear old friends, and my faith. If I had any more, I would be spreading myself too thin."

Bennett then spoke of the cornerstone of his life, his faith. "I know that the good thing about my involvement with coaching is that it has kept me closer to my relationship with Christ."

Wait a minute! Hadn't he just said that basketball pulled him away from a Christian life? "You know, because I was always praying," Bennett continued. "I found my faith experience developing ever more strongly because of my job. I hope it is more than a foxhole mentality, but that is how it has always been developing."

It is difficult to have heard about Dick Bennett and not also about his faith. But how much of a need did he have to "spread the word," the doctrine of evangelism that is so closely tied to a number of Christian denominations?

"Do you consider coaching as your ministry?" I asked.

"I don't view it that way, but it has become that. I never intended to use basketball as a platform for my faith, but as I have matured, I realize it has become that. Though when people view me in that capacity, claiming we need more people like me in coaching, it makes me extremely uncomfortable."

He then shared a subtle insight into his life. "For those who know of my faith, including my players, my ministry is in getting to know the real me. Seeing how much I want to be like Christ, but also seeing how much of a struggle it is for me. That is why my ministry is aided by my failures and my attempts to get it right after those failures. You see, when I profess to be a Christian and then fail in my efforts, they can see what is important about Christianity. They come to understand that the process of continually rising, falling, and then starting over, is acceptable. That is my ministry." He wears a constant reminder of that mission on his right wrist. A black band inscribed with four white letters, WWJD, which is an acronym for "What Would Jesus Do." It was a gift from his son and daughter-in-law.

Bennett turned and looked at the large clock behind his desk, noting that he had other commitments to attend to. Before departing, however, there was time for one more hypothetical question.

"What would you have pursued if you had not gone into coaching?" I asked.

"I really liked teaching English. I'm not the brightest fella and I'm not as well read as most, but I really like literature."

"I think you are much more intelligent than you give yourself credit . . ."

"No!" he interrupted, "I've seen the results of the tests. I know how I struggle to understand basic simple things. I've gotten lost driving to my TV show more times than I would like to admit. I just can't figure things out."

I sat patiently as he unsuccessfully tried to convince me of his intellectual limitations. Yet, a passage from the book *The Art of War* by Sun Tzu kept running through my mind: ". . . feign weakness when you are strong." The four-thousand-year-old manuscript instructs that in preparing for a battle, it is wise to keep your true abilities a secret from your opponent.

"Maybe it is not that you fail to comprehend, but rather you have no interest," I suggested.

A broad smile broke out on his face as he sheepishly retorted, "True, I know what I need to know in my profession."

He had nothing else to add, and so we ended another session. I walked out of the office complex entrance onto the crusted ice which blanketed the walkway. I thought out loud to myself, "So single in purpose that he overlooks simple details in his deep concentration, maybe. Clever enough to sheepishly feign ignorance for a competitive advantage, also maybe. Intellectually inferior, doubtful."

What comes first, success or team chemistry? That conundrum can be hotly debated to support either side. Nonetheless, the events which played out on the Badgers' team strongly favored one particular take. Several of the players had accepted their new and sometimes diminished roles on the team. There was no mistaking that many wanted to become more central figures during games, but the recent success of the team made it difficult for them to make a case for more playing time, at least outwardly. The on-court bickering between teammates, which occurred occasionally during the tough losing stretch, was a thing of the past. Compliments and encouragement became the norm. Would that have happened had the team continued to lose? So which comes first, success or team chemistry?

Bennett did not ponder why unity became an adjective used to describe his team. He concerned himself, rather, with what it would take to extend their winning streak to four, to place them in a position to make a legitimate run at a top-five finish in the conference—a preposterous idea only two weeks earlier. The only hurdle left in their way was Gene Keady and his underrated Purdue Boilermakers.

"Don't accept in victory that which you would not accept in defeat," Bennett reminded himself at Thursday's staff meeting, on the morning after the Illinois victory. Bennett, therefore, focused on continual improvement. He noted, "I am happy with how we are playing. I am just concerned about Sam. We have to get him more cognizant of moving without the ball as opposed to holding it. He is really disrupting the flow of the offense. It is hard to deal with him because he is so valuable. He was classic in the first ten minutes of the game. He either made a great play or a terrible play. There was not anything in between."

Shawn Hood pointed out that Sam moved well in the 5-on-0 practice drills. Bennett responded with a relaxed laugh. "When we go 5-on-0 in practice, it is a picture of perfection. We are probably the best 5-on-0 team in the country. It is when we get a defense in front of us that we struggle."

Bennett went on to point out that Sam had improved significantly in his sophomore season. He was a much better team player, his rebounding and defense were vastly superior now, compared to his freshman season. Still, his offense lagged behind. His screening and movement without the ball had not improved. His double-figure scoring average was due primarily to his superior athletic ability, not his skill. Nonetheless, Bennett was reluctant to make any additional changes with the offense or the personnel.

Purdue University:
Saturday, February 15, Madison, Wisconsin

The 1996-97 season was to be a rebuilding year for Purdue after winning three consecutive Big Ten Championships. "Bulldog" Keady, however, didn't see it that way and once again had his young team playing competitive basketball and hovering among the league leaders in the standings. Indiana's Knight may be best known for the ferocity of his side-line outbursts, but when it comes to the frequency of sideline antics, Keady has no equal. At the beginning of the game, once again, he spent the majority of his time airing his dissatisfaction with the officials as his seven-foot center Chad Miller picked up two quick fouls. While Keady vented, Okey hit his first two shots and the Badgers grabbed an early 7-5 lead. Purdue answered with six points of their own, and took a lead into the first official time-out. Calderwood came out of the break and hit a three from the corner and a breakaway lay-up to spark an 8-0 Wisconsin run. Keady was forced to take his second time-out in seven minutes with Wisconsin leading 16-11.

Purdue came alive as they turned up their defensive pressure and turned to their senior star Chad Austin for instant offense. The Boiler-makers used a variety of defenses to slow Wisconsin's offense. Austin scored fourteen points as Purdue regained the lead, 21-19. At that point, Bennett looked to his bench for help. Auriantal, Kosolcharoen, and Booker joined Calderwood and Daugherty on the floor and proceeded to build a 33-28 halftime lead, thus demonstrating yet another benefit of having Burkemper in the starting unit—a deeper and more experienced bench. In addition, Coleman added a fourth big man that Bennett had at his disposal, and his presence made the other three have to work hard to maintain their minutes on the floor.

To start the half, the Badger starters picked up where the reserves had left off. Their defense forced two turnovers and four missed shots, as they slowly increased their lead. Grant drew Miller's third foul on a strong move to the basket, and after completing the three-point play, Wisconsin led by 38-28, with three and a half minutes gone. Purdue then closed the gap to five in the next ninety seconds, so Bennett went back to the lineup that had finished out the half. He sat Okey, Grant, and Burkemper down, and replaced them with Kosolcharoen, Auriantal, and Coleman. Auriantal scored the next eight points as that group forced two consecutive Boilermaker mishandles, and the lead jumped to 45-32.

The starters returned soon after, but again gave ground. Purdue's Brian Cardinal sent Daugherty crashing to the floor with an elbow to the head, then stepped into shooting range and drained a three-point shot, reducing the lead to eight. For good measure, a feisty and competitive Cardinal gave Daugherty a slap on the back of the head as he converted back to the defensive end of the floor. Okey's left hand dunk and a fifteen-foot jump shot sparked the Badgers, and they regained their momentum. Moments later, with under eight minutes to play, Auriantal stole the ball, drove the length of the floor, and converted a three-point play. The lead swelled to fourteen, 55-41.

Purdue scored only one basket in the final nine minutes of play as Wisconsin pulled out an impressive 69-52 win. Once again, the Badgers put the clamps on their opponent in the second half, holding the Boilermakers to just four field goals on 23 percent shooting. Okey found the movement that Bennett had hoped for and led the Badgers in scoring with twenty points in only twenty-nine minutes of playing time. This was Bennett's first victory over Keady as the Badgers' coach. The win also moved their Big Ten record to 8-5, and tied them with Purdue and Illinois for second place.

The resurgence was due in large part to a new-found team identity, great team defense, patient offense, and depth. The equation for the players was simple: understand your role, play hard in your role, and play unselfishly. To the players' credit, whether on the floor or on the bench, they had learned to accept those criteria. Bennett finally had a full arsenal of players and he remarked about the change in his team at the Monday morning staff meeting.

"I do not want to miss the significance of what has been happening since the Ohio State game. There has been a change. David has changed the chemistry of the team. Son of a gun, we are playing good basketball with him out there. And I'll tell you something else, Burkemper will not go quietly into the night. He is not going away and the other guards better know that!"

In the Burkemper (and Coleman) era, the team had been transformed from a schizophrenic pretender into a legitimate tournament contender. Although the staff prepared themselves for their next opponent, conscious of being single-minded in purpose, they also began to discuss the countdown to the NCAA tournament. After all, they were tied for second place in the conference and ranked second in the nation in defensive efficiency. With just over two weeks remaining in the regular season, the tournament drive was under way in earnest.

Big Ten Standings, 2/17/97

	Conference		Season	
	W	L	W	L
Minnesota	11	1	22	2
Illinois	8	5	18	7
Wisconsin	8	5	15	7
Purdue	8	5	13	10
Michigan	7	5	17	7
Iowa	7	5	16	8
Indiana	7	6	20	7
Michigan State	5	7	12	9
Ohio State	5	7	10	11
Penn State	2	11	9	13
Northwestern	1	12	6	16

Chapter 17

Subtle Empowerment
and the Courage of Inactivity

Penn State University:
Wednesday, February 19, University Park, Pennsylvania

How long could the magic carpet ride continue? Bennett hoped for at least one more game. The cycle of winning "just one more big game" had become so redundant that it became humorous. Bennett laughed when he heard himself make the declaration once again. Penn State, second to last in the conference, posed a new threat. To date, with the exception of the game at Illinois, the road had proved to be a momentum-stopper for the Badgers, and Bennett worried that his team might let down against the Nittany Lions, thus denying themselves an NCAA at-large tournament invitation. Bennett eloquently summed up the situation.

"I will be glad when this one is over, because it has all the signs of a stinker."

His prophecy was borne out less than forty-eight hours later. Penn State opened the game with a lob dunk to lanky Calvin Booth. Wisconsin, on the other hand, had a less auspicious beginning. Calderwood's first two passes landed in the laps of a couple spectators and he took a seat next to Bennett. Ryan Bailey, Penn State's freshman point guard who had been abused by the Badger defense in Madison, got into the action early. He "juked" Burkemper out of position twice and drove to the basket for uncontested lay-ups. After his second penetration, Penn State led 8-5 and David joined Ty on the sidelines.

Calderwood returned to the game soon after, but turned the ball over for the third time. The Nittany Lions converted the error into a lay-up off their flex offense. The basket increased the lead to six points. It also increased Penn State's confidence. They looked more like the team that was 8-5 in the conference and playing for an NCAA bid, than did the Badgers.

Awakened after a time-out tongue lashing, the Badger starting unit pulled back to within two, when Grant hit a short bank shot. The teams then began to exchange baskets. With six minutes to go in the half, Penn State still maintained a 17-15 lead. Bennett went back to the bench at the next break in the action. Calderwood and Daugherty were the only starters who remained on the floor. They were joined by Coleman, Kosolcharoen, and Auriantal. However, that unit failed to produce any points when Calderwood missed three shots, Coleman traveled, and Daugherty shot a seventeen-foot air-ball.

The next dead ball brought even more substitutions. Grant replaced Coleman while Duany replaced Calderwood. Bennett was again on a substitution merry-go-round; never a good sign for his team. The starters ended up closing out the final two minutes of the half, but were outscored 5-2 and went into the half trailing, 24-17. The deficit was a true team effort. The Badgers had committed eleven turnovers and shot only 38 percent from the floor, against an average half-court defense.

Wisconsin was awful at the start of the second half. Their incompetence on offense continued and they became soft on defense, leading to the short end of a 7-0 Penn State run. The score stood at 31-17. Just seventeen points in twenty-four minutes! The game had all the earmarks of another devastating loss. Their NCAA bubble had seemingly burst. Only then, after another torrid time-out, were they shocked back into the reality of the situation. Bennett put the lineup of Burkemper, Auriantal, Duany, Okey, and Grant on the floor, with his team's tournament aspirations dangling perilously. On the Badgers' first possession, Okey was fouled and converted both free throws. They then forced a turnover, and Okey scored another two points on a tip-in off Grant's miss. Finally, Duany caught the ball on the right wing and drove hard to the baseline for Wisconsin's sixth straight point. The run was stopped, unfortunately, when Grant played behind Booth on the block and let him catch the ball in deep. He wheeled hard to his left and drove recklessly to the basket. Grant tried to stop him, but drew his fourth foul. Paul headed to the bench as Booth sank both charity tosses. Okey threw up an air-ball on the other end of the floor. Penn State had withstood Wisconsin's surge, sustaining a comfortable 33-24 lead with thirteen minutes left in the game.

Okey then threw up his second air-ball in a row, but was bailed out when Daugherty collected the errant shot, was fouled, and converted both free throws. Nonetheless, Penn State increased their cushion on two Bailey jump shots. Bennett jumped to his feet and called a twenty-second time-out as the second shot dropped through the net. The scoreboard displayed 12:22 and also Wisconsin's dire predicament: Penn State 37-Wisconsin 26.

Calderwood replaced Auriantal and Coleman replaced Okey coming out of the break, but the situation worsened. Calderwood forced a bad shot, which was blocked by two defenders, while Daugherty stood unguarded on the baseline. The ball was knocked into Bailey's hands, who triggered a three-on-two fast break for another Nittany Lions basket. The lead climbed to thirteen and the clock ticked away the seconds. Undaunted by his earlier miss, Calderwood pushed the ball back up the floor and pulled up for a long three-point attempt. The ball banged hard off the back of the iron, as Coleman leaped high into the air and pulled the ball away from two Penn State rebounders with his left hand. He spotted an open Duany and kicked the ball back out to the wing. Duany lifted above the approaching defender and drained a three. Stopped action at the defensive end of the floor allowed Bennett to put his starters back on the floor.

Booth immediately recognized that Grant was back on him and took the ball right at him, forcing contact on the shot. The official did not blow his whistle and Grant came away with the rebound. The action then returned to Wisconsin's end of the floor where Daugherty threw up a seventeen-foot shot that drew nothing but air. Okey chased down the ball as it sailed across the endline. In midair, he found Grant and passed it back in play. Grant pivoted and let go of a fall-away jump shot that missed. Daugherty, making amends for his miss, crashed the offensive glass and kept the ball alive. The ball finally landed back in Grant's hands and he connected on his second scoring opportunity. The deficit was back down to single digits, 39-31. The rally energized the Badgers and they further tightened their defensive stranglehold. In the meantime, Daugherty and Grant kept crashing the boards and the lead shrank to five, 40-35.

Duany then came off the bench and fueled the comeback. Grant took a pass from Okey on the right baseline and drove hard under the basket.

Out of control, his momentum was taking him out-of-bounds. He spotted Duany on the left wing and heaved a desperation baseball pass from behind the backboard, just before he landed out of bounds. Duany backed up behind the arc as he caught the ball and calmly registered his second three-pointer of the half.The lead was only two. Finally, after a time-out, a long defensive stand, and an air-ball, Calderwood collected himself and hit a three-point basket from his favorite spot, the left high elbow, which put Wisconsin up by 41-40.

Penn State, however, had no intention of playing that hard and that well, and then just giving up when they fell behind. They reclaimed the lead with a Rahsaan Carlton dunk that fouled Paul Grant out of the game. Moments later, Daugherty tied the game with a free throw, but Pete Lisicky drained a long ball and pushed the lead back to three, with just under four minutes to play. The atmosphere grew tense as the seconds ticked off the clock. Calderwood narrowed the gap with a pair of free throws, but Wisconsin turned the ball over on their next two possessions and could gain no further ground. Nonetheless, their fierce defense forced Penn State into badly missed shots and turnovers to keep their hopes alive. With 1:09 remaining in the game, and down by one point, 44-45, Auriantal subbed for Kosolcharoen. Wisconsin patiently turned over their offense, looking for the good shot and the go-ahead basket. Cut by cut and pass by pass, the shot clock wound down. When no good shots became available, Duany was forced to take a long three as the time clock expired. The ball skipped off the rim and landed fifteen feet from the basket on the right baseline. With the entire Bryce Jordan Center crowd momentarily frozen, Auriantal charged in from the wing, scooped up the ball, and drove to the rim for the go-ahead basket. Penn State rushed down the floor determined to retake the lead; instead, Duany stole a pass to the wing and drove the length of the floor for an uncontested dunk which sealed the victory. Daugherty closed out the scoring with a free throw and the Badgers sneaked out of University Park, Pennsylvania, with a 49-45 win.

The Burkemper era stood at a perfect 5-0. In reality, neither David nor Booker had contributed significantly to the victory over Penn State, but they were not alone in that distinction. Most of the team played poorly on offense and had it not been for their exceptional defensive effort they would have had no chance to steal the game as they did.

Bennett was visibly exhausted following the game. Sean Daugherty gave him a small hug to indicate that he should not have worried, they had it under control the whole time. He appreciated the gesture, but he did not share Sean's confidence. The team had come full circle since the debacle in Columbus. Little was said to the team following the game. Experience told Bennett that it was better to just let this one be. The team had been playing well and it was obvious to them that they had not been terribly effective that night. Nonetheless, the plane ride home was filled with anxious conversation among the coaching staff. Bennett lamented, "We are not as good as our record and I have no confidence in us. Every game we go into, every practice, is a mystery! I have no idea what is going to happen." Brian Hecker best summed up the game when he added, "The only difference between the Ohio State game and the Penn State game was Penn State." It was a very astute observation. He understood that a better team would have beaten the Badgers badly.

The weekend was tough on Bennett. At the Monday morning meeting, he was as distraught as he had been all season. In a moment of unchecked self-doubt, he proclaimed, "The game and the players have really changed and that is disturbing me. It is so different. I tell myself that the game has passed me by." His critical assessment came from a deep internalization of the team's poor offensive performance. The team ranked last in the conference in offensive production (points scored and field goal percentage), and that weighed heavily on his mind. "I have adjusted my defense to adapt to the way teams play now, taking away penetration, but I can't come up with an offense to meet our players' needs. Don't get me wrong, I'm happy to be where we are, but I want to continue to make positive changes and do things that can help us. I just don't know what that is."

The team's offensive ineptitude and lapses of passion had taken him to a "dark night of the soul." He had internalized the quandaries to a point that led him to a deep level of despair. His face looked weary and he sat listless at the head of the table. "I remember my dad saying to me that it was hard to get old because everyone's ideas change. I'm not old, but I am for my profession. My ideas, the way I think, is not the way people think anymore."

His assistants were quick to assure him that the profession had not outgrown him. Still, the fact of the matter was that the Badgers found themselves on two totally different ends of the spectrum when it came to offense and defense. They led the Big Ten in defense, but were last in offense. Bennett tried to understand the discrepancy. "We play defense with great heart and that starts in practice. We have no in-between defensive drills, and we do not do any defensive drills without great heart. Everything else, however, is not satisfactory." Bennett's dejected mood had infected the entire staff, who sat emotionless as he spoke. "On our best offensive days, when we shoot over fifty percent, we can't score seventy points. It is just so ugly! Quality basketball is paramount, and I just do not see it!"

Bennett shook his head after nearly two hours of venting, which had done him some good. His diatribe had released him of the burden he carried after the Penn State game. He then moved on. "I ask myself how we can be in second place. I believe the Lord has a hand in it." He looked around the table, thanked his assistants, and withdrew into his office to ponder the offensive riddle. Time was running out on finding the answer for this team. Still, a six-day reprieve before the start of the final push of the season provided valuable time to tinker. The Badgers' season schedule ended with a home game against Iowa, road games at Michigan State and Indiana, and a home game against Minnesota in the regular-season finale.

Bennett was grateful for the extra time to prepare for Iowa. The Hawkeyes were tied with Wisconsin for third place in the conference. Minnesota had run away with the conference championship and Purdue had worked its way into sole possession of second. The extra time also provided an opportunity for him to reflect on the events of the past few weeks. With Bennett himself stymied by the polar performances of his offense and defense, third-person observation seemed uniquely appropriate. That analysis began with the quote, "We do not do any defensive drills without great heart." The extremes of the team's offensive and defensive performances in the Big Ten revealed a major philosophical difference in Bennett's coaching (and leadership) style.

He is very definitive about his defensive philosophy. His defensive system emphasizes individual skills and rules. His players have a little freedom, but for the most part every player is held accountable for his own performance as dictated by the structured system. Therefore, it only seemed natural that Bennett would carry this strategy over to the offensive end of the floor. Surprisingly, he did not. A close look at his offensive philosophy reveals a significantly different approach.

Several months earlier, I had asked Bennett how he settled on his offensive system. "I never liked patterns," he answered. "I thought they were too restrictive. I thought I could build a system around rules, and still have the discipline I wanted, so that's what I did. I think that philosophy gives the players the freedom to play, but still restricts them from just running wild."

The theoretical foundation for Bennett's "blocker-mover" offense, a motion offense with designated screeners and designated cutters, is based roughly on the Bob Knight's passing game. The approach each uses to teach the offense, however, is radically different. Knight approaches offense in much the same way Bennett approaches defense. Knight is meticulous in teaching individual skills, such as cuts and screens. In addition, he demands strict adherence to the offensive principles of his passing game system by his players. Coincidentally, Wisconsin's defense improved at approximately the same rate that Indiana's offense improved throughout the season. So the natural progression of thought was to wonder if Bennett would adjust his teaching method, and thus implement the same highly disciplined approach on offense that he used to instruct defense. After all, they were dead last in the Big Ten in offensive production. What was there to lose?

Bennett refused to alter his methods throughout the season and there was little reason to believe that would change. Yet there had to be a reason beyond that which Bennett had previously noted. While discussing his basketball philosophies earlier in the season, he had said that he used a less structured offense because he did not have the intelligence to emulate Indiana's offense. I doubted the authenticity of that rationale then, and I still did. Bennett had shown all too often the depth of his understanding of the game. The idea that he can be an ingenious defensive coach and at the same time an inept offensive coach seemed preposterous. There had to be more to it. My search for the reasons underlying his unrelenting stubbornness about his offensive philosophy continued.

Could it be tied to the "prepare not to lose" strategy he had adopted early in the season? That consisted of preventing turnovers, taking good shots, making free throws, not giving up uncontested shots, not fouling and negating pressure, and not allowing second shots for opponents. But that wasn't it. Three of the six keys were defensive in nature, and of the three offensive markers, successful completion of two of them would actually increase scoring. Only "take good shots" had the potential to reduce scoring because it required the offensive players to be more patient in searching for that good shot. No, playing "not to lose" was not the answer, or at least not all of it.

I considered Bennett's comment on practicing defense "with great heart" next. Indeed, his team rarely practiced offense with the same intensity as defense, especially during shooting drills. The team members showed little effort and concentration while they practiced their shots. Bennett rarely seemed bothered by their lack of effort when shooting, however. If it were a defensive drill, their lackadaisical approach doubtless would have drawn his wrath. That dichotomy had been apparent for most of the year. That approach, however, exemplifies his offensive philosophy. At the core of the mysterious contradiction in styles is this principle:

The way to get the players to achieve their highest level of success is to create an environment in which they must define their own roles and take responsibility for developing their own talents.

In other words, Bennett relinquishes the responsibility for developing the offensive skills of his players and places it directly in their own hands. He does so because he realizes how little he can truly affect their offensive skill development during the season. He chooses, rather, to influence the offense through his use of the individual players. He does this by positioning the players in a manner which allows them to play to their strengths and away from their weaknesses. This is why he continually tinkers with the blocker-mover alignments and the substitution rotations.

A review of his past teams indicates that this approach is successful, or at least had been, for Bennett. His UWGB teams were very successful both offensively and defensively. His Phoenix teams *averaged* 49 percent shooting from the floor over a *nine year* period! Three of those teams, 1988-89 and 1990 through 1992, had season averages over 50 percent. Indeed, his own son holds the NCAA career three-point accuracy mark at forty-nine percent. Tony averaged nearly twenty points a game over his four year career at UWGB and never shot less than 52 percent from the floor for a season. In addition, his teams averaged sixty-seven points a game during a six-year stretch between 1988 and 1994, nearly ten points higher than the 1996-97 Badgers.

In Madison, his teams and individual players had rarely approached such high levels of efficiency. There is one glaring reason why. The players have found it difficult to either define their own role, or when they do, they have difficulty accepting that role. Sam Okey exemplified the dilemma, though he was not alone in the struggle. The problem in a nutshell, was that he was having difficulty finding a place in the offense. He wanted to play on the perimeter, and Bennett obliged, but Okey did not yet have the shooting or ball-handling skills to be effective away from the basket. As a result, the season was one of transition for Okey as he found himself caught between two positions, neither of which he was fully committed to or effective at playing. With several other players struggling through the same growing process as Sam, having to back up to move forward, the offense just didn't have enough consistency to thrive. Only Grant in the post and Calderwood at the point had proven to be steady performers for Bennett. Not coincidentally, they clearly understood and accepted their roles in the offense, which leads to the second major observation of the week.

Bennett's offensive philosophy, whether intentional or not, is the same approach he uses to manage his entire program. He gives those around him great freedom to define their own roles and work habits. He does not routinely delegate tasks specifically to his assistants, secretaries, or managers. His actions mandate that everyone involved with the program assume responsibility for defining his or her own job. His only concern is that his staff provide him with what he needs to be successful, but he is ambiguous as to just what that might be. Nonetheless, he holds each member of his staff accountable for his or her performance, based on that person's ability to satisfy his needs as the head coach. As with the offense, this leadership style is not without its struggles. Each of the assistants has expressed or demonstrated frustration over this cryptic approach and the inherent potential problems—lack of direction, overlap of responsibility, hierarchy of power, and accountability. How then could the staff and the program be expected to excel if not given clearly defined roles by their leader? Nearly an entire season passed before the answer revealed itself.

Bennett's method is completely harmonious with the revolutionary management theory of Total Quality Management (TQM). Indeed, a leader of the TQM movement, the late Dr. W. Edwards Deming, noted in his book *The New Economics* that, "A system is a network of independent components that work together to accomplish the aim of the system." For a college basketball program, one of those aims or goals is to produce a winning basketball program, and all those involved work toward that one goal.

Deming goes on to explain. "The components (roles) need not all be clearly defined and documented: people may merely do what needs to be done. The secret is cooperation between the components toward the aim of the organization." Thus, mandated job descriptions and assigned responsibilities by the head of the organization (Bennett) do not guarantee a unity of purpose in a group.

But what is so bad about having clearly defined job descriptions or player roles? Wouldn't that simply expedite the process? Not necessarily. In good times, all members can join in taking partial credit for success, and rightfully so, because they dutifully completed their assigned tasks. During times of organizational chaos and failure, however, those well-defined roles can divide and compartmentalize the individuals in a group. The different individuals can claim they are not responsible for the failure because, after all, they performed their duties as assigned. The natural progression is to insulate oneself in performance appraisals that are tied directly to specific responsibilities (roles) and to seek out the guilty party to blame for failures. When such events occur, division of the group is inevitable. As an example, for the basketball staff assigned tasks could include scouting, recruiting, tape preparation, and/or position coaching, to name just a few. These responsibilities could easily be delegated by Bennett, but the successful completion of any of those tasks on an individual basis does not in itself guarantee success for the program. So Bennett gives his staff the freedom to assume the roles naturally which fit them best. As already noted, this is not a particularly easy process, but it is a method that allows each assistant the opportunity to identify personally and take responsibility for his own role. Ultimately, those involved must accept Bennett's approach, and thus they must accept responsibility for the entire program. If they fail to do this, and thus fail to function as a cohesive unit, Dick Bennett's career at the University of Wisconsin would come to a quick end, and potentially, so would theirs.

After examination of Bennett's leadership style with his staff, the parallel to his offensive philosophy becomes readily evident. For the team to excel on offense, the individual players must become a symbiotic unit efficient at passing, screening, cutting, dribbling, and shooting. All basketball players are not created equal, and therefore, each member of the team assumes a role based on his individual strengths, which helps the team achieve its offensive goals. Once again, this is not a particularly easy process in Dick Bennett's system. The players initially seek guidance in the form of rules and well-defined roles from Bennett, but when little help is forthcoming, the growth process begins. Success is attained only when each member of the team identifies his role and accepts responsibility for it. To achieve this, Bennett adamantly refuses to clearly define assignments for his players on offense. By defining their role for them, he would be giving them a built-in excuse when the unit failed as a whole. That is why they must do it themselves. Only when everyone assumes this *individual* responsibility, will each individual then also be equally responsible for the success and failure of the *team*. That means no designed plays and no clearly defined roles. Additionally, it means no excuses or finger-pointing.

There is just one problem with the philosophy. It assumes that the members of the group have the maturity and ability to identify correctly not only their own roles, but also those of every member of the organization. In the absence of such ability, the group of disjointed individuals will flounder, unable to accomplish some of the most basic tasks. That had indeed been a problem for Bennett's current team. Despite their successes, that group of players continued to struggle in identifying and accepting their roles. That observation explains their terrible inconsistency on offense. In seasons to come, however, that same process will likely build Bennett's team back into one of the most efficient in the country.

———————

The Badgers faced a four-game season, arguably the toughest stretch of all remaining Big Ten games, and they needed a split to guarantee an NCAA tournament bid. Game one featured the Iowa Hawkeyes, who were obviously not distraught over Wisconsin's offensive plight. Dr. Tom Davis would bring his team into Madison with a vast array of trapping defenses in search of his 500th career victory and sole possession of third place in the conference. Bennett knew his team *had* to beat Iowa to have any chance for a split.

Thursday's practice, the first of five before the Iowa contest, brought the possibility of a major setback for Wisconsin. Okey again suffered back spasms and left the floor with head trainer Andy Winterstein. Bennett went right back to work. In his mind, there was only one thing left to do—place the burden on Paul Grant's broad shoulders. Moments later, Bennett challenged Grant in a stern voice after he missed a "gimmie" in the paint during the scrimmage.

"Paul, it is time you step up. You are seven feet tall, you are a fifth year senior, you have four games left to play and we are playing for an NCAA bid! It is time you step up and carry this team!"

The message was loud and clear, not only to Paul, but to the entire team. Over the next week of practice, even upon Sam's return, Paul continued to be the "go-to" guy. In addition, Bennett broke from the tradition of the season and emphasized working on areas that Iowa had exploited in their first meeting in early January; inbounding the ball on the endline against Iowa's zone, attacking the press, and player movement against the 1-2-2 zone. After all five practice sessions had been completed, all that was left to do was to play the game.

Bennett was relaxed and in good spirits on the unseasonably warm February morning, as he explained his "tournament push" strategy to his assistants. "I am going to try to get the players to look at these four games as a test of our system, particularly our willingness to accept our intangible concepts of humility, passion, unity, servanthood, and thankfulness." He then pulled out the base of his sweatshirt, which had the 1996 NIT logo printed on the front. "I want to stay focused on what is really important. That is why I wore this shirt today, and also why I am going to give them a passage from Philippians, which basically says to be content in all circumstances."

> *Not that I speak from want; for I have learned to be content in whatever circumstances I am.*
> *I know how to get along with humble means, and I also know how to live in prosperity; in any and every circumstance I have learned the secret of being filled and going hungry, both of having abundance and suffering need.*
> *I can do all through Him who strengthens me.*
>   Philippians 4:11-13

He again looked down at the logo on his chest. "If this is what is going to be, then we have to be grateful. We are not going to focus on the end, we are going to focus on the process, the quality, and relinquish control of the end result." His assistants were quick to agree with his strategy.

It did not take long for Bennett's own thankfulness to be tested. Shawn Hood informed him that Sam would be showing up for the game with a tattoo. Shaking his head slowly, he furrowed his brow, squinted his eyes and whispered, "What? He is getting a tattoo?" Shawn laughed at Bennett's response and added, "Yeah, he is getting a cross and the Bible passage Isaiah 40:31 tattooed on his right shoulder."

> *But they that wait upon the Lord shall renew their strength; They shall mount up with wings as eagles; They shall run, and not be weary, and they shall walk, and not faint.*
>
> Isaiah 40:31

Bennett's reaction was tempered by the fact that he had given Okey the passage. "He loves that one. I gave that to him." He then smiled and shook his head in disbelief. "The Lord does not need to be glorified in that way."

Bennett summed up the morning's meeting with a short lesson for his staff. "Sometimes, as coaches, we have to stand back and just let some things be. We can't control everything. There comes a point where you have to say, 'Fine, if you want to look like that and act like that, fine.'" He was obviously not happy with the new development, but there was a more important issue at hand, namely, beating Iowa.

University of Iowa:
Wednesday, February 26, Madison, Wisconsin

There is something about playing games of great importance that brings out the best in a crowd. The Field House crowd was no exception. Although Stu Jackson had brought a few of those games back to Madison, the Badger faithful were eager to cheer on their new contenders, and the game provided plenty of opportunities to do just that. The crushing defeat in Iowa City was a distant memory as the Badgers took the floor to battle the Hawkeyes. Both teams entered the game with identical 9-5 conference marks. The standing-room-only crowd hung on every movement as the teams played to a virtual standstill through the first eight minutes of the action. Iowa's Andre Woolridge repeatedly tested his less-heralded defender, David Burkemper, but found the going more difficult than he anticipated. In turn, he began deferring shots to his teammates.

Meanwhile, Wisconsin followed the game plan Bennett had set for them, and undaunted by Grant's misfires, pounded the ball into him as much as possible.

Trailing 10-8, Bennett went to his bench and inserted a lineup of Auriantal, Calderwood, Kosolcharoen, Coleman, and Daugherty. Dr. Tom, not respecting the shooting of that group, immediately went to the 1-2-2 half-court zone. Auriantal sliced right through the zone for a floating jump shot that tied the game at ten. Then Iowa took command of the game when their zone shut down Wisconsin's offense. The Badgers were held in check even when Bennett went back to his starting unit. A perfectly executed jump shot pass lob dunk extended Iowa's lead to 23-12. A routine post feed and jump shot made the score 25-12 thirty seconds later. Badger fans throughout the Field House grew quiet. On the very next possession, the score took on blowout proportions, 27-12, on a Woolridge seventeen-foot jump shot. Bennett called time with 1:47 remaining in the half. The bleeding was stopped momentarily when Calderwood hit a three-pointer and Duany converted one of two free throws to draw the Badgers to within eleven at the half, 27-16. Wisconsin's meager 21 percent shooting from the floor had quieted the home crowd, who sensed that their beloved Badgers were on the verge of NCAA elimination.

Daugherty stirred the emotions of those gathered when he hit from behind the arc to open the second half scoring. His second attempt from the left wing, however, fell short. Nonetheless, Sean played well in the opening minutes, scoring eight points (ten if you count the basket he tipped in for Iowa) and pulled down three rebounds. Meanwhile, Iowa's strategy of running the clock down for twenty seconds before isolating Woolridge at the point was not working. Back-to-back three-pointers by Duany, a plethora of points for the sparse offense, tied the score at 36-36 with nine minutes remaining, and brought the crowd raucously to their feet.

The game settled into a free throw contest for the next three minutes, from which the Hawkeyes reclaimed a two-point lead. Iowa's Woolridge then found the range on a fade-away jump shot and the fans nervously settled back into their seats with five minutes remaining and an Iowa lead of 42-38. Grant answered by scoring four points in the next minute to tie the game. The Badgers followed that with three unproductive possessions, while Iowa converted four of six free throws, and the lead was again four. Ryan Bowen out-hustled three Wisconsin players for the rebound off the last missed free throw, which compounded the Badgers' tenuous situation. The Hawkeyes had the ball, a fresh shot clock, and a four-point lead with 2:29 to play.

Davis' team went for the throat, but in retrospect used poor judgment. After having used less than fifteen seconds off the shot clock, they attempted another jump shot pass for a lob dunk. Darryl Moore shook free from Okey, but failed to convert on the play. Had he caught the ball, Iowa would have been up by six. As it turned out, Wisconsin had the ball with twenty more seconds to get back in the game. In addition, Moore compounded the situation when he fouled Grant going for the loose ball, another mental error. Grant walked to the line and reduced the deficit to two, 46-44, without moving the clock.

Woolridge took his time on the offensive end of the floor. With the shot clock winding down, Calderwood forced him into Auriantal's area as he drove for a shot. The ball caromed off the bottom of the rim directly into Daugherty's hands. Wisconsin advanced the ball into their offense end of the floor, looking for the tying basket. Calderwood chose to go for the lead, but his three rattled in and out. Iowa regained possession of the ball with under a minute to play, still leading by two. Woolridge again chose to run the shot clock down before taking another contested jump shot. Grant fought hard for the rebound, only to knock the ball across the endline.

The consensus of thought was that if the Badgers could not steal the inbound pass they would have to foul immediately and force Iowa to win the game at the line. Indeed, that was Bennett's intent. Kent McCausland called a time-out when his teammates failed to free themselves from the Badger defenders. On their second effort to inbound the ball, Okey and Daugherty trapped Ryan Bowen in front of the Iowa bench. Bowen tried to free himself, but Okey reached in to tie up the ball. The whistle blew as Calderwood threw up his hands indicating a jump ball, but the official saw it differently. The official called Okey for a foul. Bowen made both free throws and the lead was again four, 48-44, with just 25.8 seconds to play.

Calderwood took an inbound pass and advanced the ball to the top of the key, where he hesitated momentarily, then blew by his defender for a soft left-handed lay-up. He signaled for a time-out immediately, even before Iowa could get the ball out of the net. Bennett gathered his players on the sideline for instructions. He sketched the press alignment on his clipboard, before he instructed the players to let the ball be passed in near the baseline, then trapped instantly. They were to foul only if a pass was completed out of the trap. Bennett's goal was to force a turnover and convert it into a quick basket to tie the game at 48-48.

The players took their positions on the floor. Okey pressured the inbounder, while Auriantal and Kosolcharoen formed the second line of the press at the free-throw line so the ball would be entered in front of them. The official handed Kent McCausland the ball and he waited for his teammates to break open. He spotted Andre Woolridge open under the Badgers' basket. The ball and Auriantal arrived at Woolridge at the same time. Auriantal slapped the ball away from Woolridge toward the baseline, where Kosolcharoen dove on the ball before it could touch the endline. Okey called for time with Kosolcharoen sprawled at his feet. The crowd was delirious as Bennett again huddled with his players with 15.8 seconds on the game clock and his team down 48-46.

True to his philosophy, Bennett wanted the ball in the hands of his best ball handler, Calderwood, at the top of the key. The three post players, Okey, Grant, and Daugherty, were to free up Duany, breaking off their screens. Ty had the task of delivering the ball to the player with the best scoring opportunity. Bennett ended the huddle with a reminder that they were out of time-outs, so they had to get the ball in bounds on the first try. The official pointed Okey to his inbounding position, handed him the ball, and started his five second count. Calderwood was not open on his cut off a Daugherty screen, so Okey had to force a high pass to Daugherty, who had broken back for the ball. Daugherty fielded the dangerously high pass by tipping it to himself as the five count expired. He then relayed it to Calderwood near the point. Calderwood dribbled to the top of the key and surveyed the action. Okey and Grant settled in on the blocks while Daugherty tried to free up Duany. Ty became his own best option when no one else broke open. He gave a little stutter step, which caused his defender to back off in anticipation of a drive. Ty saw the opening and rose up from beyond the three point arc and drained a three-pointer with seven seconds remaining to give his team a 49-48 lead.

The Field House turned into thunderous bedlam. Woolridge secured the inbound pass and drove the ball the entire length of the floor, out-maneuvering Calderwood, then Okey, on his way to the basket. There stood his last obstacle, seven-foot Paul Grant. Grant had sprinted back to protect the basket as the crowd erupted in celebration after Calderwood's go-ahead basket. His hustle paid off. Woolridge pulled up for his shot, double clutched to avoid Grant's outstretched arms, and released a seven-foot bank shot. The shot caromed off the rim and Daugherty slapped the ball out to half-court to end the game. Calderwood was smothered by his elated teammates in celebration of a victory that had truly been snatched from the jaws of defeat. After the stack of bodies unpiled off Calderwood, he walked the length of the floor with his arms held up in a victory salute. He reveled in the elation of the moment, the victory. Okey swept him up in his big arms and carried him off the floor as the celebration continued in the stands.

Bennett also joined in the festivities as he walked of the floor. He raised both clenched fists to the ceiling and then punched the air in front of the camera, as he broke into full stride to join his team in the locker room. The suddenness of the victory left him nearly speechless in the post-game interview. Though nothing was said about the challenge that had been issued to Grant six days earlier, he had indeed carried his team on his back. He scored twenty-three points on his way to setting a school record for consecutive free throws in a game, fifteen, and also pulled down ten rebounds. The win, the team's tenth conference victory, marked the first time since 1951 that the Badgers had won six straight games in the Big Ten. Not bad for a team that was still operating with virtually no offense. They had shot only 30 percent from the floor, but they had also held Iowa to only 36 percent. More important, they committed only six turnovers for the entire game. Grant, with a little help from his friends, extended the Burkemper era record to a perfect 6-0.

Did anyone outside the state of Wisconsin know about the resurrected Badgers? I turned on ESPN radio on my drive into the morning meeting following the win, curious as to the answer to that question. To my surprise, there were two calls into a national program during the thirty-minute commute. The consensus of the host was the same as Bennett's. They still needed one more win to solidify an NCAA bid. Their next chance, and seemingly their best, came three days later when they traveled to Michigan State.

Michigan State University:
Saturday, March 1, East Lansing, Michigan

The Badgers went into the Breslin Center in East Lansing and proceeded to fall flat on their face. Wisconsin inexplicably returned to their former individual play as the game started. Okey, who had been held to two points on one of five shooting against Iowa, forced three poor shots on the team's first six possessions. When he threw a pass across half-court for a turnover, he joined Bennett on the bench. Wisconsin fell behind 13-4, but after a heated twenty-second time-out with Bennett, the Badgers became more team-oriented. Okey, who had been reinserted into the game, played well for a time. He passed, screened, rebounded, and only then looked to score. In turn, Wisconsin narrowed the Spartans' lead to 15-12 after eleven minutes of play.

As the game continued to unfold, however, there were indications that Michigan State wanted the game more than the Badgers. There were no particular plays that pointed to that conclusion, just subtle indications—getting to all loose balls, securing offensive rebounds, producing open shots out of their offense, dominating the defensive glass, and playing with visible emotion and unity. Wisconsin displayed the opposite. With 1:45 remaining in the half and trailing 29-17, Okey epitomized this lack of unity. He took a pass on the wing, the first of the possession, put his head down, and forced his way across the lane with four pounding dribbles. He eventually traveled as he tried to force up a shot. All four of his teammates dropped their heads and went to the defensive end of the floor without saying a word. Okey was playing poorly, for sure, but he certainly wasn't alone, as both Calderwood and Daugherty had virtually disappeared in the first half. Only Grant and Burkemper played with the consistency they had during the six-game winning streak. As a result, Wisconsin trailed at the half 33-22.

The second half was much the same as the first. The Spartans extended their lead and Wisconsin never challenged. Cleaves took an outlet pass and advanced the ball to the free throw line for an uncontested jump shot. That play broke Bennett's first rule of defense, STOP THE BALL. The basket put Michigan State up 63-40 with 3:27 to play. There was one second half highlight, however. The blowout allowed Bennett to play Matt Miner, a practice player who had been added to the team in midseason, for the final forty-six seconds of the game. Matt took a pass at the point and dribbled into the left gap against the Spartan's 2-3 zone. He left his feet to make a pass, but the lane closed down, so he sent a double-clutch "leapin' leaner" toward the basket. The ball hit off the backboard and settled into the hoop. With that basket, he had scored more game points than Calderwood, Burkemper, and Duany combined. He also had a Big Ten memory to share with his grandchildren. The final score was a disheartening 68-49.

Wisconsin's trademark defense had evaporated. The Spartans scored at will and shot over 50 percent for the game. Bennett had spent an inordinate amount of time over the previous two weeks in practice working to generate offense, yet against Michigan State all that did was weaken the defense. Bennett found himself at odds with his team once again at Monday's meeting, but the six-game winning streak made him more reflective than he had been after other bad losses.

"The game is like a book, and there are chapters in that book. Some chapters have to be shorter than other chapters. Some chapters are losing chapters, but are nonetheless important in the completion of the book."

Though he was speaking of David's role with the team, his comments could easily have been directed at the last two games of the season. There was no telling what was going to happen. But one thing was certain, the last week of the season would be extremely important for the program, win or lose. Brad Soderberg assessed the situation.

"Coach, the bottom line is that we have to score more than fifty points to win one of the next two games, and we are not going to do it with Sam as a motion player. He needs to be on the lane."

Bennett began to respond to Brad's contention, "Well, that is one reason, Shawn . . ." he hesitated, searching for the right name, "I mean Paul . . . Sean . . . Brian . . . Brad . . . whatever your name really is!" Laughter broke out as Brad interjected, "It's March, Coach. It is almost over."

In Brad's humorous comment was the unstated truth. The year had been difficult and stressful for the staff. The end of the season would provide a welcome rest. However, the staff did not want the reprieve just yet, not until after a successful run at the tournament, so the discussion turned back to the task at hand. Bennett spoke up again, "I'm going to tell Sam that he really belongs along the lane. If he is going to be really good, he has to play to his strength and not his weakness, and right now that is on the post. If he really wants to, he could become the greatest rebounder and screener this school has ever had."

Bennett clarified Okey's role in the offense over the next two days of practice. He put him on the low post and made sure that he understood exactly what was expected of him: screen, rebound, and then score. Once again the Badgers spent most of their practice time trying to improve their offense. Even though Bennett did not want to leave the defense unattended, he had little choice, as they had no chance to win in Indiana's Assembly Hall if they did not score more points. Just before the team departed for the airport, Bennett proclaimed, "This is a business trip if ever there was one. This is a time when we've got to come together. This is when we have to circle the wagons and prepare for the finish. Every voice and every set of eyes is important at this point in the season." The team headed to the airport as I pulled my Jeep Cherokee onto I-94 for the six-hour drive to Bloomington.

The drive allowed me time to reflect and contemplate. I had made the same drive exactly three years earlier, having just finished my first year coaching the men's basketball team at the College of St. Scholastica. The year of leading a poor Division III program in the hockey belt of northeastern Minnesota had drained my enthusiasm for the game. I was thankful, therefore, that my athletic director, Kevin Snyder, allowed me to take a few days to get away to my basketball mecca. Knight had given me permission through his secretary to sit in on the week's practices. The disappointment of the 5-22 season and arctic temperatures of Duluth were a million miles away as I sat on the front steps of a friend's home, slowly drank a cup of coffee, and took in the beautiful warm spring day. It felt great to be back in the heart of basketball country.

My mornings during that visit were spent working out and honing my jump shot at the Monroe County YMCA, while in the afternoons I sat among the national championship banners and thousands of empty seats and lost myself in the IU practices. After Friday practice session, I headed east to Columbus, Ohio, to watch the week's preparation in action, as IU took on Ohio State in the regular season finale.

As it turned out, I had an unexpected change of plans while in Columbus, and never did get a ticket. More significantly, the events of that weekend began the three-year journey that ultimately brought me back to Bloomington. The memories of those years swirled through my mind as I drove directly to Assembly Hall to join the Badger team for practice. My legs ached as I stepped onto the gravel parking lot. A large portable sign in front of the arena read, in bold letters "BEAT WISCONSIN." I made my way to the small bleachers which surround the court and watched the team go through a ninety-minute practice. Ironically, I barely noticed that they were there. I spent most of that time in "thankful" thought for the difficulties of the previous three years and the generosity of the entire basketball staff for letting me get so close to this process we call coaching. As practice closed, I walked silently into the drizzle of the Indiana night.

The following morning I made my way to the local bakery for a bagel and a cup of coffee before heading to shooting practice. Assembly Hall was obviously built for only one purpose, Hoosier basketball. The architecture suggests that the designers admired the small cracker-box gyms of rural Indiana. There are four rows of wooden bleachers that line the floor, basketball stanchions to support the backboard from Knight's own playing era, and a white concrete block wall that separates the floor from the 16,000 cascading theater seats. The scorers' tables and banners promote just one product—Indiana Basketball. The whole environment created a very nostalgic atmosphere for me.

The Wisconsin players quietly strolled in to begin their forty-five-minute workout. The light practice consisted of shooting, free throws, and a little 5 on 0. As the session drew to a close, Bennett walked to the top of the baseline bleachers and admired the five national championship banners hanging directly above him. He called to his players who were still out on the playing surface. Then, replaced hips and all, he jumped as high as he could in an attempt to touch the banners. He repeated the leap three times. The players smiled and laughed softly among themselves. His message was clear. "Reach for the dream!" That would be no simple task on this day. The Hoosiers were sure to be ready for the game after their embarrassing blowout in Madison.

Indiana University:
Wednesday, March 5, Bloomington, Indiana

Bennett had made one significant change for the Indiana game. He put Sam on the low post and moved Daugherty out to the perimeter in the double low-post offense. In addition to playing to Okey's strength on the post, the move also benefited Daugherty. Sean was freed up to move on the perimeter to get screens and look for his consistent outside shot. The move had one other potential advantage. Daugherty rebounded very well from the perimeter, slicing his 6'10" body toward the basket on nearly every shot. The running start enhanced his vision and jumping ability, as opposed to those players who were battling for position under the basket.

The opening tap was an event in itself. Grant and Indiana's Andrea Patterson tangled arms with each other on the first three attempts, before the official simply let the two hack each on his fourth toss, just to get the action started. Patterson effectively tied Grant up on his running jump and secured the tap. Both teams hacked and slapped on defense, which created sloppy play on both ends of the floor. Okey found himself on the bench less than two minutes into the game, with two fouls. Duany replaced him in front of his hometown crowd. Wisconsin's Indiana transplants, Daugherty and Duany, got the Badgers offense going with the first two baskets of the game. But the team struggled mightily to score points thereafter, despite executing well on offense with their quick cuts, solid screens, and good shot selection. Indiana spurted to an eight-point lead over the next two minutes. The run was capitalized by seldom-used Larry Richardson's long three-pointer, and the score stood at 16-8 with 9:05 remaining in the half. Kosolcharoen then came off the bench to score five points, which helped cut the lead to 18-17.

The first half was like watching a mirror image. Knight and Bennett had their teams playing nearly identical offenses and defenses. Indiana, however, hit a few more shots in the friendly confines of Assembly Hall and took a 25-21 lead into the locker room. Grant played a superb defense to complement his six points and six rebounds. Nevertheless, he would need help in the second half if the Badgers were to pull out a victory.

The second half started out well for Wisconsin. Okey scored four quick points and Daugherty hit from the baseline for two more. Indiana, however, reeled off seven unanswered points to take their biggest lead of the game at 37-27. Daugherty and Okey, determined not to let the game slip away, both grabbed two rebounds and scored five points to claw back to 40-37 with thirteen minutes to go. Wisconsin's relentless defense and crisp offensive movement finally paid off. Kosolcharoen hit a running seven-footer off a curl cut, Okey added a turnaround jump shot off the glass, and the Badgers took their first lead of the game. The 16,000-seat arena became as quiet as a practice gym. The Badgers gained confidence as they scored points at a rate they had seldom experienced all season. Still, Indiana kept pace. Calderwood's two free throws with seven minutes remaining gave Wisconsin a 53-50 lead. Then, without warning, someone turned off Wisconsin's spigot. That someone, of course, was Indiana's defense.

The Badgers went scoreless for three and a half minutes, during which time the Hoosiers re-established a six-point lead. Grant finally got things flowing again with an eighteen-foot jump shot from the left wing.

Back on defense, the ball skipped through Patterson's hands and out of bounds. Wisconsin had a chance to trim away at the lead once again. Okey drove hard to his right and was fouled. He failed to convert the first bonus free throw and the team retreated back to defense, where IU regained a six-point lead. Determined to make a play, Okey again drove hard off the wing and again was fouled. Once more, he missed the front end of the bonus. Indiana had the ball and a 61-55 lead, with 2:15 remaining. Patterson posted up Okey on the left block. He received a pass, and when Okey lunged for the pass, he spun to the baseline for a reverse lay-up and drew the foul. Patterson converted the free throw, and the lead was nine.

Wisconsin did not concede the game. Kosolcharoen drove the paint for a lay-up, then, following an A.J. Guyton miss, Calderwood delivered a three-pointer from his favorite spot. The scoring gap was four, 64-60, with 1:15 to play. Bennett called a time-out to set up the press. Michael Lewis took a pass in the right corner and sprinted up the floor. Kosolcharoen jumped in front of him, which sent both of them crashing to the floor. The official called a charge on Lewis and Wisconsin had the ball back. Calderwood penetrated to the basket but his shot was blocked. He hustled after the deflected shot and went up a second time with no better results. Another stuff resulted in a jump ball, and all eyes turned to the possession arrow. It pointed toward Wisconsin. The Badgers finally ran their offense, which opened Daugherty up in the right corner. He launched a long three-pointer. The ball hit the back of the iron and ricocheted back and forth in the cylinder before finally popping out. Wisconsin had to foul and the game was essentially over. Indiana hit all six of their free throws down the stretch to seal the 70-66 victory.

The loss, although turning the Minnesota game into a must win situation, had a bright side. The team's offense had finally come alive as Sam settled into his role on the low post. He had eleven points on four for five shooting, and six rebounds. Even in the costly stretch late in the game, he was simply trying to do what he had been asked to do—score. If he had been able to convert his free throws, he might have been the hero of the day. Yet when the game was on the line, it was Andrea Patterson who stepped up and finished the deal. Still, Grant, Daugherty, Calderwood, Okey, and Kosolcharoen had all played well in the loss. If the team could duplicate that performance against Minnesota, and get a little help from Duany, Auriantal, Burkemper, or Coleman, they had a legitimate chance of knocking off the number two team in the country and earning a trip to "The Big Dance."

Bennett's behavior made it obvious that he relished the challenge. He was upbeat, even jovial, as he prepared his team for the game. At Friday's meeting, just one day prior to the game, he reminisced about the season. It had been an exceptionally challenging five months for everyone involved with the program and it was simply time to sit back and enjoy the drama of the situation. Brad Soderberg added to the levity of the moment. "Coach, I just won't feel right if we do not at least talk about how we are going to adjust the offense today." The staff broke out in rousing laughter which set Bennett off on an hour-long monologue about his journey to Madison.

"You guys have no idea what it was like in the beginning. I took a six-thousand-dollar pay cut when I went from Eau Claire Memorial High School to Stevens Point. For that I was rewarded by having to teach seven credits a semester, but I wasn't allowed to teach the basketball theory course. I functioned as the entire department's sports information director, coached basketball, and also had to be working on my master's degree!"

Paul Costanzo seriously interjected, "What was your master's in?"

"I have a MSPD, a Masters in Personnel Development." Looking intently at Costanzo, mimicking his serious nature, Bennett asked, "Do you know what that is?" Costanzo shook his head. "No."

Bennett broke out in laughter as he proclaimed, "Neither do I." There would be no more serious questions on that day.

The impromptu comedy routine included tales of house bats, mice, and failed gardens. Hidden in the jocularity of the moment, however, was a keen lesson. When all was said and done, when this season had become a memory, the struggles that the staff endured would be the memories they would cherish in the future. Someday, when they sat amid their own staffs, the young coaches would look back on these days with Bennett and the 1996-97 Badgers with fondness.

University of Minnesota
Saturday, March 8, Madison, Wisconsin

The Wisconsin-Minnesota game had become the toughest ticket in town. The "old barn" would host arguably the biggest game in the history of Wisconsin basketball. There were forty minutes left in the 1996-97 Wisconsin Badgers' regular season. Forty minutes that would decide whether all the offensive adjustments had worked. Forty minutes that would determine whether this team had developed the mental toughness Bennett had questioned on so many occasions. Forty minutes that would determine whether this team belonged among the elite sixty-four teams in the country. Forty minutes that would determine whether Dick Bennett could indeed coach "at this level."

Bennett's relaxed demeanor was yesterday's memory as he took the floor just prior to tip-off against Clem Haskins' 27-2 Golden Gophers. A short ceremony to recognize Paul Grant as the lone senior allowed the game-day anxiety, which Bennett had struggled with his entire career, to build to a crescendo. Bennett sat motionless on the bench as his players were introduced. Only when Grant was again summoned by the public-address announcer did he stir out of his meditative state. He reached over and patted Paul softly on the back before Grant rose to his feet and joined his teammates in the middle of the floor.

The number two-ranked Gophers were all they were billed to be—big, strong, quick, deep, and talented. The Field House crowd was in hysteria before the game even started. Meanwhile, Grant was so energized that when he out-jumped John Thomas to start the game, he swatted the ball over Okey's head and into the lap of the shot-clock operator. Sam Jacobson, the Gopher's talented small forward, elevated from the left corner for the game's first shot. The ball skipped off the rim and Burkemper chased it down in the opposite corner. Four free throws, two apiece by Okey and Grant, gave the Badgers an early 4-2 lead, but Okey was just getting warmed up. He grabbed his third rebound, converted to offense, and posted up Courtney James on the left block. His pump-fake got James into the air where he had no choice but to come down on Okey. Both free throws found the net, to make the score 6-2. James answered with a put-back of his own at the opposite end of the floor, before the teams traded misses. Okey collected for his fourth rebound of the game on Minnesota's miss. He took James out to the three-point arc, and when James refused to defend him that far away from the basket, he elevated and swished a three-pointer. The score was 9-4.

Both Bennett and Haskins went to their benches at that point. Minnesota's depth, however, got the edge on the Badgers. Charles Thomas and Quincy Lewis hit back-to-back baskets to tie the game at nine. Then, after being quiet for most of the first nine minutes of the game, Daugherty answered with five points of his own—two free throws and a three-pointer. The Badgers reclaimed the lead at 15-10. Haskins went to a zone defense after Daugherty's one-man run. The zone, a defense that exploited their weakness as a team, again grabbed a stranglehold on Wisconsin's offense. Other than a Daugherty bank shot breaking the press, Wisconsin failed to score against the 2-3 defense over the next four minutes, and they fell behind, 22-17.

Calderwood shook off the effects of a twenty-four-hour flu and picked up the slack. He hit a three-point shot and a pull-up jumper, which reclaimed the lead at 26-23. Haskins again changed his defense, opting for a 1-2-2 zone, which triggered his team into a 13-0 run. An errant field goal attempt by Minnesota, and a last second three-pointer by Calderwood, was all that kept the game from becoming a rout. Minnesota led 36-29 at the half. Wisconsin had to play catch-up ball after they had shot just 27 percent from the floor. Several Golden Gophers raised their fists to the sky when they ran off the court, prompting the biased crowd to shower them with a chorus of loud boos. Indeed, they had looked impressive in the first half but a little humility would have served them better than premature celebration and taunts.

The second half began in a blur of ferocious defense by both teams. Wisconsin, however, came out of the locker room determined not to go down without a fight. Bodies dove and scrambled for loose balls on at least five occasions in the early minutes of the half, and the Badgers locked up the possession on each scrum. That fire carried over to their offense, as they converted three of their first five shots. With nearly five minutes gone in the half, however, Minnesota still held a 43-39 lead. A technical foul on Gophers' Bobby Jackson gave the Badgers the break they needed to turn the momentum in their direction. Three "steel trap" defensive stands by Wisconsin, a couple of charity shots, and a stone-faced three-pointer by Kosolcharoen gave Wisconsin their first lead in nearly ten minutes, 44-43. A deafening roar engulfed the Field House as Haskins rushed to call a time-out.

Haskins became animated during the break, but his impassioned words did not slow Wisconsin. They shut down the Gophers and forced a shot-clock violation on the first possession out of the huddle. Unfortunately for the Badgers, they then stopped their own momentum with a pair of turnovers. Nonetheless, Minnesota still could not crack the fervent

Badger defense. Grant finally broke the scoring drought when he stepped out to the point in the Triangle offense and nailed an eighteen-footer to build the lead to three.

Then the real battle began. Each successive possession took on increased importance as spectacular play on the floor fostered bedlam in the stands, and vice versa. The next six minutes produced seven lead changes and three ties. The Field House fell deathly quiet as Auriantal's driving lay-up skipped off the front of the rim with ninety seconds left to play. But chaos once again prevailed when Daugherty, Okey, and Auriantal swarmed Minnesota's Jacobson for the rebound. Jacobson wheeled away from the trio, and both he and the ball went flying out of control. An official's whistle stopped the action and all eyes turned in his direction. He threw both his arms in the air, indicating a jump-ball. Whose ball?! Again all eyes were riveted on the official, waiting for his signal. Cheers rang out when he pointed emphatically toward the Wisconsin bench. Calderwood took the inbound pass and drove into the middle of the lane. When his defender tripped and fell to the floor, he pulled up and drilled a pressure packed seven-foot jump shot.

Calderwood's basket tied the score for the last time at 62 with 1:15 remaining in the game. Okey, Calderwood, and Grant, each of whom had played nearly every minute of the emotionally and physically exhausting game, showed no signs of fatigue as they converted back on defense. Jackson yo-yoed the dribble at the point, before driving Auriantal to his left. He stopped hard in his tracks and pulled up for a fifteen-foot floater, but the shot caromed off the left side of the basket. Daugherty was fouled by Courtney James in a mad scramble for the rebound. He walked to the line with the weight of the entire season on his shoulders, and sank both free throws. The Badgers were up by two, 64-62, with a fraction under a minute remaining.

The Big Ten champions were not about to roll over and die. Sam Jacobson took a pass on the right wing and drove hard off a ball screen. When Okey got caught on the screen, he watched helplessly as Jacobson's shot sailed over his outstretched hand and settled softly into the basket. The long-range bomb gave the Gophers a 65-64 lead. Wisconsin converted back on offense without calling a time-out. Seconds ticked off the clock while they ran their offense, looking to take the first good shot, but the offense stagnated. Okey drove hard to his right but could not free himself for a shot. Instead, he was stuck along the right side of the lane with no dribble, no shot, and no time. He looked frantically for an open teammate, then finally spotted Calderwood breaking hard to the corner.

Ty had created just enough space between himself and his defender to field the pass from Okey and collect himself for a hurried shot. The ball barely reached the rim, but as it turned out, he was hit on the elbow by Minnesota's Eric Harris. The official was standing less than ten feet away and blew the whistle immediately. The clock showed 11.8 seconds remaining. Wearing the blank stare of an assassin, Calderwood went to the line and sank his first free throw to even the score at 66. Haskins called time out to freeze Calderwood and strategize with his team. Calderwood relished moments like that, so with ice *already* in his veins, his second shot barely disturbed the net. Wisconsin led by one.

The Minnesota Gophers and 11.8 seconds were all that stood between the Badgers and a trip to the NCAA tournament. Minnesota's Eric Harris advanced the dribble up the floor just left of the key area and passed to Jacobson, who had broken open at the top of the key off a John Thomas screen. Okey, Jacobson's defender, was not about to let his man shake him again. He worked his way free from the screen and rapidly closed the gap on his man. Jacobson instinctively put the ball on the floor to clear himself. In doing so however, he drove right into Calderwood, who knocked the ball away into Okey's hands. Okey pulled it in, while tripping over the prone Jacobson. He tossed the ball ahead to Calderwood before he hit the floor himself. Ty chased the ball down and threw it high into the air as the buzzer sounded. Wisconsin had won, 66-65!

The already ecstatic crowd exploded in celebration and rushed the floor. A mass of humanity covered the playing surface, many of the partakers holding small signs that read, "We're Dancing!" The players stayed out on the floor and joined the festivities. Bennett, however, was nowhere to be found in the post-game spectacle. He had quietly made his way to the sanctity of the locker room to be with his own thoughts. Later that day, his brother Jack would lead his UW-Stevens Point team to an upset victory over UW-Platteville in the second round of the NCAA Division III national tournament. For the Bennetts, however, March 8 was a special day for reasons that extended beyond the basketball floor. The date was also the late John Bennett's birthday.

Bennett later talked about the importance of the Minnesota win. "The kids experienced what I wanted them to experience. My hope is that they will be different, maybe not incredibly different, but that experience will change them. Their character, their confidence, and their concentration will be better when playing under that kind of pressure. That game was as tough as it gets! Now the kids can relax."

There was every reason to be optimistic heading into post-season play.

Final Big Ten Standings

| | Conference | | Season | |
	W	L	W	L
Minnesota	16	2	27	3
Iowa	12	6	21	9
Purdue	12	6	17	11
Illinois	11	7	21	9
Wisconsin	11	7	18	9
Indiana	9	9	22	10
Michigan	9	9	19	11
Michigan State	9	9	16	11
Ohio State	5	13	10	17
Penn State	3	15	10	17
Northwestern	2	16	7	22

Chapter 18

One Final Lesson is Really Just the First

Rain fell as morning broke over Madison on selection Sunday. The precipitation signaled the advent of a new season. The grass started to turn green, buds began to appear on the trees, and the remains of winter were washed away in the warm spring shower. In addition to changes of nature that accompanied the approaching vernal equinox, however, was another new season at hand, playoff season. The NCAA post-season tournament (a.k.a. March Madness or The Big Dance) was about to get underway. The top sixty-four teams in the country would partake in the most popular single-elimination tournament in the United States. The Wisconsin Badgers would be one of those elite teams for only the second time in half a century. The win over Minnesota had all but guaranteed an at-large bid. What was not known, though, was who, when, and where they would play.

Rain gave way to brilliant sunshine later in the day as the players, and the staff and their families, gathered together at the Bennetts' home to watch the NCAA Tournament Selection Show. There were no outside distractions. Bennett had refused requests by CBS and ESPN to televise the occasion. He did so for two reasons. First, as he had indicated just days earlier, this was the time of the season to circle the wagons and band together as a unit. Wisconsin fans could celebrate and enjoy the "hoops hysteria" of the tournament, but the team would stay true to its philosophy of attending only to what truly mattered. Second, the memory of a similar event with his 1991-1992 UWGB team was still fresh in his mind. That team had finished the regular season 25-3, winning the

Mid-Continent Conference regular season title. Despite their failure to secure the NCAA automatic bid by losing in the MCC conference tournament, Bennett and his team felt confident that their performance over the entire season would get them an at-large bid. A large crowd of Phoenix supporters and the entire UWGB staff and players gathered at The Fifty Yard Line Bar and Grill to watch the selection show. A television crew had been dispatched to the location to capture their reaction as the brackets were announced. Unfortunately, the excitement of the day abruptly gave way to despair as the brackets were read. UWGB was not among those listed. The pain of that moment became indelibly etched on Bennett's memory. It is highly unlikely that he will allow such an event to occur again as long as he is in coaching.

This day was different. Anne prepared pizza and hot fudge sundaes for everyone. Bennett's only worry of the day was centered around how high a seed his team would get. Clusters of players and staff gathered around one of the three television sets in the Bennett home to watch the proceedings. Bennett knelt on the floor and leaned over a foot stool to get a closer look. The clan did not have to wait long to know their fate. Applause broke out as the second bracket flashed across the television screens. The number seven seed in the East Regional, the University of Wisconsin, was pitted against the number ten seed, the University of Texas. Pittsburgh, Pennsylvania, was the host city for the East Regional first-round game. The date of the contest was set for Friday, March 16. Dick Bennett was going home.

Bennett congratulated each player on the successful season, but also planted a seed that it was time to get back to work. The gathering eventually broke up for the evening and Bennett went right to work. His first course of action was to review his season-long journal in search of clues that might help the team prepare for their first-round opponent.

Tom Penders' kids from Austin were a formidable opponent. Athletic, fast, aggressive, and experienced, it was exactly the type of team that had given the Badgers so much trouble during the regular season. Only against Illinois had they shown the ability to outplay such a team. In addition, there was an immediate match-up problem that had to be addressed. Reggie Freeman, a lanky and talented 6'6" guard/forward, would be too quick and agile for Okey to handle, yet he was too big for any of the smaller guards. Bennett summarized the dilemma, "the bar has definitely been raised." Indeed, the entire staff knew that the team would have to be better prepared for this game than for any other during the season. The monumental win against Minnesota was already a distant memory. Such is life in athletics.

The basketball staff was in a blur of non-stop activity on Monday morning. Bennett's presence, however, was a calming influence in the midst of the pre-tournament fracas. He had been in this position before and fared well, as everyone was aware. Therefore, it came as no surprise when his leadership style changed in the post season. He led from the front. The coaches' discussions were replaced with proclamations. In one short statement he made it perfectly clear that things were not business as usual.

"I have decided to go with the small lineup, and I am going to make the change immediately. I don't think we have a choice against Texas or, if we are fortunate enough to win, against South Carolina. We just cannot play big against their quickness, so I am going to move Kosolcharoen into the lineup. I was going to ask you guys about this before I changed, but I decided this is not one where I have to ask. I am not interested in feedback. I am just going to do it."

Tuesday brought less enthusiasm than Monday. The joyous mood of the tournament week began to sour when Bennett received a call from the University of Wisconsin Chancellor's office. They had received a complaint from the Madison chapter of the Freedom From Religion Foundation, expressing concern about a recent newspaper article that detailed Bennett's Christian faith. The complaint specifically noted that the voluntary Bible studies, which Bennett occasionally holds in the locker room, violated the constitutional amendment for the separation of church and state. In the article, Bennett had explained that he will periodically play Christian music and study the scriptures as they relate to basketball. He does so primarily for himself, but others are welcome to attend if they so desire. The letter, implying that Bennett's position of authority coerced his players into participating, was erroneous; nonetheless, he was visibly troubled by the call. As it turned out, that would not be the only unsettling event of the day.

The staff, and specifically Bennett, faced an ethical dilemma. They were in a position to recruit, and probably sign, a talented junior college guard who could step in and help the team for the 1997-98 season. Shaddrick Jenkins, a 6'3" guard out of Coffeyville Community College in Coffeyville, Kansas, was strong enough to excel defensively in the Big

Ten. He also possessed enough offensive skill to become the perimeter scoring threat that the team so desperately needed. The situation was complicated, yet simple. For Wisconsin to offer Jenkins a scholarship, Mosezell Peterson would have to relinquish his athletic scholarship and go on a medical scholarship. That decision was really Mosezell's alone, because in doing so, he would be resigning hopes of ever playing basketball again. While Mosezell had responded well after the surgery to repair his badly damaged knee, his injury was so extensive as to cast doubt on whether he would ever compete at such a high level again.

Brad pressed Bennett for clarity on his intent to offer Jenkins the scholarship. "We have to decide whether or not we are going to go forward with Shaddrick. If we wait any longer, our inactivity will have made our decision for us." Brad went on to explain that time was running out for an official visit because Jenkins indicated that he would make his final decision on the national signing date, less than three weeks away.

"What can I do!?" Bennett responded. "This is a medical issue. Mosezell's situation will be resolved in time, but maybe not on the timetable we want. In addition, there are other issues here, too. Mike Kosolcharoen and David Burkemper, who are good enough to start an NCAA Tournament game, are going to be bypassed. That is what I am wrestling with."

Seeking to clarify the situation, head trainer Andy Winterstein was called into the meeting for an update on Mosezell's recovery. Andy was reluctant to give a definitive answer, explaining that the final decision to give up his athletic scholarship was Mosezell's to make. His point was well received by Bennett and his staff. Upon Winterstein's departure, Bennett noted, "This is one of those occasions where the right thing to do is not the best thing to do. By my personal code, there is an obligation to do the right thing. This is my call, and nothing should change my standards. If I value winning over doing the right thing, then the decision is easy enough to make. We offer Shaddrick the scholarship. But if I value doing the right thing over winning, though I wish to win, the decision is not complicated, it is just hard to make."

That afternoon's practice did little to soothe Bennett's spirits. The small unit of Mike, Ty, David, Sam, and Paul proved to be hopelessly incompetent on offense. Each possession was a battle of futility. The group scored only a handful of baskets in over thirty minutes of scrimmaging. Bennett said little during the practice. He didn't have to. His displeasure showed intensely on his face. Finally, with only a few minutes left in the practice, he shouted across the gym to Soderberg, "I have made my decision!" The players look dumbfounded, having no idea what he meant, but Brad simply nodded his head in agreement. His comment was really twofold: he would be returning to the big starting lineup, and he would offer the scholarship to the junior college recruit.

Bennett realized he also had an obligation to himself. He absolutely had to get more depth at the guard position to take the program to the next level. A year of frustration had taught him that. Bennett called the team together in the locker room at the end of practice. He was left ill at ease with their poor practice. He let them know that their preparation, to that point, was unacceptable. They had not elevated their level of play, their intensity, or their focus. To borrow an old coach's axiom, by failing to prepare they were preparing to fail!

Only twelve hours after the players left the locker room, they returned for one final early-morning practice before their flight departed for Pittsburgh. The players were quiet and passive as they went through their warm-up drills. That inattentiveness carried over into the defensive drills, at which time Bennett began to reproach them for their lack of purpose. However, the players seemed to have turned a deaf ear to his comments, which were growing more intense with each minute. Okey finally turned to Bennett with a scowl and questioned, "What is going on?" His question was genuine, as he could not understand Bennett's displeasure with the team.

"You guys have a comfort zone that you play in, but the regular season is over! NCAA tournament basketball has a whole different ceiling! It is played at an entirely different level of intensity. You guys don't know that, but I do!" He stopped momentarily to look into the eyes of each starter. Only then did he walk off the court to resume practice. The players finally understood and immediately elevated their intensity level to match Bennett's. But was it too little too late? The tumult of the past few days was forgotten as the players left the floor. There was nothing left to do but play the game.

Once again, it was late afternoon by the time I pulled my weary Jeep Cherokee onto I-94 and headed southeast. The mapped-out route to Pittsburgh would veer slightly south, through Indianapolis, Columbus, and Wheeling. Not the quickest and most direct route, but making good time was not the motivation. Bringing back memories and contemplating the wisdom locked within the Badgers' mystifying core was my goal.

The trip had been a success as the gentle, rolling farmland of central Ohio gave way to the steep bluffs of the Ohio River valley and the Appalachian Mountains. With each passing mile, however, I thought more about watching the practice sessions of the afternoon. The NCAA tournament took on a new perspective in my mind, by the time I arrived at the Pittsburgh Civic Arena, better known to Pittsburgh natives as "The Igloo." Under all the hype, all the publicity, and all the fanfare are two unmistakable truths: one, only those who have sacrificed and paid the price get to participate; and two, only those who have given themselves to something greater than themselves will advance to the future rounds. In that light, the tournament was more a celebration of life than just a bunch of games.

The dramatic topography of the area was surprising to me. Equally impressive was the sensation of passing through a tunnel cut through the mountains and coming out on the other side to see downtown Pittsburgh spread out in front of me. My vertigo did not subside until I was firmly seated in the arena at mid-court. A loose and carefree Coppin State team went through a scrimmage before Wisconsin took the floor. Bennett led his team through a full complement of defensive and shooting drills. The intensity of the defensive drills, especially, caught the attention of the several hundred onlookers in the stands. The precision teamwork by the players spawned a few rounds of spontaneous applause. Bennett used his full hour for preparation, and when the horn sounded the players jogged off the court to one final ovation. By all impressions, they looked prepared. Those close to the program, however, again had the lingering doubt as to whether their focus had arrived too late. They needed a week of that kind of concerted effort, not an hour.

Game day got off to a shaky start when Ty Calderwood was late for the team meal. He had overslept. Though he was only eight minutes late, Bennett enforced the few rules he had set for the team. Calderwood would not start. The time and the reason for his tardiness were of very little concern to Bennett. A precedent had been set for being late to a team meal when Grant was held out of the lineup against Providence. Besides, Bennett understood that if he was going to have team rules, he had to be ready to enforce them when they were broken and to accept the consequences. Bennett took no pleasure in benching Calderwood. He knew that

Calderwood's lateness was a simple oversight. Nonetheless, he also realized that both Ty and the team had to be held accountable for the oversight (or oversleep).

University of Texas:
Friday, March 16, Pittsburgh, Pennsylvania

The afternoon session of the tournament was not a complete sellout. While less than half of the large facility was filled, there was a large throng of supporters, clad in red and white, sitting in the sections immediately behind the Badger bench. The first game of the East Regional got under way just after noon, Eastern Time. Texas won the opening tap. Ten seconds later the ball went sailing out of bounds and the Badgers had their first crack at offense. Auriantal, who had replaced Calderwood in the lineup, took the inbound pass and carefully assessed the press. His careful approach backfired when he picked up the ball, was trapped immediately and called for a ten-second violation. Texas went back on the offensive. Kris Clack, an athletically gifted forward, went high in the air for a backdoor lob dunk. Grant hit him in mid air and sent him crashing to the floor. Clack picked himself up and converted both free throws to open the scoring. Texas was well prepared and had no intention of waiting for Wisconsin to run their patient offense. They trapped the ball on three consecutive passes as the Badgers advanced it toward the baseline. Only when the ball was thrown back out to Auriantal at the top of the key did they fall into their half-court man. By that time, however, the Badgers had less than twenty seconds to turn over their motion offense. Burkemper got the first open shot for Wisconsin. He hesitated because he knew that his role was not to be the scorer, but the shot clock was approaching zero. Texas dared him to shoot, which he did, but the ball hit off the back of the rim and a high-flying Clack pulled it in. The Longhorns pushed the ball up the floor. Reggie Freeman set up on the left wing and lofted a soft left-handed twenty-one-foot jump shot. Burkemper tried to close ground and contest the shot, but he didn't get there in time and the score went to 5-0.

Wisconsin was extremely tentative on offense. Their cuts were slow and without purpose. Furthermore, there were only two screens during the first three offensive possessions. Grant's first shot boomeranged hard off the backboard without touching the rim and the Badgers began to dig a deep hole for themselves. Daugherty finally broke the ice on their next possession when he faked a screen and slipped to the basket for an easy lay-up off an Okey feed. That momentum lasted all of nine seconds. Texas again pushed the ball up the floor searching for a quick score. Clack received the pass at twenty-two feet, elevated over Okey, and drained the three. The lead became 8-2. Bennett had seen enough. Calderwood made his first appearance in the game at the next dead ball.

Texas began to trap the ball on every pass in Wisconsin's offense. The Badgers' best bet to beat that strategy was to penetrate to the basket when the ball was passed out of the trap, thus catching their opponent out-numbered and out of position. A seven-foot center, however, was not the best player on the team to do so. Grant's drive from the corner resulted in a charge that gave the ball back to Texas. Wisconsin held defensively, but when the ball skipped through Duany's hands and into his defender's, the turnovers began to mount. The Longhorns wasted no time in capitalizing on the errors. Freeman took the ball at the top of the key and drove Duany hard to the basket. He scored and was fouled. The lead swelled to 15-3.

Wisconsin's future grew more bleak with each passing second. Calderwood was a bit too aggressive on defense, trying to spark his team. He picked up his third personal foul with 11:30 remaining in the half. Bennett had no recourse but to bring him back to the bench. Then finally, Wisconsin began to play with the drive that had gotten them to the tournament. Even though the scoring gap initially reached 25-11, Texas' shooting eventually cooled in the face of Wisconsin's improved defense. The Badgers chipped away ever so slowly at the lead. Two Kosolcharoen free throws with 3:58 remaining in the half reduced the deficit to seven, 27-20. However, costly turnovers stopped the Badgers' 9-2 run and Texas re-established a nine point lead at the half, 33-24.

The Badgers big three had kept Wisconsin in the game. Okey had five points, three rebounds, and four assists; Grant added six points to go with his four rebounds and a block; and Daugherty accumulated seven points and two rebounds. The only blemish on the trio's performance was the four Okey turnovers, but even those were committed while trying to make good plays. The guards, on the other hand, labored against the attacking Longhorn defense. Calderwood, Auriantal, Burkemper, Kosolcharoen, and Duany had only six points, five rebounds, and one assist among them. They simply had to have a greater impact on the game for the Badgers to make a comeback.

The second half started well for the Badgers. Okey took a pass out of a Texas trap and drove straight to the rim for a dunk. Burkemper came away with a steal on the defensive end of the floor, and the Badgers had a chance to close to within five. Calderwood's three rimmed out and Texas relentlessly pushed the ball up the floor in search of quick scores. Clack pulled up for a transition three-point shot, but was fouled. He made all three of the free throws and the lead was back to ten, 36-26. Then, as Bennett had feared, Freeman became unguardable. He used his superior size on the smaller Wisconsin defenders to score seven of his team's next nine points. His play forced Bennett to go to the 1-2-2 zone in an attempt to slow him down. Moments later, the situation worsened, when Grant went to the bench with his fourth foul at the 11:58 mark. Even with Grant on the bench, the zone slowed Freeman down and the Badgers chopped the lead back to nine. Bennett then went back to the team's strength, man-to-man defense.

Over the next several minutes of play, Calderwood and Okey cut the lead to eight points on three different occasions, but Wisconsin just didn't have an answer for Freeman. He scored eight straight points and prevented the Badgers from building any momentum. Okey's driving dunk, which came with 7:23 remaining and made the score 58-50, turned out to be the Badgers' last serious challenge. Texas pulled away on the strength of Freeman's thirty-one points for a 71-58 victory. The red team—Matt Miner, Adam Schafer, Matt Quest, Brian Vraney, and Booker Coleman—played out the final twenty-six seconds of the season.

Bennett was visibly distraught as he made his way off the floor and into the post-game press conference. His comments were cordial and complimentary to Tom Penders and his Texas Longhorns, but internally he was crushed. His team, in the greatest showcase for college basketball, had failed. That meant only one thing to him at that point—he had failed his team as their coach. He lamented his inability to convey the importance of exceptional effort and unity in such an intense environment. They had played hard, but not every minute, and they wanted to win the game, but turned inward for the victory instead of relying on the potential of the unit. Always the teacher, he again circled his students around him, and taught a lesson that mirrored the thoughts of Ralph Waldo Emerson. Emerson wrote in his essay *Friendship:*

There are two elements that go to the composition of friendship. One is truth. A friend is a person with whom I may be sincere. The other element is tenderness [love]. When a man becomes dear to me, I have touched the goal of fortune.

Bennett instructed, "It is amazing how close you guys are off the floor. You really like each other. But the thing you lack for one another is a real love. You do not love one another to the point where you will say the things that need to be said, because you do not want to ruffle each other's feathers. Well, that is just not good enough . . . *I do not wish to treat friendship daintily, but with roughest courage.* . . If you truly loved one another, you would make each other do what has to be done. In this case, you would chase each other down if someone was going to be late for a meal. You can't always be best buddies and look the other way. Sometimes love is not always kind, it is tough. Until you experience that, you will not come together for a single purpose."

Though Bennett lamented that the Badger players had a propensity to avoid confrontation with each other, he knew his meeting had no impact on that day's events. Still, he wanted the seed to be planted for the future growth of the team. The 1996-97 season was history.

———————

Sitting in my hotel room later that evening, I found myself asking, "What is the tangible lesson that could be learned from this devastating loss?" Left to contemplate that question alone, as Bennett had retreated into the solitary sanctity of his suite, only one conclusion seemed appropriate. This team had learned to be accountable only on one level, to themselves. This is an extremely important step in Dick Bennett's program. However, that is really just the first step of accountability, especially within the dynamics of a team. What they had failed to do all season long was to take their accountability to the next level, to give themselves to something greater than themselves, and to become accountable as a whole, as a team. Bennett understood this from the start, as he yearned to bring the group together and make *the whole greater than the sum of the parts*. After all, that is what had made Bennett's former teams so successful. That is what he knew, but his Wisconsin players still did not.

Does this make these young men bad people or bad players? Of course not! Their accomplishments throughout the season were miraculous and they can take great pride in their admirable feats. Yet, to stay true to their foundation concept of thankfulness in all situations, they must seek the wisdom in the disappointing loss. Again, that wisdom is to be accountable to something greater than oneself. It was readily evident that each member of the team became more accountable for his own behavior and to himself throughout the season. However, each member of the team is not an island onto himself and is uniquely joined with the other members, both on and off the court. Each player's actions directly affect not only himself, but also his teammates. There is no such thing as neutrality on a team. Accountability to the team then, includes being accountable for the actions of each member of the team.

Dick Bennett holds himself accountable on three levels, and all three mirror his priorities in life. He is first accountable to his faith, secondly to his family, and finally, he is accountable to his basketball team. With this high level of personal and professional accountability, the next time the Badgers earn a berth in the NCAA tournament, accountability will be a strength of this team, and the potential of the team will be without limits.

Equipped with that knowledge, the Wisconsin basketball team can then move forward and grow as a unit. That is the beauty of college basketball; there is always another season just around the corner. Each member of the program, staff and players alike, get the opportunity to start all over again in six months. If they are truly thankful in all situations, they will seek the wisdom in the crushing defeat. Having done so, they can only conclude that they must continue to improve, both individually and as a unit, to reach the next level of play. No area of that improvement is more important than their accountability *to* the team and collective responsibility *for* each other. Ultimately, the Texas loss may prove to have been the most important game of a tumultuous season by providing ample fodder for improvement.

That last step, that type of accountability, takes a fairly high degree of genuine integrity, a characteristic that Erik Erickson suggested only develops in the later stages of personal development. Therein lies one of the most important lessons that Bennett's players can learn from their coach, although it is a revelation they would have to come to on their own. Giving of yourself to something greater than yourself has no guarantees of personal reward, yet when everyone in the group does so, the potential for the unit is limitless. Dick Bennett is a patient man, a teacher who

Conclusion

The players finally got a chance to get away from Madison, the university, and Badger basketball. Spring break provided them the chance to be ordinary college kids and enjoy time off relaxing with friends. The coaches, on the other hand, returned to the office and wrapped up the season. Finally, even they enjoyed a few days of relaxation at the Final Four in Indianapolis. Lute Olson's Arizona Wildcats captured the national championship, and within days Bennett and his staff were back at work chasing their own elusive dream.

The events of the past seven months were quickly becoming a memory. Individual meetings were conducted with each player to discuss his past performance and establish new goals for the off-season. Mosezell Peterson would not be setting any new goals. He had come to the painful realization that his injured knee would prevent him from ever playing competitive basketball again. A healthy Mike Kosolcharoen would also not be setting any new goals for his basketball career, as he informed Bennett that his "fire" for the game was gone, and thus, so was he. Shaddrick Jenkins, the Coffeyville JC recruit, would not be taking either of their places, as he had decided to return to his native state and attend South Florida University. Paul Grant, meanwhile, was busy impressing NBA scouts in the pre-draft camps with his tireless work ethic and athletic body. (Minnesota selected him in the first round, twentieth overall, in the June draft.)

Bennett took a break from his routine for one final conversation about the season. The sparkle was back in his eye as he sat at his desk with the stress of the season behind him. Asked to give one final appraisal on the season, he sat forward in his chair, rubbed his chin slowly, and looked into space through squinted eyes. He remained in the pose for several long moments before he abruptly sat back in his chair.

"My final assessment would be that it was a remarkable season," he said, nodding his head affirmatively. "This team accomplished so much in terms of moving up the ladder that it has to be respected for that. We can talk about how we never came together as a unit, or how we never got a cohesive offense, but in spite of that, we were a team good enough to win some big games and to put up one of the best records in the history of the school. That was a remarkable accomplishment the players can be proud of."

Their accomplishments, going 18-10 and making it to the NCAA tournament, were even more impressive when put into historical perspective. With their eighteen regular-season victories, they equalled the total of the 1915-16 squad, the only other team to achieve that many wins in nearly one hundred years of basketball at Wisconsin. In addition, the eleven conference victories were the highest total since the 1941 national championship season. Thus, Bennett's comments were obviously not idle praise.

Despite those accomplishments, however, a still greater one may be in the legacy they had started to build. Their coach, for one, understood that.

"Going into the season, I did not know for how much longer I would want to continue coaching. There were so many times that I thought that maybe the game had passed me by. But this season, and especially the way it ended, has lit a fire in me to keep going."

> *Though much is taken, much abides; and tho'*
> *We are not now that strength which in old days*
> *Moved earth and heaven, that which we are,we are;*
> *One equal temper of heroic hearts,*
> *Made weak by time and fate, but strong in will*
> *To strive, to seek, to find, and not to yield.*

From William Tennyson's poem *ULYSSES*

Glossary of Basketball Terms

Assist—a pass that leads directly to a score by a teammate.

Ball handler—a player who is controlling the ball on the dribble.

Ball side—the side of the court in which the basketball is located.

Baseline—the line at the end of the court that runs parallel to the backboard; also a term used to describe the area on the playing surface near the end line.

Block—the area of the free throw lane nearest the baseline. Named after the rectangular block located at the base of the free throw lane.

Block-out—a rebounding maneuver, typically done on defense, in which a player positions himself between the basket and an opponent in an attempt to secure the ball on a missed shot.

Blocker/mover offense—the free-lance offensive system that Dick Bennett has developed throughout his coaching career.

> **Blocker**—a player designated to operate primarily as a screener in the offense, continually looking to block the path of the defensive players guarding the movers.
>
> **Mover**—a player designated to move freely in the offense, continually looking to rub his defensive player off the screens set by the blockers.

Center—the pivot or post, typically the tallest player on the team who plays along the free throw lane.

Conversion—a term used to describe the process of changing from offense to defense.

Cutter—a player moving off a teammate's screen toward the basket or the ball looking to receive a pass.

Dead ball—one of two situations; either an offensive player who has used his dribble and picked up the ball, or the times when the ball is not in play.

Fast-break—quickly advancing the ball up the floor in an attempt to catch the opponent in an out-numbered situation for an easy basket.

Field goal—a term used to describe the action of making a basket during regulation play; can be worth either two or three points.

Field goal percentage—number of baskets made divided by the total number of shots attempted.

Floor burn—a surface abrasion of the skin caused by the exposed skin sliding across the surface of the floor.

Forward—a term used to identify a player who typically plays on the perimeter and the post.

Free throw—a shot taken without any defensive pressure 15 feet from a line directly in front of the basket.

Free throw line—a line 15 feet from the basket behind which players take foul shots.

Free throw percentage—number of free throws made divided by the total number of shots taken.

Help and recover—a defensive maneuver in which a player leaves the man he is defending to stop the ball handler, and then moves back to his own player.

Help side—the side of the court opposite the basketball.

High post—the area around and near the free throw line.

Inbound pass—the action of throwing the ball into play from out of bounds.

Jump ball—used to start each game, and overtime if necessary. The official tosses the ball into the air between two players at the center circle. Each player attempts to tap it to one of their teammates to secure possession of the ball.

Jump-hook—an offensive shot in which the offensive player turns his body sideways to the basket (using his body to shield the defender from the ball), jumps into the air, and releases the ball toward the basket with one hand.

Jump shot—an offensive skill used to throw the ball to the basket in an attempt to score. The player jumps off the floor and releases the ball at the peak of his jump.

Lay-up—a shot made from very close range, usually while moving directly to the basket on the dribble.

Leapin' leaner—slang, a shot taken while floating sideways through the air.

Low post—the area along the free throw lane closest to the basket. Generally extends a few feet off the lane and approximately half-way up the lane toward the free throw line.

Man-to-man defense—each defensive player is assigned the responsibility to defend one specific offensive player.

Match-up zone defense—players are designated an area to guard on the floor, yet each defensive player always has responsibility for an offensive player. The match-up changes alignments depending on the alignment of the offensive players.

Off-the-ball screen—an offensive maneuver in which an offensive player (screener) attempts to block the path of a teammate's defender to keep the defender away from the ball.

On-the-ball screen—an offensive maneuver in which an offensive player without the ball attempts to obstruct the path of the defensive player defending the player with the ball (ball handler).

On-the-line—a man-to-man defensive term which describes the position in which the defensive player positions himself directly on the imaginary line between the ball handler and his offensive player.

Out of bounds—area outside the playing surface. Also a term used to describe the action of throwing the ball into play from outside the playing surface.

Perimeter—the area outside of the free throw lane.

Pivot foot—an offensive player must keep at least one foot continuously in contact with the floor when not dribbling the ball.

Point—the area just above the top of the free throw lane.

Point guard—primary ball handler in the offense, the "quarterback" of the team.

Post—the area along the free throw lane closest to the basket. Generally extends a few feet off the lane and approximately half-way up the lane toward the free throw line. Also a term sometimes used to describe a player who plays in the low post area. "Paul Grant is a post player."

Press—the defensive team extends their defense to the half-court line (half-court press), to their own free throw line (three-quarter court press), or all the way to their own offensive baseline (full-court press).

Press-breaker—an offensive scheme designed to break an opponent's defensive press.

Rebound—the action of securing possession of the ball off a missed shot attempt, either when playing offense (offensive rebound), or when playing defense (defensive rebound).

Rhythm shot—a coaching term used to describe the action of catching a pass and going directly up for a field goal attempt without being distracted by the defense.

Screen—an offensive maneuver used to block the path of a defensive player.

Screener—an offensive player who is attempting to block the path of his teammate's defensive player.

Second shot—a shot taken after an offensive rebound.

Shot selection—a term used to describe the ability to identify a good shot, which means a field goal attempt that has a good chance of going in.

Steal—taking the ball away from an offensive player or team.

Strong side—the side of the court in which the basketball is located.

Tip-in—an offensive act of directing the ball into the basket off a missed shot without regaining total possession of the ball.

Three-point line—a semicircular line that runs around the perimeter of the court and which is 19'9" from the basket.

Three-point shot—a field goal attempt from beyond the three point line.

Top of the key—the area just beyond the top of the free throw circle.

Trap—two or more defensive players surround the ball handler and attempt to force him into a mistake with the ball.

Traveling—an offensive violation which results in a turnover. An offensive player takes more than one step or lifts their pivot foot without dribbling the basketball.

Turn-around jump shot—an offensive skill used by a low post player to throw the ball toward the basket in an attempt to score. The offensive player receives the ball with his back to the basket, pivots half-way around toward the basket, and jumps into the air before releasing the ball at the peak of his jump.

Turnover—giving the ball back to the opponent without taking a shot. A turnover can occur because of a bad pass, fumbling the ball, or committing a variety of offensive infractions (offensive foul, traveling, three-second lane violation, etc.).

Up-the-line—a man-to-man defensive term which describes an imaginary position between the ball handler and another offensive player. Also commonly called the "Ball-You-Man" position. The defensive player moves away from his player "up the line" toward the ball.

Weak side—the side of the court opposite the basketball.

Wing—the area located on the side of the playing surface from the free throw line toward the sideline.

Zone defense—the defensive players are assigned the responsibility of guarding an area of the court as opposed to a specific offensive player.

About the Author

Born in Fargo, North Dakota, in 1962, Eric Ferris spent the first twelve years of his life growing up in the tiny blue-collar town of Downer, Minnesota. Potato storage sheds and a local concrete plant were the cultural centers of the village, which was home to fewer than a hundred inhabitants. Childhood games were the center of activity for the neighborhood children, which included Ferris and his two brothers and a sister. In 1974, when Eric was twelve, his family moved to the farming community of Barnesville, Minnesota. He graduated from Barnesville High School in 1980.

Four years, two knee surgeries, and three colleges later, Ferris graduated from Valley City State College (North Dakota), in the spring of 1984 with a degree in physical education. That fall, after spending the summer driving a gravel truck for his father's road construction crew and contemplating his future, Ferris began graduate school at the University of North Dakota. It was then, while conducting research and writing papers for his courses, that he discovered an interest in literature and writing. That curiosity continued to develop as he began his professional career.

Over the next eleven years, Ferris' resume grew as he sought out new experiences to fulfill his coaching aspirations. He served as a women's basketball assistant at Montana State University and Weber State University before taking his first head coaching job at Moorhead State University (Minnesota) in 1988. He left the profession one year later, disillusioned, and ran a YMCA in Fargo, North Dakota, for two years. The pull of coaching was unrelenting, however, and he returned to the sidelines when he took over the women's basketball team at the college of St. Scholastica (CSS) in Duluth, Minnesota. Two years with the women's team, one with the men's, and finally, two years at Detroit Lakes High

School in Northwestern Minnesota, could not extinguish his desire to study and write.

He succumbed to his desire in the fall of 1996 and decided to combine his two passions, basketball and writing. He enrolled at the University of Wisconsin-Madison to pursue a PhD in educational administration, to examine the leadership methods of UW basketball coach Dick Bennett, and to document his findings.

This book is the result of that inquiry.